American Catholics and Social Reform

THE NEW DEAL YEARS

David J. O'Brien

New York
OXFORD UNIVERSITY PRESS
1968

To My Mother and Father
Who Know What It Means
To Be Catholic and American

Preface

When Catholics speak of the social thought of the Church, they usually have in mind the encyclicals of recent Popes dealing with "the social question." These writings, most notably *Rerum Novarum* of Leo XIII and *Quadragesimo Anno* of Pius XI, have been concerned explicitly with the problems of modern society, particularly the existence of clearly defined social classes, the relations between these classes, and their ultimate relationship to society as a whole. In recent years Pope John XXIII and Pope Paul VI have broadened the scope of Catholic social doctrine to cover the peculiar problems of affluent Western nations and particularly the relations between these countries and the poor nations of Asia, Africa, and Latin America. Historically, however, the emergence of a distinct urban working class preoccupied Catholics interested in social problems; indeed, until recently, the Popes have appeared to consider the terms "social question" and "labor question" interchangeable.

Catholics who consider economic, social, and political questions from a consciously Catholic point of view frequently look to the encyclicals for guidance. This study is concerned with the process of referral, the manner in which American Catholics in the 1930's interpreted and applied the social teachings of the Church to American problems. Catholics possess an authoritatively formulated body of social doctrine developed independently of the American experience and based on principles derived from revelation and natural law. In addition, Catholics are part of an international hierarchical organization designed to make them aware of the Church's teachings and to enforce its religious and moral discipline. On the surface, at least, these things distinguish Catholics from their fellow Americans. The fact of difference is not necessarily harmful to society; the American experiment surely is based on the opposite assumption. Nevertheless the problems of religious pluralism have been particularly acute for Catholics, and examination of their attempts to relate themselves and their faith to the American situation can be significant for an understanding both of the American experience and of the contemporary dilemmas of Christianity. The objective of this study, therefore, is to gain some insight into the meaning of the dual tradition, national and religious, of American Catholics through an examination of the social ideas and attitudes of Catholic spokesmen in the New Deal years.

To accomplish the objectives set for this study, research has been directed to those published writings that interpreted encyclical teachings and applied them to the United States or attempted to evaluate American developments in terms of Catholic thought. This method has a number of limitations. For one thing national periodicals and the writings of Catholic intellectuals and publicists do not necessarily reflect in any exact way the opinions of the Catholic community as a whole. And their influence on the political and social behavior of Catholics at large is not subject to precise measurement. Fully aware of these limitations, the reader can derive value from a study based on the ideas of articulate Catholic spokesmen. Catholics have tended to give due weight to authority and, in moments of crisis particularly, they will often turn to the pronouncements of Popes and bishops and the writings of authoritative Catholic leaders. Further, the awakening social consciousness of American Catholics in the 1930's led them naturally to the encyclicals and their better known American expositors. The analysis of Catholic social teachings was encouraged by the Pope, and the ensuing discussion was one of which educated and self-conscious Catholics were well aware.

Most important, the significance of this study lies in the interaction of Catholic and American traditions, and this implies that the people discussed were seriously and consciously Catholic. Those who were serious about their Catholicism did listen to the bishops and did read the Catholic press. It is on the level of books, magazines, and newspapers that the intellectual dialogue between the Church and the rest of society was carried on, a level distinct from that of the sociological conflicts between the Church and her organizations and other political, social, and religious groups. These serious, articulate Catholic leaders included bishops, priests, and laymen whose motives and concerns covered a wide spectrum, from an anxiety to prove that the Catholic Church was loyal and patriotic to an equally intense passion to remake America as a truly Christian society. Whatever their reasons for entering the intellectual controversies of the day, all had to face the major problem of every religious and ethnic group in the nation: the definition of the meaning of the American experience. Frequently confused, often blind to the social forces behind the ideas they expressed, they nevertheless addressed themselves to real problems, and their effort was important for themselves, for their country, and for those who would follow.

Several institutions and many people assisted in the preparation of this book. A dissertation fellowship from the Woodrow Wilson Foundation allowed me an extra year of graduate study during which research on the subject was carried out. The Canada Council and the administration of Loyola College assisted further research and provided secretarial assistance in preparation of the manuscript. Librarians at the University of Rochester, the Franklin D. Roosevelt Library, the Catholic University of America, and Loyola College were always generous with their time and skills.

Mrs. Gwen Holden typed the manuscript and Allen Reznick assisted in the preparation of the index. The *Catholic Historical Review* granted permission to reprint my "American Catholics and Organized Labor in the 1930s" (*Catholic Historical Review*, LII, October 1966, 323–49), which appears in revised form as Chapter V. The *Catholic World* permitted me to revise portions of my "American Catholics and Anti-Semitism in the 1930s" (*Catholic World*, CCIV, February 1967, 270–76), for inclusion in Chapter VII.

The Reverend Thomas T. McAvoy, C.S.C., Professor Walter Gray, and the late Professor Aaron I. Abell of the University of Notre Dame first introduced me to the study of American history; Professor Glyndon Van Deusen, Willson H. Coates, and Hayden V. White deepened my interest at the University of Rochester. These men provided me with more than an education; they were models of dedicated scholarship and genuine commitment to the values of rationality and freedom. I owe a special obligation to Professor Milton Berman of the University of Rochester, who directed this work in its earlier stage as a doctoral dissertation. He encouraged me to enter a field in which few historians have worked, and he provided exactly the correct portions of encouragement and criticism. Philip Gleason of the University of Notre Dame, William Miller of Marquette University, William Akin of Harpur College, and John F. McGovern of the University of Wisconsin at Milwaukee have read all or parts of the manuscript and provided invaluable advice and encouragement. My colleagues Geoffrey Adams, Robert Ruigh, and J. Terry Copp have done the same, and the Reverend C. B. O'Keefe, S.J., Academic Vice President at Loyola College, has been a constant source of moral support and material assistance. Monsignor John Tracy Ellis, the foremost living historian of American Catholicism, has kindly encouraged my efforts in this field.

Most important, my children bore the burden of an historian

father with patience and in the process taught me much of life and of faith. Their mother's contribution to this book and its author can hardly be stated; she will know how important her presence has been. Finally, this book is dedicated to my parents, who remain for me models of all that is best in American Catholicism, the tradition I have chosen for study and for life.

David O'Brien
Loyola College
Montreal, Canada
April 15, 1968

Contents

American Catholics
and Social Reform

I

Catholic Social Thought

When American Catholics looked to their Church for guidance in attempting to deal with the economic and social issues of the 1930's they found, sometimes to their surprise, that a large body of teaching on such subjects existed, including elaborate pronouncements from the Church's highest authority. For some the encyclicals of Popes Leo XIII and Pius XI served as a starting point for the evaluation of society and its problems, but for most American Catholics the Church's teachings were but one element in a complex of factors and loyalties that shaped their attitudes and actions. In any case, American Catholics who took their religion seriously came into contact with Catholic social doctrine either directly from the encyclicals, or indirectly from interpretations presented by the American hierarchy, the local bishop, priests, and teachers, and the Catholic press. Before examining the character of these interpretations one must look at the nature of Catholic social thought and the content of papal teachings on social questions.

In the words of Pope John XXIII, the Catholic Church regards itself as "Mater et Magistra," mother and teacher of all men. It has been charged by Christ with the mission of carrying to men the "good news" of his salvation message, a responsibility to be accomplished within history by close attention to living men working out their salvation in concrete historical circumstances. The central Christian doctrine of the Incarnation, that Jesus Christ was at once God and Man, means that there can be no escape, no retreat from the world. Creation must "return to God not by retracing its steps, not by moving backward toward Christ at the intersection of the old and the new . . . but rather by moving forward with Christ in the continuing action of the Incarnation." [1] The Church must fulfill the promise of the Incarnation by winning men to Christ, striving always to make the Christian message meaningful to each age and to every society.

This understanding of the role of the Church, revitalized in recent years by the pastoral message of Pope John, nevertheless continues to coexist with another point of view, one which emphasizes the more negative and defensive responsibilities of the Church derived from its role as the divinely constituted guardian of the truths of Revelation and the moral law. Frequently the Church has neglected its dynamic teaching function and drawn in upon itself, seeking to protect its doctrine against error and its institutional power and prestige against attack. The development of a defensive, introverted posture in the post-Reformation period, for example, corresponded with the decline of Catholicism as a meaningful, positive force in Western life. Fearful of liberal attacks from without and modernist accommodation within, the Church reacted by overemphasizing its role as a vehicle of salvation, obscuring the mysterious character of its life and ignoring the inevitable effects of its temporal, historical involvement. When the Church is seen as the only link between spheres of nature and grace, when it is viewed as having a monopoly of the means of divine assistance, then Catholicism easily deteriorates into ideology, presenting a rationale for ecclesiastical interests. The institutional, historical existence and welfare of the Church take on absolute value, before which all human values pale into insignificance. If the Church's objective is not the life of grace, but belief, allegiance, and loyalty, then, as Lord Acton saw, ignorance is easily affirmed to be "quite as serviceable as knowl-edge" and the Church must "unite with any cause whose alliance promises most profit." [2] Exclusivism, clericalism, and self-righteousness all follow from the view of the Church as a "perfect society" never in need of substantial reform or development.[3]

The institutional character of the Church offers a permanent temptation to confuse institutional self-interest and divine mandate. Nevertheless the Christian message is personal and must enter the life of man from within. "The fact is that her presence is brought about by the rebirth and resurrection of each person in Christ," Pope John wrote. Whatever the practice of the past, the Church has no mandate to force external conformity. "A society which claims to teach—but with a sovereign authority—only what is contained in the natural and moral law, may act as regards other societies only by the formation of conscience." [4] But the Christian message is also social, and acceptance of Christ must influence men's behavior in society, "for when men become Christians," Pope John stated, "they feel bound to work vigorously for the improvement of institutions in the temporal environment, trying to prevent them from debasing the dignity of man, or to eliminate all obstacles in the way of a wholesome life and multiply incentives and initiatives to its attainment." [5] Definition of the relationship which should exist between the individual Christian, the Church, and the broader society within which both live, constitutes one of the central themes of Christian history and lies at the heart of the revolutionary developments in Roman Catholicism in the years of *aggiornamento*. While some theologians now argue that "Catholic social thought" is redundant, because Catholicism is a social and political faith, most continue to think of it as a statement of the "social implications of a religious faith," [6] implying a distinction between religious and social dimensions. Certainly in the period under consideration here the spirit of social Catholicism combined a hopefully realistic assessment of social, economic, and political life with the Church's unique view of man and his end drawn from natural law and revelation. "Nothing is more useful than to look at the world as it really is," Leo XIII wrote in *Rerum Novarum*, "and at the same time to seek elsewhere for the solace of its troubles." [7]

Attempts to make religious faith relevant to social life have been continuous in Christian history. In the primitive Church, for example, although the existence of rich and poor was accepted as permanent, millenarian hopes impelled renunciation of the world and of material goods. In the second century, however, Christian thought drifted away from Scriptural literalism and found in the concepts of detachment and stewardship suitable substitutes for voluntary poverty. Property could then be held with good conscience, but the rich would have to place their surplus wealth at the disposal of the poor. Emphasis on stewardship created tension in Christian life, evident in the constant revival of a "mystique of poverty [as an] expression of the Christian impulse to trust only in Providence and as a reaction against the universal tendency of men to assert themselves by relying on material goods and material security." [8] This tradition provided a standard against which to judge the world and the Church, but it never became dominant—in part because its demands on human nature surpassed the expectations of realistic Church leaders. Moreover the revolutionary implications of radical renunciation conflicted with the demand for adaptation and compromise necessitated by the increasing political, social, and cultural activities of the Church. [9]

The process of adaptation reached its peak in the Middle Ages and found expression in the writings of Thomas Aquinas, who provided a philosophical framework long taken for granted by Catholic thinkers. [10] Until very recent years Catholic social thought in general and papal teachings in particular were clearly based upon Thomistic categories and assumptions. [11] Man possesses inherent dignity, consequent upon his rationality and his creation in the image of God, and natural rights, of which he cannot justly be deprived. The most fundamental of these are the right to seek salvation and the right to life and the means to sustain it. Because common ownership of property would bring social disorder and violence, material goods should be held in private; their use should be considered common, for they were created for the maintenance of all men. Property in land and tools, therefore, should not be used in such a way as to deprive others of the means of earning a livelihood, while superfluous goods, beyond personal needs, should be placed at the service of the poor.

Catholic social thought combines a powerful emphasis on natural rights with a view of society as an imperative of nature itself, indispensable for the full development of man's personality and the attainment of his salvation. The individual, endowed with rights independently of society, is simultaneously bound to pursue the good of society, which he depends on for the provision of those conditions necessary for his own self-fulfillment, "for by his innermost nature man is a social being, and unless he relates himself to others he can neither live nor develop his potential." [12]

Society, to function effectively, requires two virtues of its members, justice and charity. General justice directs men toward the attainment of the common good. Particular justice, governing relations between individuals and groups, is subdivided into commutative justice, which demands fair and equitable exchange, and distributive justice, which requires of those charged with the administration of public societies a fair and equitable apportioning of social benefits and obligations. [13] Justice is the observance of reciprocal rights and duties and is necessary for social order and peace. It presupposes a fundamental equality of individuals and considers them to be separate one from another. Alone "it cannot bring about the unity and harmony which will make society a smoothly functioning body." [14] For this, charity is needed, love of men for one another as sons of a common Father. Justice considers men as persons, charity as sharing a common nature, destiny, and end. Only love based upon recognition of brotherhood and human dignity, can bind men together in prosperity, harmony, and peace.

When men recognize the demands of justice and charity, society achieves an organic unity, expressed by universal devotion to the temporal common good, itself ordered to the attainment of the ultimate goal of salvation. Within such a unity a rich, pluralistic group life is possible; guilds, estates, religious orders can all organize and operate freely within a broad juridical structure. For medieval Christianity a hierarchical conception of society rising from the individual through a pyramid of organized bodies to the summits of Church and State, each supreme in its own sphere, seemed natural, assuming the existence of a consensus of ultimate ends and values. At the same time, limits on economic expansion inhibited social mobility, while the personal appeal of Christianity rendered class and status religiously unimportant. Medieval social thought provided a static society and economy with a framework of reciprocal rights and obligations within which justice and charity could be realized. The ethic of worldly success implicit in the stewardship idea did not disappear but was placed within the context of an ordered and organized society. The right of each man to work and to receive an income sufficient for his maintenance in decency and in accord with his status in society was upheld, as was the obligation of his superiors to provide the means needed for its realization. A relatively simple and immobile society was a fit setting for the application of more detailed norms; commutative and distributive justice could be defined in terms of just prices, just wages, specific duties and obligations resting on each and every group in society.

In modern times, a number of new forces challenged the assumptions of the classic Catholic social teachings of the Middle Ages. For one thing the modern, contractual concept of society differed from the Christian notion of a necessary functional organism. The development of a "civilization of plenty" occasioned by technological breakthroughs in agriculture and manufacturing made it possible to envision an end of poverty and want, a change that naturally challenged traditional concepts of property and justice developed during an age of scarcity.[15] A third fact of importance was that these developments took place apart from, even in spite of, the influence of the Church. From the Reformation onward Catholicism was preoccupied with the defense of dogma and privilege and gave little attention to social questions. Economic changes progressed most rapidly in those countries of northern Europe that were no longer Catholic; many Catholic countries were not affected until well into the nineteenth century. The Papacy, concerned with more immediate problems, gave little indication that it was aware of the meaning of the Industrial Revolution. Further, Catholic theology in the post-Reformation era was weak and apologetic. The spirit of the modern Catholic Church appeared to be primarily that of a besieged garrison, holding fast to the truth and decrying "progress, Liberalism and recent departures in civil society." [16]

The predominantly negative character of Catholic thought in the nineteenth century did not imply that Catholics were not concerned about the problems raised by industrial and political revolutions but that they continued to interpret these problems on the basis of assumptions no longer adequate to reality. Thus Catholic thinkers located the source of modern problems in secularism, particularly in the divorce of political authority from its divine foundations and the separation of economic life from moral and ethical influence. Excessive individualism had destroyed the rich group life of the Christian era and left men at the mercy of the absolute State and irresponsible Capitalists. Catholic leaders, both liberal and reactionary, agreed that contemporary problems could be overcome by a restoration of organic unity and direction to modern life through the reconciliation of society and culture with the Church. As part of their attempt to bring about this reunification, Catholics developed a number of approaches to the "social question," ranging from integralism, which totally rejected the values of contemporary culture and called for retrenchment and reaction as the best means of realizing the Christian mission in a world which had rejected the Church, to modernism, which accepted the liberal view of progress, gave absolute value to liberal institutions, and called upon the Church to reform itself in essence as well as in expression and life.[17] The critique of modern thought that Catholicism provided was often valid and valuable, but it gave little positive assistance to those seeking to realize the promise and potential of modern life.

Nevertheless, by the time Pope Leo XIII turned his attention to the social question, organized Catholic social action had developed in most European countries. In France, Joseph de Maistre and others had provided an interpretation of the French Revolution that emphasized the central importance of restoring the Church and particularly the Papacy to a central position in European society, a reactionary point of view that powerfully influenced later Catholic social thought. The liberal Catholic movement, led by de Lammenais, Montalembert, and Lacordaire, also desired for a time to increase the power of the Pope, but liberal Catholics hoped for a reconciliation of Church and society on the basis of endorsement by Catholics of many of the ideals of the revolution.[18] This disagreement reflected the profound division of French society in the nineteenth century, which led most Catholics to concentrate on political problems, particularly the relations of Church and State. Of the early figures only Frederick Ozanam, founder of the St. Vincent de Paul Society, devoted much attention to social and economic questions. Ozanam advocated a living wage and labor organization, but his major efforts were devoted to charitable activity aimed at the alleviation of misery and the easing of class antagonisms.[19] Later, Catholic aristocrats organized study clubs of workers and employers in the hope of overcoming class conflict and restoring medieval guilds with capital and labor. Others, unsympathetic with this counter-revolutionary corporatism, concentrated on developing co-operative and copartnership schemes through which workers would be given a sense of status and responsibility and an effective participation in economic decision making.[20] Political preoccupations plagued French Catholic social action, divided Catholic leaders, and brought official condemnation to the more venturesome. The idealistic efforts at social and political reform of the Liberal Catholic movement of 1830–31, of the Christian Democrats of the 1890's, and the *Sillon* in the first decade of the new century, all came under strong criticism from conservative Catholics and all were rebuked by Rome.[21]

In Germany, political divisions were less intense, and dogmatic, revolutionary corporatism was replaced by moderate, reformist participation in the liberal society even before the publication of *Rerum Novarum.* The pioneer of German social Catholicism, Bishop Emmanual von Ketteler of Mainz, like most other Catholic social critics of the period, believed that a revised guild order of joint organizations of workers and owners, inspired by Christian principles, would restore the institutions of function and status. Organized on the basis of vocation, or occupation, not on the basis of class, such institutions would restore the unified and organic structure of society, lessening class antagonism and ending the alienation of men from one another that liberal individualism had created. However, recognizing the impossibility of establishing a corporate social order in the near future, Ketteler, without abandoning his theoretical objective, gradually turned to State action to alleviate immediate economic abuses. In 1873 he wrote of the re-establishment of vocational groups: "It is a heavy task and I fear we are a long way from its accomplishment. We must be content with collecting materials for future construction." [22] Acutely aware of the responsibility of Christians to work for immediate alleviation of suffering and injustice, Ket-

teler eventually supported industrial legislation and trade unionism as the only methods of overcoming the causes of poverty and
insecurity in a reasonable amount of time.[23]

After Ketteler the chief Catholic exponent of a moderate
program, was Franz Hitze who organized study groups to propagate knowledge of Catholic social teachings and assisted the growth
of educational and benevolent organizations aimed at the formation
of a Christian social conscience among the workers. He pioneered
in the organization and training of the Catholic labor movement
and worked with the Center party for the implementation of the
moderate reform program which Ketteler had drawn up for it in
1874. Although first attracted by corporate anticapitalism, Hitze
and the Center party increasingly called for State action to assist
labor and worked simultaneously for the development of social
attitudes necessary for a vocational group system. Hitze felt that
the State must "awaken a consciousness of Christian solidarity,
ultimately acting . . . to give legal expression to this consciousness." [24] Ketteler and Hitze, by responding realistically to the
pressure of events and the needs of the working class, changed
the conception of the vocational group order from a reactionary,
counterrevolutionary notion to a vision of the gradual and evolutionary integration of the workers into a changing capitalist
order. Fully committed to the guild objective and still suspicious
of State power, they nevertheless were determined to work for
practical reforms to alleviate suffering and injustice.

Romanticism strongly influenced early Catholic thought in
Austria where the ever-present tendency to idealize the Middle
Ages was encouraged by the persistence of guild and craft organizations, carryovers from medieval times, and the popular association of capitalism with the Jews, a phenomenon that made
anti-Semitism an explicit element in Austrian Catholic social
thought.[25] The so-called Vienna school, led by Karl von Vogel-
sang and several prominent Dominicans, held capitalism to be
fundamentally usurious, condemned economic competition as

unchristian, and aimed at a restored guild order with political representation along functional lines. They called for an exclusive Catholic labor movement and a political party under clerical control, on "the assumption that there existed a specifically 'Catholic' order of state and society, even a 'Catholic' economic system, totally opposed to all relatively autonomous formations in the modern state, economy and society." [26] By posing a thoroughgoing challenge to the liberal capitalist order, the Austrians forced Catholics who were engaged in social activity to reexamine their reformism in the light of the ultimate objective of a Christian social order and to be wary of overly increasing the authority of the no longer Christian State. They confused sociological and theological categories and lacked a dynamic conception of history, but these tendencies were present in most Catholic writing and accounted for many of the ambiguities and much of the ineffectiveness of modern Catholic social thought.

Catholic social thought in the nineteenth century began within a traditional frame of reference, and its leaders were prepared to overhaul society in order to re-establish a medieval guild order. Under the pressure of events, Catholics in France and Germany gradually moved away from doctrinaire corporatism to a moderate program of social reform and worked through private organizations to change the ideas of the population in such a way that the people would allow the substitution of some form of organized and co-operative structure for the competitive individualism of liberal capitalism. In Austria the Christian Social party carried on the tradition of a dogmatic and authoritarian corportism, but elsewhere, as small and medium-sized firms were displaced by monopolies and cartels and as a large class-conscious trade-union movement developed, the attainment of a vocational group order seemed less simple and, in some cases, less desirable.

This trend was accelerated by the publication in 1891 of Leo XIII's *Rerum Novarum*. Like his predecessors the Pope hoped to reconcile the Church and modern society, but he also wished to divorce the Church from particular political arrangements and to turn Catholic attention to social action as a means of re-Christianizing society and overcoming the dangers of secularism. Leo offered no program of corporate reconstruction but concentrated on immediate problems. Locating the source of the social question in a class structure founded on greed and exploitation, Leo condemned economic liberalism and unchecked individualism, both of which were rooted in the disappearance of the guilds and the divorce of social life from moral and ethical considerations:

> . . . by degree it has come to pass that the workingmen have been surrendered, isolated and helpless, to the hardheartedness of employers and the greed of unchecked competition . . . the hiring of labor and the conduct of trade are concentrated in the hands of comparatively few; so that a small number of very rich men have been able to lay upon the teeming masses of the laboring poor a yoke little better than that of slavery itself.[27]

But Leo condemned socialism as well, for no system which destroyed the right of private property could better the workers' conditions. Only the possession of property could provide security and integrity for individuals and families and render men independent of the play of economic forces. At the same time Leo insisted that the right of private property, like the economy as a whole, was limited by the moral law and, in particular, by the right of every man to provide a decent living for himself and his family.

In enforcing recognition of this and other rights the State played a crucial role. It was obliged to actively assist the working classes, for they had no adequate means of defense and their rights would otherwise be systematically violated.

> Whenever the general interest of any particular class suffers, or is threatened with harm, which can in no other way be met or prevented, the public authority must step in to deal

with it. . . . The limits must be determined by the nature of
the occasion which calls for the law's interference—the principle being that the law must not undertake more, nor pro-
ceed further, than is required for the remedy of the evil or
the removal of the mischief . . . when there is a question of
defending the rights of individuals, the poor and badly off
have a right to special consideration. The richer class have
many ways of shielding themselves, and stand less in need of
help from the State; whereas the mass of the poor have no
resources of their own to fall back upon, and must chiefly
depend upon the assistance of the State.[28]

Specifically the State was to safeguard private property, protect
the public against the evils of strikes, especially by helping to
remove the causes of industrial unrest, prohibit Sunday labor,
regulate the hours of labor for women and children, and assure all
of a living wage. Discussing the issue of wages in detail, the Pope
concluded that "each one has a natural right to procure what is
required in order to live, and the poor can procure that in no
other way than by what they can earn through their work." [29]
Consequently, Leo rejected the liberal doctrine of the free contract and attacked the basis of economic individualism:

Let the working man and the employer make free agree-
ments, and in particular let them agree freely as to the
wages; nevertheless, there underlies a dictate of natural justice more imperious and ancient than any bargain between
man and man, namely, that wages ought not to be insufficient to support a frugal and well-behaved wage earner. If
through necessity or fear of a worse evil the workman accepts harder conditions, because an employer or contractor
will afford him no better, he is made the victim of force and
injustice.[30]

Worker themselves could assist in attaining high wages by association for mutual aid. Leo endorsed the labor union principle
and upheld the natural right of association, to be protected by the
State. In addition, he hopefully envisioned the time when workers and employers, inspired by Christian principles, would be

organized in supplementary joint bodies to settle matters of common interest. On this point the Pope was not specific, for he desired to center Catholic attention on immediate injustices and their alleviation rather than on long-range objectives. But the direction was clear: as economic and social disorder stemmed from the breakdown of medieval organizations, organization according to class and function would restore harmonious social order. Finally, the Pope recognized the primacy of moral reform for any genuine solution of the social question, and he accordingly stressed the necessary role of the Church in social reform and reorganization.

The period which intervened between the publication of *Rerum Novarum* in 1891 and *Quadragesimo Anno* in 1931 saw major changes in the expression of Catholic social principles and in the character of the social question itself. In both France and Germany a gradual change took place in Catholic thought, from a stress on the complete overhaul of existing society to a more gradual, reformist approach. In Germany, the Center party played an important role in the politics of the Weimar Republic, recognizing fully the political supremacy of Parliament and working within this structure for a gradual reform of economic life through political action and private education.[31] In Austria, on the other hand, the earlier stress on the financial injustice of the capitalist order, the rejection of interest and credit as Jewish-inspired, and the dream of a corporate, clerically dominated social order remained strong. Extreme rejection of capitalism also developed in England where the distributists, Hilaire Belloc, G. K. Chesterton, and Father Vincent McNabb, advocated the rejection of machine technology and urban civilization in favor of a frank return to a peasant, handicraft society. But in England as elsewhere others took a more realistic attitude and, through the Catholic Social Guild and labor schools, sought to educate the workers toward Christian reform and co-operation.[32]

World War I brought major changes in the European economy as well. The decade of the twenties was characterized by increasing concentration of capital and finance in larger units controlled by ever-fewer men, giving the economy an impersonal and bureaucratic character less susceptible to change through religious exhortation and moral reform. Parallel with this was the growth of a large, class-conscious trade-union movement, and, in Italy, the appearance of the authoritarian, fascist State. Finally, the menace of socialism which had concerned nineteenth-century Catholics had taken a threatening concrete form in Russia while another segment had modified its attack on religion and the family in such a way as to appear attractive to many Catholics. In 1930, there was an extensive world-wide depression, adding immediate privation and suffering to the structural and moral elements of the general social question.[33]

It was this increasingly complex socio-economic and political situation which served as the setting for the second of the major social encyclicals, *Quadragesimo Anno*, published in 1931. Pope Pius XI began by tracing the changes since Leo's time, noting the progress in social legislation and the acceptance of papal teachings. He praised the growth of labor organization and reaffirmed the decision of his predecessor, Pius X, that although confessional unions were to be preferred generally, circumstances might make it advisable for Catholics to join neutral unions, provided provisions were made for their education in Catholic social teachings.

The Pope then launched into a sweeping condemnation of both individualism and collectivism, each of which stressed but one aspect of labor, property, and society. Following the middle road, Pius denied with Leo that either labor or capital had exclusive right to possession of the product of their joint efforts. The exact distribution should be guided by "social justice":

> Therefore, the riches that economic-social developments constantly increase ought to be so distributed among individual persons and classes that the common advantage of all . . . will be safeguarded; in other words, that the com-

> mon good of all society will be kept inviolate. By this law of
> social justice one class is forbidden to exclude the other
> from sharing in the benefits.[34]

The common good therefore was the major standard for judging
all social activity and had to be considered at all levels of economic decision making.[35]

Pius directed attention to an aspect of the labor question that
Leo had mentioned but not developed: the existence of a proper-
tyless proletariat when the possession of property was essential to
the full development of personality. The goal of Catholic social
action, for Pius, was "the redemption" of the laboring classes
through the redistribution of property "in ample sufficiency
among the workers." This could come about only through the
wage system:

> those who declare that a contract of hiring and being hired
> is unjust of its own nature, and hence a partnership-contract
> must take its place, are certainly in error. . . . We consider
> it more advisable, however, in the present condition of
> human society that, so far as possible, the work-contract be
> somewhat modified by a partnership-contract. . . . Workers
> and other employees thus become sharers in ownership or
> management or participate in some fashion in the profits
> received.[36]

Wages should be sufficient to meet the needs not only of the
worker himself but of his family, so that the labor of women and
children would not be necessary for the family's maintenance. It
should further be a full employment wage, one balanced with
prices and salaries in such a way as to provide the greatest number of jobs for the population. Finally, it should be a saving wage,
allowing the thrifty worker to provide against unseen contingencies and to gain some property of his own. A full employment
wage necessitated some new mechanism for economic planning
and control, implying the need for structural reform and reorganization. The principle of a saving wage and the use of the term

"social justice" as the principle for the distribution of the product of industry introduced a dynamic element into wage discussion; wages became the method through which men could share in the increasing prosperity and higher standard of living made possible by technological innovations.[37]

Catholic writers had long recognized that the practice of justice between employer and employee assumed the presence of a framework of general or social justice. By introducing the element of the common good into discussion of wage policy, Pius XI recognized the necessity of such a framework and he went on to outline in a general way its character, so that his encyclical was justly titled "The Reconstruction of the Social Order." For such a reconstruction, Pius wrote, "two things are equally necessary: reform of institutions and correction of morals." As regards the reform of institutions "the State comes chiefly to mind," Pius wrote,

> not as if universal well-being were to be expected from its activity, but because things have come to such a pass through the evil of what we have termed "individualism" that, following upon the overthrow and near extinction of that rich social life which was once highly developed through associations of various kinds, there remain only individuals and the State. This is to the great harm of the State itself; for, with a structure of social government lost, and with the taking over of all the burdens which the wrecked associations once bore, the State has been overwhelmed and crushed by almost infinite tasks and duties.[38]

Concerned with the increasing role of the State the Pope went on to reassert the traditional principle of subsidiarity:

> Just as it is gravely wrong to take from individuals what they can accomplish by their own initiative and industry and give it to the community, so also it is an injustice and at the same time a grave evil and disturbance of right order to assign to a greater and higher association what lesser and subordinate organizations can do.[39]

If this principle were applied, the State would delegate to subordinate bodies those tasks which "dissipate its efforts greatly," leaving it free to "do all those things which belong to it alone because it alone can do them: directing, watching, urging, restraining, as occasion requires and necessity demands." [40] The State's immediate task, therefore, was to see to it that "a graduated order is preserved among the various associations in observance of the principle of 'subsidiary function.'" The Pope was even more specific:

> First and foremost, the State and every good citizen ought to look to and strive toward this end: that the conflict between hostile classes be abolished, and harmonious cooperation of the Industries and Professions be encouraged and promoted. The social policy of the State, therefore, must devote itself to the re-establishment of the Industries and Professions. [41]

Only through these "Industries and Professions" in which men would be ranked not by their position in the labor market "but according to the function which each performs," could the conflict of classes be resolved. Those who followed the same industry or profession, either as employers or employees, were to be joined together in "guilds or associations [which were] if not essential, at least natural, to civil society." [42] The unifying force in such bodies was not only their activity but the common good, in the achievement of which all groups should co-operate. Capital and labor would continue to have their own associations to deal with matters of group interest. All associations were to be free, with the members able to join or not, and the groups able to adapt their rules and structure to the purpose for which they were organized.

One object of social reorganization was to restore a "directing principle" in economic life. Free competition "while justified and certainly useful provided it is kept within certain limits, clearly cannot direct economic life—a truth which the outcome of the application in practice of the tenets of this evil individu-

alistic spirit has more than effectively demonstrated." Neither
could this directive function be carried out by "the economic
dictatorship which has already displaced free competition." The
only true principles of direction were "social justice and social
charity." The former should penetrate all the institutions of social life, establishing "a juridical and social order which will, as it
were, give form and shape to all economic life" and aid the
fulfillment of the common good. Social charity should be "the
soul of this order," binding all together in a spirit of brotherhood
and mutual love and assistance.[43]

Pius took pains to distinguish his proposals from the existing
system of Italian fascism, which despite its "obvious advantages,"
he regarded as substituting political domination for free activity.
With an involved bureaucracy, it "rather serves particular political ends than leads to the reconstruction and promotion of a
better social order." [44]

Social reorganization could not be brought about "without reform of morality," the Pope believed. He emphasized the point:
"the first and most necessary remedy is a reform of morals."
Before social reconstruction was possible "there must be a renewal of the Christian spirit . . . lest all our efforts be builded
not on rock but on shifting sand." Greed, especially, led to social
irresponsibility and stood as a bulwark against the establishment
of a just social order. No genuine cure was possible "unless all
men returned openly and sincerely to the teachings of the Gospel." All institutions and laws, Pope Pius wrote, have

> the principle foundation of their stability in the mutual bond
> of minds and hearts whereby the members are united with
> one another. . . . And so, then only will true cooperation be
> possible for a single common good when the constituent
> parts of society deeply feel themselves part of one great fam-
> ily and children of the same heavenly Father.[45]

The role of Catholic Action, a great project of Pope Pius's pon-
tificate, was to train Catholic laymen in the knowledge and practice of their faith so they would diffuse the spirit of the gospel

throughout the world. Lay apostles, recruited and trained from the working class, should, in co-operation with their bishops, strive for the restoration of Christian principles to the pinnacle of social life.

The exact assent which Catholics must give to the encyclicals is unclear. The popes have no particular authority on technical matters, which they try to avoid, but their moral teachings are part of the general teaching office of the Church, and therefore must be taken most seriously by Catholics. The formal conditions under which papal definitions are considered infallible are ordinarily not present in an encyclical letter. Most authorities agree, nevertheless, that Catholics are usually bound to give such pronouncements at least external assent, with the requirements of internal assent, without reservations, to be determined by the Pope's intention as seen in the context of the document.[46]

In any case, the application of the encyclicals to particular historical situations is left to individual Catholics and their bishops. The distinction between doctrine and application is often vague, but the history of modern social Catholicism indicates that a very wide range of choice remains open. Only in a few instances have the popes given authoritative interpretation of parts of the social doctrine or condemned certain Catholic movements. Numerous schools of thought have developed that differ substantially in methods and objectives, but they all claim to base their programs on papal pronouncements.

One major conflict in Catholic thought has centered on the relative importance that should be assigned to moral reform, as opposed to economic and institutional changes. Many argue that the roots of social disorganization, and thus of any reform or reorganization, lie in sin and are therefore moral and religious. Accordingly, fundamental solutions can be sought only with the help of the Church, which alone brings true spiritual reform and regeneration. It was the rejection of the Church and its moral sanctions that created the modern social question and is "the

source of every laxity and every abuse." A recent writer, Father
Daniel O'Connor, puts this point of view most forcefully:

> It is very true that disorder in human life has resulted from
> the rejection of universally valid moral norms. That has
> occurred progressively: first, the Reformation destroyed the
> faith in the true Church, then deism and rationalism rejected
> faith in Christ, and finally atheism came and chased God
> from public life. . . . For, without faith in the Church,
> there is no faith in Christ, and without faith in Christ there
> is no true faith in God. And where faith in God has dis-
> appeared, the moral order itself is compromised. Religious
> agnosticism leads to moral and juridical agnosticism; incre-
> dulity prepares the way for social anarchy. The chaos of
> present day Western Civilization must be attributed to the
> progressive diminution of Christian influence in public
> life.[47]

While recent Catholic scholarship has taken a more constructive attitude toward Western history since the Reformation,
most modern Catholic social thought developed within an historical frame of reference similar to O'Connor's. This view of
progressive decay since the age of Christendom did not necessarily imply a static or romantic view of history attributing absolute value to medieval social forms, but a tendency to such
attitudes did exist, at least with respect to the social role of the
Church and its teachings.

The approach to social problems that would give primary attention to moral and spiritual reform had solid support in the
encyclicals. As one informed student of *Quadragesimo Anno*
noted:

> The final conclusion of the encyclical is that all these tech-
> nical questions can only be solved if there is first a moral
> reformation within men's souls which causes them to turn
> away from selfishness and greed. Without such a reforma-
> tion no economic system, however technically perfect, can
> hope to succeed.[48]

Social action based on such a view can be progressive or reactionary. Liturgists and personalists strive to permeate society with cells of committed Christians who, by their example, will "leaven the mass" and open men's hearts to love of neighbor. Others refrain from co-operative social action with non-Catholics, attack all attempts to remedy social problems by recourse to the secular State, and await large scale return to the Catholic fold as the prerequisite of true social reform. Such an attitude may be coupled with most generous almsgiving and true concern for the fate of the poor.

Although they agree that original sin inhibits utopian dreams, many Catholics nevertheless argue that the moral approach ignores the effect of custom, institutions, and poverty upon human behavior. The first step in the attainment of a Christian social order, according to the American John F. Cronin, is the infusion of justice and charity into economic groups so that "each would seek the common welfare as well as individual goals. This would *not* be primarily a matter of forming a Christian consensus among individuals," Cronin continues. "Rather it would involve a reform of the institutions of society. If the institutions of society tend towards wrong ends, the efforts inspired by personal good will are likely to be nullified." [49] The bulk of Catholic writers tend to accept the natural order as at least relatively autonomous and to seek natural causes and cures for social problems. They call for organized action, both economic and political, in co-operation with all men of good will, whether Catholic or not, to change the institutions of the distribution of wealth with the object of achieving a rational, ordered, and humane economy and society. The unique role of the Church lies elsewhere, they feel, judging and advising such movements on the basis of the eternal truths of which it is the guardian. [50]

A second, and related, area of disagreement arises in connection with the relation between social legislation and reform and the reconstruction of society. The tendency to social adjustment and moderation which followed *Rerum Novarum* sometimes obscured the long-range vocational group order to which most Catholics remain theoretically attached. Many tend to accommodate to the capitalist order—to accept a degree of competition, the soundness of the credit system, and the basic social structure of an urban industrial society—and they are able to find support for these positions in the ambiguities of *Quadragesimo Anno*. But the same encyclical provides ammunition for the opponents of gradualism who reject any accommodation to modern social forms. Agrarians, distributists, and co-operationists who look to decentralization and the restoration of farming and handicrafts as prerequisites to true reform find support in the social doctrine of the Church; doctrinaire corporatists who focus on the long-range objective and see the gap between Catholic principles and the present order as so great as to eliminate any possibility of making the compromises necessary to reform, find Church support as well.

A third general area of disagreement concerns the role of the State both in bringing about the new order and within the corporate structure itself. The function of the State has been the most persistent problem for Catholic social reformers in modern times. Traditional Catholic thought upholds the prerogatives of the political power as guardian of natural rights and the common good. Yet when speaking in these terms Catholics often have in mind the Christian sacral State which recognizes and co-operates with the Catholic Church within the context of a Christian consensus. Catholics have tended to be suspicious of the modern secular State both because of the suffering of the Church at its hands and because they carry the memory of a sacral order as an integral element of their ideological baggage.

Catholic social reformers, particularly in countries where the Church is a minority, have often found that application of the principle of subsidiarity leads naturally to the State as the only agency capable of fulfilling real and pressing social needs. Their fellow Catholics often respond with charges of "Statism," giving political authority undue control over individuals and private associations. Such charges generate emotional heat particularly where the Church as a minority fears State interference with her institutional liberties and interests. Similarly, reformers argue that the State must initiate and encourage movements leading to a vocational group order, whereas others hold that the new order must await the development of a co-operative spirit in the society, presumably following upon a spiritual renewal. In countries where the Church is a majority and where liberal institutions have never taken deep root, however, Catholic corporatists have been willing to invoke the power of an authoritarian State to restore old values and institutions.[51]

On all these divisions, clarification and development have taken place since the 1930's. Catholic political thought has been much more democratic since World War II. Catholics speak less of liberty in countries where they are a minority and have begun to emphasize rather the search for "those things which give purposefulness to life." [52] Pius XII was very much concerned with the wider distribution of productive property and the participation of workers in industrial decision making in order to give men more independence, freedom, and status.[53] John XXIII wrote with a similar stress on the spiritual freedom and dignity of man, and, recognizing the increasing complexity of economic life as the result of historic necessity, he assigned the State an ever-increasing role: "The human dignity of man will not be respected, his personality will not be developed, his liberty will not be protected, unless the state actively works with private enterprise to further the common good." [54]

The increasing willingness of the Church to respect the autonomy of the secular order, and the pervasive sense of history so evident in the writings of Pope John, are recent developments. For Catholics in the 1930's things were far different, and the great question of the nineteenth century regarding the stance they should adopt toward a society that was no longer Christian remained uppermost in their minds. Secular society, especially the State, still appeared hostile and foreign, and the tendency to withdraw from modern society in the hope of a restored sacral and clerical order remained strong. Reformers often accused their fellow Catholics who stressed charity rather than justice in social action of being tainted with the liberal individualism condemned by the popes. Their attitude was probably better understood in terms of the post-Reformation heritage, which identified the Church with the defense of dogmatic truth, Church property, and clerical privilege. In those nations where these medieval remnants remained strongest, the papal social encyclicals met with their least enthusiastic response. The same tendencies existed where Catholics were a minority, but there, many were anxious to reach an accord with their society, they found leaders prepared to deal with secular problems on their own terms and, gradually, to adapt the traditional teachings to the modern social situation.

This adaptation and attempted reconciliation of Church and society had been the basic objective of Leo XIII and Pius XI. Gradually Catholics have come to realize that the process is a continuing one and can never be completed in history, for no society or civilization can be fully Christian. Natural law principles are static and indicate nothing of concrete economic or historical possibilities. As history is dynamic, there can be no single Christian program for society, no single Christian civilization or culture. "It is never possible simply to deduce from Christian principles any one single pattern of the world as it ought to be," theologian Karl Rahner writes.

> It is possible to reject certain conditions, tendencies, endeavors and actions as contradicting the Christian laws of faith and morality. . . . But it is never, in principle, possible to say in the name of these principles that the world is or has got to be "thus and so" when "thus and so" means something

ultimate, positive and individual. . . . Christians *as such* do not have any ready made concrete program for the conduct of the state, or of culture, or of economics, and in fact *cannot* have one. . . . It is now coming to be gradually clear that the gap between universal Christian principles and the putting of them into practice in any one of a number of possible forms is a gap as wide as the possibilities now opening before us.[55]

While the Christian and the Church must always seek to realize spiritual values in history, neither has the power to control or dominate the historical process and as long as men are free they will resist the imposition of specifically Christian forms on their institutions.

So, although there is such a thing as Catholic social doctrine, although indeed Christianity may be a social doctrine, there can be no single Catholic program for the organization of government, economy, and society. Catholics have often tried to give their proposals the same dogmatic force as the religious doctrine on which they were based, but such efforts have generally proven ineffective. The Christian message remains both personal, the free commitment of men to Christ and to their fellow men, and social, the dedication to building the Kingdom of God. Social reform and reconstruction necessarily follow upon Christian commitment, but the Christian profanes his faith when he assigns absolute value to temporal, historical forms rather than to the men they are designed to serve. Realization of this, and of the profound dilemmas confronting the Christian in society, were clear to Protestants like Reinhold Niebuhr in the 1930's, and are increasingly clear to Catholics in the days of Vatican II. For American Catholics of the 1930's, however, this awareness was at best hesitant, inconsistent, and incomplete.

II

Church and Society
in the United States

The papal encyclicals highlighted a growing body of social and political thought that represented the Catholic Church's response to the emergence in Europe of modern urban, industrial civilization. Leo XIII and Pius XI attempted to guide Catholics along lines consistent with Church doctrine in order to counter the spread of radicalism and restore the Church to a position of prestige, power, and influence. They carefully refrained from presenting clear and specific directives for social action, however, and left Catholics free to interpret and apply the norms and principles of the encyclicals in concrete local and national circumstances. English, French, German, and Austrian Catholics found in papal teachings support for widely differing political and social programs; so did Catholic aristocrats, employers, workers, and farmers. Nations, classes, and individuals who read and analyzed the encyclicals were bound to be influenced by factors other than religious zeal or ecclesiastical interest. The result was that Catholicism, despite its appearance of rigid control from the top after the Vatican Council of 1869–70, presented a multiplicity of views on social, political, and economic questions.

This contrast between ecclesiastical uniformity and internal diversity was particularly apparent in the United States. Anti-

Catholic hostility and minority self-consciousness combined to intensify centralization, but ethnic rivalries, organizational immaturity, and extremely rapid growth prevented the development of a truly unified, coherent American Catholicism. Preoccupied with the problem of providing for the spiritual and material needs of hundreds of thousands of immigrants amid indifferent if not hostile surroundings, the leaders of the American Church devoted little time or effort to the problems of modern society which so concerned Leo XIII. Lacking the solid middle-class families that provided cultural leadership for American Protestantism and possessing no counterpart of the Catholic aristocracy that served the function in Europe, American Catholicism failed to develop a vigorous intellectual life or a meaningful understanding of the significance of its own experience.[1] As an integral part of immigrant communities, the Church responded to Protestant proselytization and the distractions of potential mobility with a system of separate organizations and institutions designed to prevent the growth of dual loyalties and cement the already close relationship between priests and people. "It was not enough to regard its populations as occasional participants in the rites of worship," Oscar Handlin writes. "They were to be bound together by a vigorous round of activities as a social entity within which the individual could be sheltered from an alien and hostile world." [2]

While striving to preserve ethnic and religious identity, neither the immigrants nor the Church totally rejected the society around them. Sincerely devoted to America and fearful of latent nativism, laity and clergy alike insisted on the complete compatibility of Catholicism and Americanism. Yet there were sharp contrasts between the characteristic Catholic values of order, hierarchy and status and American individualism, mobility, and faith in progress. Tension between the two traditions, Catholic and American, could have been fruitful for both. As historian Richard Hofstadter writes: "One might have expected

Catholicism to have added a distinctive leaven to the intellectual dialogue in America, bringing as it did a different sense of the past and of the world, a different awareness of the human condition and of the imperatives of institutions." Instead of engaging in such dialogue, American Catholics devoted themselves alternately to denouncing some aspects of American life as "materialistic" or "secularistic" while overidentifying with more congenial features of American society in order, as Hofstadter puts it, "to surmount its minority complex and 'Americanize' itself."[3] Only in very recent years have American Catholics begun to think seriously about that interaction between Catholicism and America which has been at the heart of the Church's history in this country.[4]

The difficulties which faced those who attempted to open up the Catholic-American dialogue in earlier years are best illustrated in the history of the controversy over "Americanism" in the late nineteenth century. The story has been told frequently.[5] One faction of the American hierarchy, led by Archbishop John Ireland of St. Paul, strongly desired to complete the adaptation of the Church to American society, convinced that America was at heart a Christian nation and that there was nothing in her political or social arrangements which could not be reconciled with Church teachings. Accordingly they sought to modify the parochial school system, Americanize the Catholic immigrants, prevent Vatican condemnations of secret societies, trade unions, and radical reformers, and carry on public discussions with Protestants. Their opponents, led by the German-American Catholics, occasionally joined by New York's Archbishop Corrigan and several other bishops of predominantly Irish dioceses, wished to retain their ethnic identity, resist dissolution by the Protestant majority, and defend what they took to be the full integrity of Catholic doctrine. Bitter conflict obscured the range of agreement that existed and when both sides began defining their positions in terms of the Church's world-wide problems, the confusion was compounded. Eventually the controversy reached France, where the ideas of Ireland and Father Isaac Hecker were seen by many as a political and religious expression of what was later called modernism. In the end Leo XIII condemned the heresy of "Americanism" while exempting prelates in the United States from direct association with it.[6]

Pope Leo's condemnation "abruptly killed off the dialogue between the Church and America . . . and dealt a blow to American Catholic self-confidence from which the American Catholic mind has never effectively recovered."[7] A "great silence" fell over the American Church, co-operation with non-Catholics was stifled, and Catholic leaders labored for years under the threat of heresy. Yet, however regrettable the results, it must be noted that Ireland's uncritical embrace of the America of the 1890's was at best only a slight advance beyond the exclusivism of his opponents. Americanization, purging the Church of its foreignness, was no more a solution to the American Catholic dilemma than was the rejection of America symbolized by the papal condemnation.[8] In both Europe and America, Catholic thought remained confined within a juridical and legalistic conception of the Church and a highly defensive attitude toward modern society. Until these could be transcended, Catholics were likely to misunderstand one another and misinterpret the significance of their own actions.

In his discussion of Americanism Leo XIII praised the American constitutional arrangements of Church and State but warned Catholics not to regard these as a model for the entire Church. Leo, and his successors, believed that intimate association of Church and State was the ideal arrangement, although separation might be tolerated in order to avoid social conflict. American Catholics seldom qualified their enthusiasm for the First Amendment, which they believed had created conditions that accounted for the Church's success in retaining influence over its people. "Let Catholics in religion stand isolated as a body, and upon as good ground as their brethren," wrote Bishop John England. "Let Catholics as citizens and politicians not be distinguishable from their other brethren of the commonwealth." [9] Although willing to speak out forcefully on public questions involving moral considerations or serious interference with the independence of the Church, the hierarchy generally abstained from political controversy and instructed their congregations to participate in the democratic process, voting intelligently for the best candidates, and avoiding partisanship or extremism.

Periodic depressions sometimes shook the middle-class assumptions of Catholic workers, but few were attracted to radical politics. Partisanship was a different story. The Irish, who dominated the American Church, became almost totally identified with the Democratic party. The urban political machines, which they joined and eventually controlled, took on many of the characteristics of Irish life: loyalty to the informal rather than the formal governmental mechanism, the hierarchy of officials, the disdain for the values of the dominant culture. Irish politics were conservative, reflecting the immigrants' desire to remove the risk from politics, to create a structure with the capacity to survive and serve family and group interests. Yet, despite their remarkable political talents, the Irish contributed little of significant value to the general betterment of society. That is, "The very parochialism and bureaucracy that enabled them to succeed in politics prevented them from doing much with government," as Daniel P. Moynihan writes. "They never thought of politics as an instrument of social change—their kind of politics involved the processes of a society that was not changing." [10]

One consequence was the isolation of Catholics from the reform movements of the nineteenth century. The institutional preoccupations of the hierarchy and clergy and the group-conscious politics of the immigrants prevented the growth of generalized social concern. Agrarian reform movements had but little appeal for largely urban-based Catholic blocs, and middle-class progressivism, with its desire to reform the urban machines and with its Protestant, paternalist overtones, conflicted directly with the loyalties of Catholic voters. When reform proposals coincided with the interests of Catholic workers or with the desires of their political leaders, a temporary alliance of reformers and machine politicians was possible.[11] But, until the 1930's, conscious identification with the reform movement was restricted to a handful of socially conscious Catholic leaders.

On the other hand, the needs of the immigrants and the competition of Protestant and secular agencies led Church leaders to establish and multiply social welfare agencies and charitable institutions under Catholic auspices. In dealing with poverty the American Church developed an activist temper very noticeable to foreign observers. Charitable efforts, such as the voluntary work of the St. Vincent de Paul Society, were highly personalized. Little thought was given to the causes of poverty or the faults of the economic system. Most Catholics seemed to agree that social distress could be solved by personal morality, a Christian upbringing, private charity, and close association with the Church.[12]

What social concern the hierarchy did exhibit in the years before World War I arose more as a reaction to labor violence and the threat of socialism than as a positive desire to apply Catholic social teachings in the United States. *Rerum Novarum,* published in 1891, was welcomed, but most American spokesmen noted its defense of private property and its condemnation of socialism. Few seemed to feel that the Pope's strictures against the excesses of liberal capitalism had any important application in the United States.[13] Those who did recognize the existence of real injustice often found adequate solutions in the practice of Christian charity, temperance, or, at best, local legislation. The "Christian solution," according to Bishop James McFaul of Trenton, involved "the elevation of the poor, the obtaining and defending of the rights of the working class and the betterment of the individual and society." [14] But neither Bishop McFaul nor his colleagues were able to offer programs for attaining these objectives beyond the voluntary practice of the works of mercy and the daily application of Christian principles in personal life. On the other hand, the Catholic clergy did not join in the widespread baptism of the doctrine of material success. The historian of the "rags to riches" myth has noted that in the nineteenth century "no eminent prelate urged the young to seek salvation along the road of wealth," a teaching which found support in nearly every major Protestant denomination.[15]

It was natural for Catholics to take a significant part in the labor movement, as they were largely concentrated in the working class. The upward movement of Irish Catholics into the ranks of skilled labor and white-collar work was rapid, but well into the twentieth century relatively few Catholics were found among the nation's business and commercial leaders.[16] By contrast, Catholics have been prominent in labor organizations from the days of Terence Powderly to the present.

The Catholic hierarchy was awakened to labor problems by the strikes of the 1870's and 1880's and the activities of the Molly Maguires.[17] Archbishop Bayley of Baltimore felt that organizations like the Irish Catholic Benevolent Union served to guard Catholics "from what is worse than the secret societies—that is the miserable associations called labor organizations." [18] On the other hand the Boston *Pilot*, under the editorship of John Boyle O'Reilly, adopted a sympathetic attitude toward the problems of labor and denounced the irresponsible actions of capital, though even the *Pilot* was slow in endorsing genuine trade unions.[19] In the 1890's there was a good deal of interest in arbitration as a solution to labor violence. Speakers at the lay Catholic congresses of 1889 and 1893 favored such action to protect the general public against the detrimental effects of strikes.

Through the decade almost every major Catholic spokesman agreed on the necessity for legally enforced arbitration to allay social discontent and industrial strife.[20]

In 1886 Cardinal Gibbons won a lasting reputation as a friend of labor by his defense of the Knights of Labor against possible Vatican condemnation. In a letter to Rome, Gibbons upheld the right of workers to organize in defense of their rights and warned of the danger for the Church if it were regularly found on the side of capital while ignoring labor's just grievances. Yet the Cardinal's actions were motivated by his desire to retain the allegiance of working-class Catholics, and he noted that the Knights of Labor was unlikely to long remain an important force in American society.[21] "Experience has shown that strikes are a disaster and at best a very questionable remedy for the redress of the laborer's grievances," he wrote some years later. "They paralyze industry, they often foment fierce passions and lead to the destruction of property, and above all they result in inflicting grievous injury on the laborer himself by keeping him in forced idleness." [22] Archbishop Ireland agreed with Gibbons's defense of the Knights, but he defended the rights of property as strongly as those of labor. A close friend of leading businessmen and a staunch Republican, Ireland was shocked by the violence of many strikes and felt that labor's recourse should be its appeal to the public conscience. "Law and public opinion," he wrote, "are the natural and ultimate remedies for social grievances." [23] While he endorsed the right of workers to organize and deplored the selfishness of some Capitalists, Ireland feared that the Church might inadvertently promote radicalism. After the Pullman strike he wrote Cardinal Gibbons: "We have been siding with labor in its grievances; the unthinking ones transgress the golden mean and rush into war against property." [24] For all his insight into the power and positive value of democracy, Ireland, with his social philosophy of thrift, temperance, and self-help, appeared to preach a "Catholic version of the old Puritan individualism." [25]

Some Catholic attention was drawn to the American Federation of Labor in the years preceding World War I because a large percentage of its membership and half of its governing board were Catholics. Yet interest was sporadic and often negative. On the local level priests sometimes took an active role in strikes and in advising Catholic unionists, but nationally the hierarchy showed little interest.[26] Several observers have attributed to Catholic influence the failure of the federation to adopt a socialist program, but, although undoubtedly of some importance, Catholic attempts to moderate the policies of the American Federation of Labor were few, and there is little evidence to offset the conclusion that the actions of Catholic members derived from secular and not religious motives.[27]

This conclusion is borne out by the career of Father Peter Dietz who in 1910 established the Militia of Christ for Social Service as an organization for Catholic members of the A.F. of L. Dietz hoped to educate the members in Christian principles and fight socialism within the federation. Unlike even his most active contemporaries Dietz saw the positive historic significance of the trade unions and believed that Catholic attention should be centered on them rather than on social legislation, co-operatives, or corporate reform. His experience with the Militia of Christ was unhappy; Catholic labor leaders gladly lent their names but, with the exception of John Mitchell of the United Mine Workers, they were unwilling to provide the money or the enthusiasm necessary for success.[28]

His labor activity was not Father Dietz's only frustration. He hoped to get American Catholics to forget local and ethnic prejudices and "adopt a common program to advance a national Catholic movement for social reform." [29] Both he and Father John Ryan saw in Europe organized groups of Catholics seeking to apply Catholic Social teachings and both tried to build similar movements in the United States. Ryan looked unsuccessfully to the Knights of Columbus for the basis of such a movement, Dietz to the German Catholic Central Verein and later to the American Federation of Catholic Societies.

The Central Verein had been established in 1855 as a federation of German Catholic benefit and insurance societies, paralleling similar organizations in Germany. In 1908 a social bureau was established under the direction of Frederick B. Kenkel, a disciple of Bishop von Ketteler and a longtime advocate of social reform. Kenkel and the Verein were the leading American exponents of a program of corporate reform but, like their German counterparts, they did not ignore immediate needs or anticipate a rapid total change. Recognizing the difficulty of implementing a corporate, vocational group order in the face of the dominant American individualism, Kenkel concentrated his efforts on restoring Christian principles and awareness of the "organic duty of mutual consideration and cooperation."[30] Beyond this he supported the A.F. of L. as a bulwark against socialism and urged action to improve the status and economic prosperity of workers through higher wages, consumers' cooperatives, and in some cases legislation by the separate states. But he was hostile to strikes, favored compulsory arbitration, urged caution in dealing with nondenominational labor unions, and rejected federal social legislation.[31]

As the basis of a national Catholic social movement the Verein was limited because of its ethnic identification and its continued use of the German language. More promising was the American Federation of Catholic Societies, a union of many Catholic social and charitable organizations. However, the constituent groups and most of the hierarchy had little interest in national action and, although Dietz was appointed director of a social secretariat and editor of a paper, he never had the funds or the audience to realize his goal.[32]

Reliance on voluntary charity had always been strong among American Catholics, and in this field significant developments took place after the turn of the century. The concept of charity was gradually broadened from a voluntary fulfilling of certain basic and permanent human needs carried out for the benefit of donor as well as recipient to a vision of charity as a guarantee of progress, an instrument for winning converts and a major tool for reforming society.[33] In 1910 Father William Kerby and a number of other leaders in the field founded the National Conference of Catholic Charities to bring order and consolidation to Catholic charitable endeavors and to enlighten the work with the findings and techniques of sociology and social work. The social problems of industrial society challenged traditional charitable practice and, increasingly, Catholic leaders were dissatisfied with a purely parochial approach which ignored the scientific study of the causes of poverty and the work of the non-Catholic and secular agencies. The efforts of Kerby and his associates were hampered by the aloofness of the religious orders, ethnic divisions, and the reluctance of Catholics to co-operate with non-Catholics in social welfare work. Kerby saw these problems as based on two fundamental prejudices: the conviction of the superiority of voluntary over professional social work and the belief that bigotry was inseparable from non-Catholic charitable activity. Kerby "more than any American Catholic before him appreciated that a knowledge of theoretical principles and a conviction of truth were not enough" for effective social action. He and the other leaders of the NCCC saw clearly that true social action had to be directed at the causes of suffering through social education and the promotion of legislation, but the problems they faced in gaining co-operation prevented effective efforts in this direction until the 1930's.[34]

Dietz, Kerby, Ryan, and a number of other Catholics working at the local level, brought about a vigorous expansion of Catholic social services in the years before World War I. They were developing a wider vision of Catholic social and charitable work, utilizing settlement houses and other agencies for the relief of distress and for the offsetting of those social pressures that could lead to the growth of socialism. Experience in such work together with the increasingly vocal efforts of Catholic publicists would eventually lead to a more positive approach to social action than the hitherto dominant antisocialism.[35]

World War I brought a real turning point in the development of Catholic social consciousness with the organization of the National Catholic War Council, reorganized after the war as the National Catholic Welfare Conference. Because it was not a canonical organization, the NCWC's decisions were not binding on the individual bishops, who remained supreme within their own dioceses. The NCWC was established to carry out the policies set at the annual meetings of the bishops, to serve as a clearing house of information for local and specialized Catholic groups, to co-ordinate Catholic efforts in various fields, and, when necessary, to represent the hierarchy's views on national affairs. An administrative board of five prelates was authorized to act for the hierarchy between annual meetings. Actual administration was handled by an executive director who presided over four departments, each headed by a bishop and administered by a director and staff. In 1919 the four departments covered the Catholic press, education, lay organizations, and social action. The task of the last department was to carry out official policies set by the hierarchy and, more important, to conduct educational campaigns to acquaint Catholics with the Church's teachings on social problems.[36] The structure of the NCWC left each department considerable autonomy and the Social Action Department, headed by the progressive bishop, Peter J. Muldoon of Rockford, Illinois, was able to adopt positions far in advance of the views of most bishops.

As director of the Social Action Department from 1919 to 1945 John A. Ryan put his personal stamp on its work. His influence was evident even before the department was established when the hierarchy published the so-called Bishops' Program of Social Reconstruction, a very progressive document drafted by Ryan and issued hastily by the administrative committee in 1919. Avoiding discussion of a "comprehensive scheme of reconstruction," the bishops instead concentrated on reforms that were "desirable and attainable." They called for public assistance to returning servicemen in finding work through a national system of employment exchanges, and urged the continuation of the United States Employment Service and the National War Labor Board. The program condemned the inefficiency and waste of monopolies, which should be abolished or controlled, and it endorsed the maintenance of wartime wage levels, equal pay for women, municipal housing for veterans, and a living wage by legislation. The bishops also supported a system of social insurance against unemployment, sickness, and old age, to be financed entirely by a tax on industry.

Such insurance, the bishops hoped, would be temporary; they looked forward to a time when high wages and a more equitable distribution of property would allow the worker to provide for himself against contingencies. The bishops further endorsed the right of labor to organize and urged the formation of joint labor-management committees that would provide structures for labor's participation in industrial decision making. Finally the program called for experiments in copartnership and in producers' and consumers' co-operatives as possible means for bringing about a wider distribution of productive property.[37]

In their annual meeting of 1919 the bishops joined in issuing a pastoral letter which dealt with many of the same issues in a tone perhaps more closely approximating the consensus of the hierarchy. Following Leo XIII closely, the bishops called for reform that would inspire men to turn away from materialism to recognition of the divine origin of man and society and the necessity for justice as the foundation of social order. Distressed by evidence of class hostility, the bishops called on workers and owners to recognize their mutual rights and obligations. Industry was defined as "a cooperative enterprise for the common good and not a contest between two parties for a restricted product." Unions should be supplemented by joint associations giving institutional expression to the mutual dependence of capital and labor and their common interest in industrial growth and expansion. The bishops condemned strikes and stated that "the public as a whole have a prior claim" that superseded the particular claims of the parties to the dispute. Accordingly, the bishops believed that when negotiations failed, labor-management controversies "should always be submitted to arbitration," for the only alternative was a contest of economic force with no reference to the demands of justice.[38]

In both documents the bishops emphasized the point that the status, dignity, and security of the workers, as well as their economic well-being, were involved in the social question. They shied away from a total scheme of reconstruction, looking to co-operation, copartnership, stock sharing, and joint organization, but not giving detailed attention to the problems of each of these methods. Similarly the need for State action was recognized and endorsed in principle, but the exact role of the State in social policy was left unclear. In general they placed more hope in private efforts and remained fearful of State power, without setting definite limits. These fears increased, rather than lessened, in the years following the war. The aged Cardinal Gibbons, for example, was no longer worried about socialism, but he was concerned about "the consolidating of the great public interests of the country in the authorities of the government itself." [39]

The publication of the Bishops' Program constituted a distinct advance on earlier American Catholic social thought, and it gave authoritative sanction to the work of the few active Catholic reformers. On the other hand it did not signal the start of a large-scale Catholic social movement. Indeed, in many ways the decade that followed was one of reaction in the Catholic community as in society at large. Conservatives denounced the 1919 statement as "partisan, pro-labor union, socialistic propaganda," [40] whereas the renewal of anti-Catholic agitation turned the attention of the bishops and Catholics generally away from political and economic problems. Even socially active Catholics became wary of association with secular liberals as issues involving the institutional rights and interests of the Church brought them into conflict and old fears of State interference in education, religion, and family life revived. In 1922 the administrative board of the NCWC issued a statement on "Paternalism in Government," which illustrated the conflict between the ideal of social justice and the fears of radicalism and the State—a conflict that characterized Catholic social attitudes. "The growth of bureaucracy in the United States is one of the most significant after-effects of the war," the bishops wrote.[41]

> This growth must be resolutely checked. Federal assistance and federal direction are in some cases beneficial and even necessary; but extreme bureaucracy is foreign to everything American. It is unconstitutional and undemocratic. It means officialdom, red tape, and prodigal waste of public money. It spells hordes of so-called experts and self perpetuating groups of politicians to regulate every detail of daily life. It would eventually sovietize our form of government. . . . The press, the home, the school and the Church have no greater enemy at the present time than the paternalistic and bureaucratic government which certain self-seeking elements are attempting to foist upon us.

The "Bolshevik menace" arising from the Russian Revolution and the "Red Scare" of 1919–20 in the United States revived deeply ingrained fears of radicalism among Church leaders. At the same time a number of domestic controversies pointedly reminded Catholics of their minority status, helping to muffle the reforming zeal of the new Social Action Department by turning attention away from public issues to matters related to Catholic security and status. The proposed child labor amendment to the Constitution, for example, was opposed almost unanimously by the hierarchy. Catholic opponents contended that the amendment was unnecessary because of the progress being made by state governments in eliminating the evil of child labor. More important, they pointed to the ambiguous wording of the amendment, which gave Congress the power to regulate the "labor" of children under eighteen. Many Catholics feared that this power could be used to interfere with domestic labor, thus undermining family life and subjecting parents to the dictation of the State. Regulation of child "labor" might also be interpreted as giving the federal government control over education, something that Church leaders had long regarded as contrary to the interests of the parochial schools. The fact that during this period the state of Oregon attempted to effectively destroy Catholic schools intensified this concern by reminding Catholics that the Protestant majority was capable of using political power to express its hostility toward the Church and its institutions. As a result, in states where Catholic political influence was significant, the full weight of the Church was thrown into the battle against the child labor amendment. In Massachusetts, for example, Boston's Cardinal O'Connell ordered the clergy to instruct the faithful to oppose the "socialistic legislation" and he attempted to get John Ryan, one of the amendment's few Catholic supporters, ousted from his teaching position at Catholic University.[42]

Ryan and his assistant, Father Raymond McGowan futilely tried to stem the tide by pointing to the continued existence of the evil of child labor and the unfair competition this brought to states with high standards. They argued that Catholic adherence to the conservative side on social issues when reform was necessary would bring them blame for the hardships that would inevitably follow, to which there would be severe anti-Catholic reaction.[43]

During the twenties other issues aggravated Catholics and raised anew the question of the compatibility of their faith with American institutions. Catholic opposition to Prohibition irritated many Protestants, and the Ku Klux Klan appeared to justify Catholic suspicions that Protestants were not devoted to constitutional guarantees. The fierce persecution of the Church in Mexico infuriated American Catholics but seemed to disturb other Americans very little, again strengthening the charges of bigotry and hypocrisy which Catholics were quick to apply to Protestants and "liberals." The stereotype of the Catholic as an ignorant tool of a selfish and power-seeking hierarchy came to be matched by Catholic notions of the Protestant as a "Tory" because of his views on Prohibition, and the liberal as a hypocrite because of his failure to denounce religious persecution in Mexico.[44]

All these sources of conflict were exposed before 1928 and Al Smith's campaign and the accompanying propaganda served to perpetuate and accentuate the isolation and insecurity of American Catholics. Individual Catholics had always seen the problem of pluralism on a practical level and thus had regarded citations of Catholic patriotism in wartime as sufficient answer to all questions regarding the possible conflicts of Catholicism and Americanism. Moreover the Catholic layman had for the most part accepted the American divorce of religious and secular concerns and had been, in his political and social views, more self-consciously American than Catholic. The impact of papal social and political teachings on bishops and priests was slight, but there was even less of an impact on the laity. It was only natural that Al Smith's initial reaction to Charles Marshall's attack on Catholicism on the basis of the political teachings of Leo XIII was to ask advisers, "Will someone please tell me what the hell a papal encyclical is!" [45] For lay people who had grown up in heavily Catholic city ghettoes the challenge to their Americanism in 1928 was the most severe of a number of shocks which retarded their mature emergence into the pluralistic structure of American religious life.

It is clear then that Catholic social thought in the United States was only slightly developed in 1929. With some significant exceptions, American Catholics were largely out of contact with American reform movements. Their knowledge of the social teachings of Leo XIII was scanty and centered on the negative aspects of his thought. The high promise of 1919 had not been realized as the hierarchy's social leadership faded in the twenties. Much of this was due to the paradoxical nature of Catholic history in America; the Church developed an isolated ghetto atmosphere, avoided contacts with other religions, and built an extensive network of Catholic schools and organizations. At the same time, it adopted many of the prevailing social and political prejudices of the society around it. Not until the tensions between Catholic and American commitments were sharpened and clarified by events would a significant number of Catholics be led to re-examine their position. Nineteen twenty-nine found Catholics more self-conscious and defensive than ever. But the end of immigration, the work of the Social Action Department and the increasing number of educated lay Catholics evident from new publications like *Commonweal, Thought,* and *The New Scholasticism* which appeared during the twenties, helped lay the groundwork for the development of the truly American Catholicism for which Hecker, Ireland, and others had struggled. It was not until the 1930's, however, "that we can really speak in realistic terms of a widespread Catholic social consciousness and with it a willingness not simply to adapt to the community life but also to work to transform it." [46]

III

Catholic Social Thought and
the New Deal, 1933–1936

The Great Depression shattered Catholic complacency and challenged the traditional confidence of Americans in the material beneficence and natural harmonies of an individualistic, free-enterprise economy. Most came to appreciate the need for change to temper the harsh effects of the competitive order, if not to fundamentally alter the structure and spirit of national life. American Catholics, heavily concentrated in the ranks of labor and the lower middle class, were profoundly shaken by the disaster. Their political leaders had never translated their highly functional approach to government into a systematic theory of reform, so that once the usual efforts of municipal relief and public works failed, they possessed no meaningful response. Church leaders had not prepared their people for political or social action, but a distinctive Catholic position did exist and after the publication of *Quadragesimo Anno* Catholics had a guide for analyzing their ills and evaluating proposals for action. In the United States, where the attention given *Rerum Novarum* had been minimal, the new encyclical was greeted in the confident expectation that the confusion and adversity of depression would provide fertile soil for the Pope's message. All seemed to agree, with typical exaggeration, that the encyclical was "one of the greatest pronouncements on the social question" to which

47

society, searching for a more just and humane order without dictatorship or revolution, would lend a willing ear.[1]

Even before the appearance of *Quadragesimo Anno* Catholic spokesmen, overwhelmed by the depth and severity of the collapse, had moved beyond the apathy and negativeness of the twenties. By 1931 Father Charles E. Coughlin had become one of the nation's most controversial men by giving clear expression to popular shock at the experience of "want in the midst of plenty."[2] He was joined by more respectable Catholic leaders like Archbishop John T. McNicholas of Cincinnati, one of the most influential members of the hierarchy, who repeatedly denounced the huge gap between "the comparatively small group possessing fabulous wealth and exercising the enormous influence that wealth confers" and those denied "the very food and shelter necessary to keep body and soul together."[3] Nothing better measured the impact of the Depression than the frequency with which Catholic leaders like McNicholas attacked "the monstrous abuses of capitalism and the injustices of our present economic system," a system which, according to Father Paul Blakely of *America*, "repudiates nearly every principle upon which [Leo XIII] lays emphasis."[4] Even Boston's conservative Cardinal O'Connell, who regarded Coughlin as a demagogue, blamed the Depression on the avarice of the rich and feared that their callous disregard of suffering would aggravate class hostility. The administrative committee of the NCWC agreed. "The real authors of violent and bloody revolutions in our times are not the radicals and communists," the bishops charged, "but the callous and autocratic possessors of wealth and power who use their positions and their riches to oppress their fellows."[5]

Most Catholic leaders initially regarded the fundamental problem as one of moral weakness. The "root cause" of the Depression, according to oil executive Michael O'Shaughnessy, was "human greed, the uncontrolled profit motive, the inordinate desire for gain," and the solution lay in personal and collective moral regeneration. Accordingly O'Shaughnessy attempted to mobilize spritual energies in a Catholic league for social justice, whose members would pledge themselves to prayer, sacrifice, and personal efforts to implement social justice in their neighborhoods and jobs. With the active support of important bishops and of the Catholic press, the league spread rapidly in the early thirties, manifesting the conviction of many that the causes of social problems were moral and religious and required corresponding means of reform and renewal.[6] As the editors of *Commonweal* put the case, "Not until the principles taught by religion guide the counsels of men will those counsels issue in the permanent improvement of society." [7]

Despite the support which *Quadragesimo Anno* gave to the argument that moral considerations were primary, Catholic leaders, like the Pope, went on to call for immediate and long-range reforms to alleviate suffering, end unemployment, and initiate recovery. Capitalism itself was on trial, and if reform was not forthcoming, the result would be "revolution or confiscation." [8] Even O'Shaughnessy, who opposed government spending, regulation of business, and social insurance, presented detailed proposals for economic reorganization through trade associations controlled by boards representing management, labor, and the public, a structure in which "cooperation in industry might take the place of competition." [9] His program, which blended the suggestions of Pius XI with schemes proposed by American business organizations, was only one of many proposals from Catholics demanding basic changes in American economic life.

Nevertheless the old fears of governmental action were difficult to overcome. Some denied that the needed "renovation and humanizing" of capitalism could be accomplished through coercion, whereas others feared that the pendulum might swing too far in a collectivist direction. With the examples of Italy and Russia in mind, many Catholics saw a threat of State absolutism

in demands for reform occasioned by the Depression. Father
Blakely of *America*, like many others, believed that the growth
of federal bureaucracy threatened personal liberty and religious
freedom. Although he denounced American capitalists as the
world's most selfish and arrogant, Blakely regarded the American government as "so ignorant and corrupt we should hesitate
long before using it as a club." [10] Regarding the Constitution as
their bulwark against potential enemies, Catholics, including
those who supported public action, held firmly to the principle
"that the good of the Union is best provided for in a regime
under which each state is encouraged to exercise the greatest
possible independence in providing for the well-being of its
population." [11]

Offsetting these fears were the pressing needs of the Catholic
population. Time seemed to be running out, Catholic charities
were swamped and discontent became more and more vocal. Led
by the bishops, Catholic spokesmen gradually put aside their
fears and turned to Washington for relief. In a pastoral letter
issued in late 1931 the hierarchy called upon the federal government to assist the unemployed and went on to urge reform along
the lines of the 1919 program.[12] As the Depression deepened,
Catholic leaders came to agree with Detroit's Catholic mayor,
Frank Murphy, that "Governments should do their best, not
least, to look after their stricken people in the time of famine,
and that is what this is." [13]

Drawing upon the long-unrecognized flexibility of the principle of subsidiarity, Catholics began to argue for government
action on frankly pragmatic grounds. "Government in the
United States is dedicated to the people and not to a theory,
however pseudo-sacrosanct," the editors of *Commonweal* stated.
"For ourselves we think that the future depends upon what use
we of the present make of our collective powers." [14] President
Hoover's failure to act decisively to allay discontent angered and
scandalized Catholic spokesmen. His policy of awaiting the

automatic operation of economic laws left him, according to *Commonweal*, "humanly speaking deeply touched by the distress but philosophically incapable of doing anything about it." [15] The 1932 election seemed a clear confrontation between those who saw the Depression as the result of economic laws beyond human control and those who felt it resulted from greed and stupidity. On this basis Catholics generally welcomed the election of Franklin D. Roosevelt and eagerly awaited his program.[16]

Many factors contributed to the favorable political response of Catholics to the New Deal. Irish Catholics had always given overwhelming support to Democratic administrations, but Franklin Roosevelt also attracted "new immigrant" groups less clearly identified with his party. In part this resulted from the fact that many New Deal programs were designed to improve the lot of those classes among whom Catholics were most heavily represented. In addition, Roosevelt recognized Catholic political power and prestige by the appointment of prominent laymen to high administration positions and by his public friendship with well-known ecclesiastics.[17] The attraction which many Catholics felt for the New Deal was reinforced by their most articulate religious leaders between 1933 and 1936, when Catholic intellectuals and publicists paid considerable attention to social and economic problems and adopted positions sympathetic to reform. The pressures of the Depression reduced minority fears and helped create a climate of opinion receptive to the use of government power to alleviate suffering, end unemployment, restore prosperity, and reform American business practices. By 1936, however, these pressures had relaxed and divisions reappeared in the Catholic community so that, during the election year, American Catholicism again spoke with many voices on the issues of the day.

Whatever differences developed later, Catholic journalists and writers greeted the New Deal with nearly universal enthusiasm,

convinced that a positive sense of justice and a desire to serve all
the people inspired Franklin D. Roosevelt and his policies.
"Practically every act of Mr. Roosevelt's has been motivated by
a Christian philosophy," wrote Patrick Scanlan, editor of the
normally conservative Brooklyn *Tablet*, while *Sign* magazine
praised the President's "forthright and genuine Christian sentiments," and added that he stood "among the rulers of the world
as one of the foremost advocates of the principles of Pope Leo
XIII." [18] Three months after taking office, the President received an honorary degree from Catholic University at which
time New York's Cardinal Hayes praised his program in glowing
terms, and pointed out its striking similarity to Catholic teachings.[19]

Such comparisons appeared frequently in Catholic circles. As
early as the Commonwealth Club speech during the campaign,
some had seen a close relationship between papal social doctrine
and Roosevelt's approach to social problems. Bishop Karl J.
Alter of Toledo thought that the President's inaugural address
"breathes the spirit of our Holy Father's recent encyclical,"
offering hope that "Christian social ideas" would replace "the
false pagan philosophy which has dominated much of our
thought and action in recent years." [20] The President himself referred to *Rerum Novarum* and *Quadragesimo Anno* when
speaking to Catholic audiences, and friendly Catholics told party
leaders that if Catholics "once understood clearly the identity of
idea between the administration's efforts and the Pope's recent
program of social justice, they would be more likely to give it
enthusiastic support through thick and thin." [21]

Catholic attention focused particularly on the National Industrial Recovery Act, the heart of the New Deal's recovery program, which appropriated $3.3 billion for public works and es-
tablished a system of government-sanctioned industrial codes
aimed at eliminating cut-throat competition and insuring minimum standards of wages and hours. Catholics predisposed to
view American developments in terms of papal guidelines were

bound to be struck by the apparent similarity of the National Recovery Administration, with its co-operative approach to industrial government, and the vocational group proposals of Pius XI. Almost without exception Catholic leaders welcomed the legislation and even those most fearful of government centralization urged their fellow Catholics to back the President.[22] *Catholic Action*, official organ of the National Catholic Welfare Conference, held it to be "a matter of some congratulations for Catholics that some of the most important proposals in the encyclical are at least partially incorporated in the law." [23] Similarly Father Francis Haas, head of the National Catholic School of Social Service, argued in numerous speeches and articles that the NRA constituted "the most momentous experiment our country has yet made in the field of industry and business" and that "in broad outline" it followed the program of *Quadragesimo Anno*.[24] Although recognizing weaknesses in the administration and urging greater labor representation and firmer control of prices, organizations like the National Catholic Alumni Federation, the National Council of Catholic Women, and the National Conference of Catholic Charities, and journals like *America, Commonweal*, and the *Catholic World* minimized their reservations and lent their full support to the NRA.[25]

The NRA drew a disproportionate share of attention but Catholic spokesmen did not ignore other phases of the New Deal. Agricultural policy interested some, and comments on the Agricultural Adjustment Act were generally favorable. Throughout the decade, however, those who were concerned with the plight of the farmer tended to give more attention to co-operatives, resettlement, and the cultural advantages of rural life, than to the concrete problems of farm prices that dominated New Deal policies.[26] Despite persisting fears of socialism, Catholics endorsed Roosevelt's program for the Tennessee Valley almost without reservation. *Catholic Action* regarded TVA as "a vast experiment in Christian sociology." [27]

The right of each person to the means of earning a decent

livelihood was a basic principle of Catholic social teachings and led most Catholics to support proposals for social insurance. Disagreement arose over the relative roles of federal and state governments and the problem of contribution. Some argued that the entire cost should be borne out of general taxation whereas others reiterated the position of the 1919 Bishops' Program that the burden should be placed upon industry. *Commonweal*'s suggestion of joint labor-management contribution anticipated the Social Security Bill of 1935 which provided a federal-state system of unemployment insurance and a federal system of old-age pensions, both financed through joint contributions of employers and employees.[28] Catholic observers praised the law as closely corresponding to the principles of Pius XI and Leo XIII. John A. Lapp, for example, thought the program "by far the greatest achievement of the present administration—or of any administration in half a century." *America* found the legislation satisfactory, although some of its provisions were perhaps unconstitutional. The *Tablet*, which had denounced the bill when first presented, thought it one of the New Deal's best measures when passed; the editor was especially pleased by the wide latitude left to the states.[29]

Throughout the first two years of the New Deal, then, American Catholicism spoke with a high degree of unanimity on behalf of social and economic reform. Interested Catholics found in the papal encyclicals ample justification for government action to check competition and end business domination. Applying the principle of subsidiarity, few could see any alternative to stronger intervention by the national government in the nation's economic life. Dean Paul Kiniery of Loyola University in Chicago argued that the only alternative to government regulation was big business domination—plutocracy—which would necessarily benefit selfish interests. Recognizing that the disruption that would result from continued distress posed a far greater threat to the Church than did a stronger national government, he felt that Catholics should present a united front favorable to social legislation.[30]

The support of some Catholic social action leaders for the New Deal went beyond education and publicity. John A. Ryan was appointed by Roosevelt to the Industrial Appeals Board of NRA and to the President's Committee on Farm Tenancy, and he was consulted on the drafting of the Social Security Act. Father Francis Haas served in a number of New Deal posts while undertaking to defend Roosevelt's policies before the Catholic public. Haas was most active on labor matters, serving on the National Labor Board and the Labor Advisory Board of the Works Progress Administration. Father John J. Burke, executive director of the NCWC, and Father Maurice Sheehy, assistant to the Rector of Catholic University, were friends of the President who occasionally undertook to smooth over difficulties between the administration and the Catholic community.[31]

Roosevelt himself carefully cultivated Catholic support. Prominent laymen like Joseph P. Kennedy, James Farley, Frank Murphy, and Leo T. Crowley served in the administration and sometimes addressed their fellow Catholics on its behalf. The White House staff was on the lookout for occasions to manifest the administration's attitude toward the Church through speeches before Catholic organizations or messages to prelates on festive occasions. Cardinal Hayes, Cardinal O'Connell, Archbishop Mooney of Detroit, and many others were recipients of presidential greetings. The best investment of this sort came in the early months of the administration when Roosevelt took the opportunity of Cardinal Mundelein's "name day" to send him a message to add to his collection of presidential autographs. Mundelein soon became the President's closest friend in the hierarchy. In 1935, when Catholics were incensed by Roosevelt's Mexican policy, the Cardinal heaped praise on him in ceremonies at Notre Dame. In other times of crisis: after Roosevelt's "quarantine speech," during the 1936 campaign, in the midst of the controversy over the Supreme Court, and again during the debate over revision of the neutrality laws, Mundelein was ready to send a message to the President, issue a carefully phrased public statement, or lunch with the Chief Executive amid proper photographic accompaniment.[32]

Yet even the most enthusiastic Catholic supporters of the New Deal had some reservations. Ernest P. Ament, a graduate student at Catholic University, presented a doctoral dissertation that summarized the position of many pro-New Deal Catholics. The Roosevelt administration, Ament argued, was bringing order out of the chaos of laissez-faire individualism and advancing toward a Catholic theory of the State as the custodian of the common good. While the "general aim and principles of the NIRA" were admirable, the program nevertheless was "shortsighted." The crisis of depression had created a widespread spirit of co-operation which might have made possible the construction of "an organic society." "But there was no clear goal of a society composed of integrated occupational groups . . . placed before the minds of the people by the leaders of the New Deal." Ament cited many specific criticisms: employer-dominated codes, wages that did not reach a level of decency and were insufficient to provide full employment, and lack of concern for a wider diffusion of ownership. The New Deal, he concluded, had been less bold than the Pope: [33]

> From an ethical point of view, the basic concepts of the Recovery Act are on the whole conformable to the ideas of social justice proclaimed by the Sovereign Pontiffs. If at times the principles are not worked out to their ultimate logical conclusions, the defect is one of incompleteness rather than contradiction with Catholic socio-economic teachings. The NIRA stopped short of genuine social reform.

This position reflected the sentiments of many who welcomed the New Deal's attempt to close the gap that existed between political freedom and economic dependence, to make concrete the abstract rights guaranteed Americans by their constitution. Those who were aware of Catholic social teachings, however, believed that something more was needed and, however laudable in themselves the objectives of the Roosevelt administration might be, the New Deal's enactments were but way-stations on the road to a just and Christian social order.

As time went on, it became clear that the NRA was not reforming the economic system, although it and other New Deal measures had relieved some of the pressure of poverty and unemployment which had been felt in 1933. This relaxation of tension was evident in mounting criticism of the New Deal in the Catholic press, criticism apparently muffled for months by the sense of crisis and emergency.

There were only a few business-oriented attacks on the New Deal in Catholic periodicals, but several prominent Catholics who claimed to be supporters of the New Deal were disturbed by attacks on business leadership by prominent administration spokesmen. Father Edmund A. Walsh of Georgetown University wrote Commerce Secretary Daniel C. Roper that efforts made by New Dealers like Rexford Tugwell to divide the American people would paralyze business co-operation with the government and hamper the achievement of the goal of social justice. Like others who adopted a similar point of view, Walsh believed that only "persuasion and enlightened social consciousness," not "compulsion," could bring permanent recovery and reform.[34] The conservative implications of this position were recognized by Father John A. Ryan, who charged proponents of personal moral reform with ignorance or a dishonest desire to prevent any significant change.[35]

More frequent were complaints about high prices and the domination of NRA by big business. Proponents of corporate reform like the strongly anticapitalist Edward Koch sharply attacked the recovery program as "a general conspiracy" to cheat the public and "retain the large owners in peaceful possession and even, by favoritism in the matter of prices, to give them a temporary advantage over the small." [36] Similar complaints came from supporters of distributism, agrarianism, and cooperation, all of whom disliked the suspension of the antitrust laws and hoped for an active policy of political and economic decentralization.

Such criticisms were of slight importance compared to the revival of old fears of federal encroachment on personal liberty and state independence. Growing concern with government centralization and the radical tone of the New Deal was reflected in reaction to the ending of NRA by the Supreme Court. Both *America* and the *Catholic World* welcomed the decision as vindicating government of laws and not of men but they warned against return to the pre-Depression situations.[37] While pro-New Deal Catholics called for constitutional amendment to allow the enactment of a new and improved NRA, others felt that it was possible to secure needed reforms within the existing constitutional framework. *America* and its columnist, Paul Blakely, the *Catholic World* and its editor, James Gillis, and the Brooklyn *Tablet*'s managing editor, Patrick Scanlan, joined Father Coughlin in a growing reaction against the New Deal.

In the early days of the Roosevelt administration, *America* consistently defended the President, arguing that despite the New Deal's shortcomings, its policies were infinitely preferable to those of the twenties. Yet the confidence of the editors that reform could be accomplished without permanently extending federal power and destroying the Constitution gradually diminished. For a time they wavered between support and opposition, but in the end they chose to abide by the Constitution, which became for them "the sole test of the validity of legislation." [38] Although the journal flirted editorially with the idea of constitutional amendment, Father Paul Blakely pointed the future direction by arguing that increasing federal authority over the economy necessarily weakened local initiative, reduced the states to dependencies of Washington, and destroyed the traditional American form of government. Instead, he insisted, the states, either acting separately or through interstate compacts with minimal assistance from the federal government, should deal with the nation's social and economic problems.[39]

Managing editor Wilfrid Parsons was far less doctrinaire than Blakely; indeed, he was one of the most balanced and thoughtful critics of the New Deal. Initially, Parsons enthusiastically endorsed the New Deal's effort to bring about a more equitable distribution of the products of industry by means of centralized planning and limitations on competition. Comparing "the philosophy of the New Deal," discovered in the writings of Henry Wallace, with that of the papal encyclicals, Parsons found many similarities: both recognized that men could no longer use or misuse their property without regard to general social consequence, and both saw the need for some form of economic control. Nevertheless, Parsons believed that the New Deal was essentially transitionary, a pause between laissez-faire and some form of collectivism. The admirable objectives of reform—wider distribution of productive property, limitation of excess profits and of competition, and economic planning aimed at the attainment of a qualitatively better life for all—could be achieved by federal action, but at the cost of individual liberty. Only a system of vocational groups could bring planning and control without regimentation. Father Parsons wished to go beyond the New Deal, but he was not prepared to do so by further increasing the power of the federal government.[40]

Parsons's doubts about the New Deal were slight when compared to those of his colleagues at the *Catholic World* or the Brooklyn *Tablet*. Father Gillis revised his views more drastically than did the editors of *America*. He defended the New Deal and the NRA for months, but by early 1936 reckless spending, the extension of executive prerogative, the leftist tendencies of some New Dealers, and in particular, disrespectful treatment of the

Constitution and attacks on the Supreme Court, all made Father Gillis extremely suspicious. Communist support for Roosevelt in the 1936 campaign intensified his fears, leading him to define the issues of the election as "the decline of democracy, the increase in centralization of government powers, and the possible emergence of the absolute state." [41] The emergency was over and Father Gillis, although not completely abandoning the President, demanded that Roosevelt reassure those disturbed by his power, his dislike of criticism, and his flirtation with the Left.

More pronounced in his dislike of the New Deal was the *Tablet*'s managing editor, Patrick Scanlan. A strong current of anti-intellectualism was evident in his paper's hatred of experts, "impractical idealists," and college professors, who supposedly controlled the otherwise moderate and sensible President. Although the *Tablet*, like other Catholic papers which criticized the administration, originally warmly endorsed Roosevelt and his anti-Depression efforts, its editor hailed the Supreme Court as "the citadel of defense of real American liberties" when it struck down NRA. The New Deal had been acceptable as long as it confined its attention to wages and hours; it had been ruined by "its adoption of so many impractical, absurd, and seemingly insane projects—most of them proposed by the so-called brains trust with the grand object of wasting millions of dollars." [42] The New Deal's job, Scanlan believed, was "to provide recovery rather than to institute vast reforms." Reform could come only from below; evils could not be eliminated by a far-away government dominated by a vast, impersonal bureaucracy.

In addition, nondomestic issues made Scanlan apprehensive. Recognition of Soviet Russia awakened the *Tablet*'s vigilance, and Roosevelt's refusal to denounce religious persecution in Mexico seemed a direct slap at American Catholics. When Notre Dame gave Roosevelt an honorary degree shortly after his refusal to answer a Knights of Columbus petition on Mexico, the paper lashed out at the university for breaking a united front of hostility toward the President. The Mexican issue, coming on top of Russian recognition and coupled with the rising prominence in the administration of such allegedly leftist advisors as Rexford Tugwell, Harry Hopkins, and Felix Frankfurter, led Scanlan into intense opposition to Roosevelt and the New Deal.[43] Although endorsing no candidate in 1936, the *Tablet* urged Catholics to resist the efforts of politicians like Farley, Kennedy, and even John A. Ryan to capture the Catholic vote for Roosevelt. Scanlan also warned that if their interests continued to be ignored, Catholics might organize and vote as a bloc.[44] On the eve of the election, Scanlan noted the support which Roosevelt received from Communists; he said that Catholics should vote only for men who would safeguard the nation and religion and should remember that the "reds" would exact tribute for any support they might bring the winner.[45]

The change from support to opposition was even more dramatic in the case of Father Coughlin, whose disenchantment with the New Deal led him to organize and direct a third party political campaign in the 1936 election. Most Catholic commentators found his economic arguments unconvincing and his political activities unwise. Nevertheless, many were greatly concerned by the priest's involvement in politics, both because of the harm he could do the President and, more important, because of the harm he could do the Church by rekindling the fires of anti-Catholicism smoldering since 1928.[46] For most leaders of the Church the best policy was one of dignified aloofness, to be broken only to deplore the occasional excesses of Coughlin's rhetoric. But some, more committed to the reforms of the New Deal, took an active course. Father Ryan rendered the most important service with a national radio address sponsored by the Democratic National Committee in which he assailed Coughlin and defended the President and his advisors against the charge that they were sympathetic to communism.[47] Bishops James H. Ryan and Bernard J. Mahoney wrote letters rebutting the allegations made by Coughlin, while Roosevelt's friend Cardinal Mundelein disassociated the Church from the Coughlinites and hinted at his own support for the President.[48] Father Maurice Sheehy of Catholic University used his influence with the hierarchy and the Catholic press to offset anti-Roosevelt sentiment, while prominent priests and laymen offered their active support to the Democratic cause.[49]

There were many reasons for American Catholics to disavow Coughlinism, but the American Liberty League, with Al Smith among its leaders, and the Republican party, were closer to the center of the political spectrum and might have offered potentially greater attractions for essentially conservative American Catholics. Their arguments against Roosevelt were expressed in traditional American rhetoric, and they strongly emphasized the constitutional factors which worried so many Catholic spokesmen. In attempting to appeal to American Catholics, however, the conservative movement suffered from serious handicaps. For one thing, American Catholics were historically weakly represented in the business class which was most directly involved in the conservative reaction. On the contrary, they had always been associated with the working class and organized labor. Although some upward ascent on the social scale was evident in the thirties, the rise of great numbers of Catholics into the middle and upper classes had only begun.[50]

Though American Catholics had shared in the worship of business that characterized the twenties, they were disillusioned like other Americans by the experience of the Depression, which had particularly harsh effects upon the economic classes to which they belonged. In addition, if they had often harkened to business rhetoric, the Coughlin experience showed an ability to assimilate Populist symbols as well. Most American Catholics tended to react, particularly in hard times, on the basis of their pocketbooks, their aspirations, and the ideology of their class and section. Problems of status, of ethnic and cultural identity, of institutional Church interests all played an important part in the social life of American Catholics in the thirties, but voting patterns indicated that economic interest and traditional loyalty to the Democratic party overshadowed these other factors in determining Catholic political behavior.

The minority of the Catholic community who sought to determine political loyalties and intellectual positions on the basis of Christian teachings, had even stronger reasons for disassociation from Al Smith and the conservative Liberty League, for they upheld those policies of the twenties, economic individualism and laissez-faire, that had been condemned by Popes Leo XIII and Piux XI. On this basis most Catholic editors denounced the Liberty League and many accepted the conclusion of Bishop Bernard Mahoney of Sioux Falls that the constitutional argument against the New Deal had no basis in Catholic teaching. "The Church, the great guardian of human liberties, sees nothing in the recent enactments over which to be alarmed," Bishop Mahoney wrote. "In fact, despite the possibility of future abuses—a possibility that will always confront us—she can safely place her stamp of approval in the interests of social justice upon the broad and human philosophy that underlies the national legislation of the changing social order of America today." [51]

The sharpest attacks on the philosophy expressed by the Liberty League came from Father Ignatius Cox of Fordham University. He berated the league's slogans of individual liberty and argued that the political freedom it so eloquently defended was meaningless without corresponding economic freedom. The "real danger" to the United States was not communism, he warned Al Smith and the Liberty League in a radio address, but "the economic liberalism you sponsor. Your system and your principles," he told them, "are the cancerous growth eating at the vitals of our American social organism." [52] Cox went beyond other Catholics in his condemnation of the greed and selfishness of "our immoral economic order," and he denounced in the strongest terms defenders of the individualism and economic dictatorship which were characteristic of that order. Cox's radio speeches in answer to Smith, together with the editorials of the *Tablet* and the *Catholic World* and the political activities of Father Coughlin and Monsignor Ryan, were symptomatic of the increasingly "bitter divisions among American Catholics on the subject of Social Justice and the papal teachings." [53]

Despite rising controversy about the New Deal, however, there remained as late as 1936 a very wide area of agreement among most Catholic social critics, with notable exceptions like Father Coughlin and the Brooklyn *Tablet*. This was illustrated by the publication in January of that year of a pamphlet, *Organized Social Justice—An Economic Program for the United States Applying Pius XI's Great Encyclical on Social Life.* Among the 131 signers of the document were Ryan and Father Raymond McGowan of the Social Action Department of the NCWC, Dorothy Day of the Catholic Worker movement, Father Gillis of the *Catholic World*, George Shuster of *Commonweal,* Edgar Schmeidler of the Catholic Rural Life movement, and Fathers Husslein, LaFarge, and Parsons of *America*. Others who did not sign, like Michael O'Shaughnessy, had only slight reservations about the document itself.[54]

The program condemned unregulated competition and urged the re-enactment of the NIRA. It called for wages and hours legislation that would insure "continuous employment, a decent livelihood and adequate security for all workers," and agricultural legislation that would bring producers similar benefits. The signers urged the government to provide for the well-being and prosperity of society as a whole, the protection of the poor and the workers, and the enforcement of the social obligations of property ownership. Significantly the manifesto concluded that "these and many other social obligations of public authority" would have to be performed mainly by the federal government since industry was "national in its scope and effects." The sole alternative to a constitutional amendment broadening the power of the federal government to deal with such matters was inaction, so that critics who hoped "that the thing can be done by the forty-eight states" were in reality upholding the continuation of laissez-faire and unlimited competition.

Yet, the program added, legislation by itself was inadequate and could lead to totalitarianism. Labor organization was a "right and necessity," while collective bargaining had to be carried forward to a system of joint organization of capital and labor into vocational groups. These groups would maintain standards of wages, hours, prices, and business practices, they would enable labor to share responsibility for industrial policy making, and they would prevent dictatorship by keeping "immediate and day to day control in the hands of the agents of production."

The object of these proposals was "to build an economic order within a governmental order," an economy of partnership between government at all levels and "the self-governing, democratically organized membership of the industries, of farming, of trade, and of the professions." If labor had been given full representation in drawing up the codes, NRA would have been "fairly comparable" to the papal program. Catholic efforts should be directed, the signers believed, at overcoming the obstacles of business hostility, incomplete organization, and constitutional inadequacy. Moral reform was recognized as necessary, but the signers professed to dislike assigning it priority; instead both moral and economic reform were needed and had to be developed simultaneously. The occupational-group system had to be sought through legislation, organization, moral reform, and education, and its realization was "the only arrangement that will hold America safe from Fascism or Communism."

Organized Social Justice clearly reflected the ideas of Fathers Ryan and McGowan, who had drafted it, and the program contained all the ambiguities and theoretical difficulties of the encyclical on which it was based. Most important the separation of economic and political life was theoretically unsound and practically impossible. On the one hand lay the danger of political domination of such a system, for all admitted that the State exercised at least supervisory authority over the semi-autonomous economic orders. In Italy and Austria similar corporate programs had in reality become mechanisms for the domination of society by a monolithic party bureaucracy. If, as Pius XI insisted in distinguishing his program from that of the Fascists, the State was to be denied any but the most general powers, the problem remained of how to enforce decisions within the economic order and, equally important, how to give central control and direction to economic activity. To avoid government or party dictation, one would have to assume a natural harmony of interests, one of the tenets of the liberal individualism which Catholics attacked. Even if NRA had full labor participation, only State authority and direction could prevent the "orders" from degenerating into mere interest groups. As the middle-class progressives had seen earlier, labor, once organized, was not averse to joining with capital to secure benefits for the industry as a whole at the expense of the consumer and the common good.

The dilemma of this kind of Catholic corporatism is inherent in its natural law basis, for like St. Thomas, modern corporatists assume a single purpose in the life of society as of the individual. Within the "common good" is included the notion of a priority of ends, the highest of which is the salvation of individuals. Men should recognize this end, and if they do, it can be assumed that the result will be a consensus on the moral values of Catholic natural law thought and this in turn will dictate agreement on the material components of the common good.[55] In Europe Catholic leaders were willing to use the power of the authoritarian State to impose moral values in the vain hope that, once society had been restored to its Christian basis, the need for State intervention in the social sphere would disappear. In countries where the Church was a minority, Catholics hesitated to give such power to the secular State and hoped instead for the development of autonomous groups by organization from below. Their problems increased because the threat of social upheaval denied them time to await widespread return to the necessary moral basis, and immediate organization of a corporate system could come only through State action or delegation of power to joint bodies of capital and labor, which lacked the disinterested concern for the common good needed for the proper operation of the new order. Thus it was that Catholic leaders who held conflicting views of the State, unions, and business could agree on the occupational group order but could never define the nature of that system or the exact manner in which it would be created.

American Catholics remained very conscious of their minority status; although they rejoiced at the recognition of their importance symbolized by their prominent role in New Deal politics, they were aware that there was no lack of evidence of continued Catholic impotence or of the hostility of important segments of American society to Catholic interests. The recognition of Russia, the apathy toward religious persecution in Mexico, and, most important, the near unanimous opposition of articulate American opinion to the Catholic position on the Spanish Civil War, all worked to perpetuate among American Catholics the sense of alienation and minority consciousness which had dominated their thought since the middle of the nineteenth century. Evidence of Catholic isolation and weakness could be found also in the increasing propaganda of birth control advocates, liberal hostility toward the Legion of Decency, indifference to demands for assistance to parochial schools, and the supposed decline in the nation's moral tone.

This situation kept alive and accentuated the fear of the secular State so characteristic of nineteenth-century Catholicism. On

the other hand, evidence of Catholic assimilation and respectabil-
ity, which could be found by those who looked for it, helped
some to overcome these fears. Thus, Catholics could and did
differ over the merits of State action on social problems on the
basis of their view of their own relative security within American society.

Papal doctrine, when interpreted in the light of differing
assessments of the empirical situation, could offer support in
both directions. John Ryan and Patrick Scanlan could draw on
the writings of the popes to justify their divergent attitudes
toward social action by the federal government. The peculiar
American federal system added to the difficulty, necessitating
interpretive application of the papal concept of the State to a
nation with constitutionally decentralized government. Given
these problems, Catholics naturally were likely to divide according to such essentially extraneous factors as economic or institutional interest, degree of social assimilation, or level of group
consciousness.

Catholic thought offered a clear mandate for action in the
crisis conditions of 1932. The situation called for, and the
bishops demanded, immediate steps to alleviate suffering and distress; few were prepared to bicker over constitutional niceties.
Questions of reform and reconstruction, however, involved no
such mandate and Catholics had to engage in the difficult process
of evaluating the demands of conflicting religious, social, and
political commitments. The most divisive aspect of the debates
that resulted from this process arose out of the conflict between
the loyalty of Catholics to ideals of social justice and their
equally strong commitment to the American Constitution,
which seemed to many to hinder the realization of these ideals.[56]
The constitutional issue went to the very heart of the problems
of the American Church in the thirties. Institutionally it had
been very successful in the United States. Despite pervasive and
often violent anti-Catholicism, the Church had succeeded in

erecting religious, educational, and charitable institutions unsurpassed in any Catholic country. The educational system in particular was a source of great pride, and the American hierarchy
and their flock were determined to safeguard it at all cost. This
success Catholics often attributed to the constitutional arrangements of the United States. They saw the Constitution as their
safeguard against Protestant and secular enemies. While most
Americans saw threats to the traditional constitutional structure
in terms of economic and civil liberty, Catholics in addition considered the effect of change upon the institutional liberty of the
Church.[57]

As for the New Deal itself, the unity of Catholic support in
the early months obscured the divisions inherent in the Catholic
community and in Catholic social thought itself, while it also
temporarily covered over old fears of the State. Disagreement
was natural and its reappearance in the middle of the decade
should not have excited undue concern. Some of the opposition
was parochial and group centered in its social views, but there
were also articulate critics who were aware of the difficulty of
reconciling Catholic social teachings with American reformism.

Supporters of the New Deal were also numerous, and they
helped soften some of the traditional American suspicion of the
Church. They also helped Catholics develop a more realistic
conception of the nature and meaning of American political and
economic life and assisted them in overcoming their fears of persecution by the non-Catholic majority. Most important, for all
their theoretical difficulties, the Catholic reformers demonstrated
that American liberalism offered concrete programs through
which moral objectives of human welfare could find at least partial practical realization.

IV

The New Deal, Communism,
and Controversy, 1937–1940

Although there were signs of an approaching break in their support of the New Deal in 1936, most American Catholics remained faithful to President Roosevelt and his program.[1] Catholic voters appreciated the benefits New Deal policies brought them, and their gratitude, along with their traditional loyalty to the Democratic party, was sufficient to offset any apprehension they might have felt about the future. Neither Father Coughlin nor the American Liberty League promised anything nearly as attractive in terms of economic advancement and political recognition. In addition, the New Deal's rhetoric and many of its policies at least superficially resembled Catholic teachings. The assertion of social values over individual values, the friendly attitude toward labor, the use of government for the protection and promotion of the common good, these were principles which were far closer to the Catholic position than were those of the old order or of the Republican party of 1936.

But there were differences as well which became increasingly apparent with the easing of the atmosphere of crisis that dominated most of the first administration. Many New Dealers gloried in being undogmatic, being tied to no set scheme and attempting to meet each problem unhampered by ideological commitments. In the early years this amounted in practice to an

attempt to hold the middle ground between reaction and revolution, a position coinciding with the general stance of American
Catholics. From the start, however, some feared increasing the
power of the federal government and were suspicious of the
political approach to reform, while others regarded New Deal
legislation as beneficial only as it contributed to the advent of
the new Christian social order outlined by Pius XI. Catholics
differed like other Americans, and the papal encyclicals provided
no basis for consensus that could inspire united social action.
The ambiguity of Catholic social doctrine and increasing economic, social, and intellectual diversity weakened the earlier
unity of the ghetto, which had been, in any case, more the
product of social conditions than of agreement on the meaning
or application of political or social principles.[2]

One reason for division was the fact that the Church's teaching on the role of the State in economic life was almost impossible to apply authoritatively to the United States. The popes
upheld the duty of the State to protect natural rights and promote the common good but restricted efforts for the general
welfare to the lowest level that could deal with problems effectively. Emphasis on the common good fitted the demands of
working-class and lower-middle-class Americans, including
Catholics, for government assistance in getting jobs, improving
economic conditions, and providing against unemployment, sickness, and old age. Insistence on protection of individual liberties,
on the other hand, encouraged the fear of big government felt
by many Americans and accentuated among Catholics by their
concern for the safety of parochial schools. Finally, the principle
of subsidiarity supplemented the strong American attachment to
the Constitution and its federal framework, which many Catholics believed protected the Church from the hostile Protestant
majority.

In the New Deal years these elements frequently conflicted
with one another. Father Coughlin played on all of them with

no attempt at reconciliation. More judicious critics, like the editors of *America* and the *Catholic World*, were aware of the difficulties of adjustment but came down strongly on the side of state sovereignty, strictly limited federal action, and rigid adherence to the Constitution. The leaders of the Social Action Department, on the other hand, looked to the federal government as the agency of reform, arguing that the states were unwilling and unable to deal with national questions and that the Constitution could be reinterpreted or changed to meet modern needs. They answered Catholic fears by arguing that developing private associations would check whatever dangers arose from increased federal power.

Very few wished to return to the old days of rugged individualism and laissez-faire. Even the defenders of the states were usually proponents of social action at every level—local, state, and federal. The sharp dichotomy between Roosevelt and the Liberty League obscured division somewhat in 1936. Father Gillis expressed the feelings of many when he told Monsignor Ryan that he admired Roosevelt, had voted for him in 1932, and probably would vote for him again, but he was concerned about the growing national debt, centralization of government, and continued unemployment, concerns which intensified in the years following the election.[3]

The constitutional dispute culminated in Roosevelt's plan to "pack" the Supreme Court in 1937. Earlier invalidation of New Deal legislation had brought varied reactions in the Catholic press: Coughlin, the *Tablet*, *America*, and the *Catholic World* supported the court, whereas *Commonweal*, Monsignor Ryan, Father McGowan, and Father Haas deplored the court's action and called for a constitutional amendment to legalize labor legislation. Roosevelt's plan went far beyond this and appeared to many to threaten the very existence of the court while granting the President vast new powers. The proposal gave further ammunition to Catholics already suspicious of his intentions and his reverence for the Constitution, and lent substance to charges of an impending loss of liberty.

Discussion of the issue had a melodramatic quality, with a new note of near hysteria infusing heretofore sober editorials. The *Tablet*'s Patrick Scanlan, for example, seriously described the plan as a brazen attempt to establish dictatorship, while *America*'s editors agreed, but argued that Roosevelt, who already had overwhelming control of Congress, now hoped to bend the Supreme Court to his will.[4] Father Gillis lamented the death of democracy, and was most grieved by the fact that Roosevelt and his "twenty-seven million supporters" did not even care.[5] Father Paul Blakely, who regretted that the court had already granted the government broad powers, expected that the President, with his "rubber-stamp Congress" would ignore the amending process and prepare the way for a dictator even if he did not become one himself.[6] Less severely, Professor William F. Sands of Georgetown University, writing in *America*, admitted the probable necessity for constitutional revision, but he believed Roosevelt's plan would destroy the separation of powers and endanger the liberties of all. All these positions reflected not only stark pessimism about the state of the nation but an extremely static view of the court's role as interpreter of the Constitution, a conception articulated by a writer in the *Catholic World:* "In theory a judge is merely a conduit for applying legal principles previously established to a case that comes before him." [7]

Nevertheless the President also had a good many Catholic supporters. John A. Ryan, who had earlier advocated amendment, supported the plan as necessary to save time, avoid crisis, and place men with correct social views on the bench. Years earlier Ryan had written that the appointment of justices was one of the President's most important duties. Fully accepting the view that the Constitution was what the court said it was, he saw the new proposal as more realistic than the slower process of amendment which would leave the problem of interpretation untouched.[8]

Commonweal agreed that there was immediate need for more balanced economic views on the court and held that minority opinions proved that the Constitution was fully adequate for the tasks of modern government when interpreted by men in tune with the "manifest will of the nation, acting to accomplish manifestly necessary measures of humane and justifiable social justice." [9] *Sign* magazine, in a perceptive editorial, argued that amendment was too slow a process, given the immediate need to re-enact many New Deal laws. To a large extent the Supreme Court had become a legislative body, the editorial continued, and a good case could be made for having it reflect the will of the people on legislation which was not clearly unconstitutional. The *Christian Front*, a newly established offshoot of the Catholic Worker movement, endorsed the plan as a reasonable and sensible effort to make the social views of the justices conform to the evident needs of society.[10]

The anticlimactic outcome of the "court fight" revived the opposition's faith in democracy, although the President's supporters pointed to the changed attitude of the court as evidence of victory.[11] The major effect of the episode on the Catholic community was to bring criticism of the New Deal more clearly into the open, make it respectable, and increase suspicion of the administration. In the future Catholic opponents of Roosevelt would easily find further evidence of the President's disregard for American traditions and Catholic sensitivities. Hugo Black's nomination to the Supreme Court, for example, infuriated many Catholic critics. Black was severely attacked as an enemy of Negroes and Catholics because of his earlier membership in the Ku Klux Klan.[12] A presidential plan to reorganize the executive branch of the government, coming on the heels of the court fight, seemed a further attempt to undermine constitutional government and create an arbitrary, all-powerful federal bureaucracy capable of crushing religious liberty and educational freedom.[13] *America* saw similar dangers in Roosevelt's attempt to "purge" wayward Senators in the 1938 election.[14] The apparent movement of New Deal advisors to the Left, the interference of the President in elections, and his general disrespect for the rights of the states incensed Father Gillis, who also blamed the administration for the "smell of Sovietism" in the new c.i.o. unions, and for the "cowardly" way in which the Catholic Governor of Michigan, Frank Murphy, dealt with the sit-down strikers. Anticipating Roosevelt's dark intentions as early as 1938, *America* stated its vigorous opposition to any hope the President might have for a third term.[15]

During this period real hatred of Roosevelt appeared in the Catholic press for the first time. The *Tablet* and Father Coughlin long detested many New Deal policies but they usually painted a picture of a well-meaning President surrounded by wicked advisors. Coughlin became more bitter after the election, but there were even more extreme attacks. Father Gillis of the *Catholic World*, now an opponent of Roosevelt on most counts, foreign and domestic, usually was respectful and reasonable in his criticism. Yet he printed in his paper two articles by Arthur Stanley Riggs unsurpassed in their nostalgia for lost American innocence and their hatred of Roosevelt, John L. Lewis, and the working class. The 1936 election, according to Riggs, was "a dark and irremediable blot upon our political history, an ominous commentary upon the stupidity of the electorate, some of whom refused to 'shoot Santa Claus' and many of whom regarded the candidate with the worship of dogs toward humans." Riggs went on to identify Christianity with capitalism and progress with the incentives to private gain. He attributed low moral standards to "the wholesale education of the unfit" and to population increases in the "lower strata of intellectual and earning power." [16] Riggs made no attempt to justify his position on the basis of the encyclicals, but his articles indicated the changed atmosphere of the later thirties when the Catholic sense of alienation intensified and hatred and bitterness came into the open.

The extent of *America*'s alienation from the New Deal became clear in its reaction to the Wages and Hours Act of 1938. *America* had supported the rights of labor for a generation, emphasizing the need for minimum-wage and maximum-hour legislation, preferably, but not necessarily, on the state level. On the eve of the bill's passage *America* announced that its hope for a sane and equitable national labor policy had been disappointed, for the bill had been emasculated by sectional interests and labor factions. Later *America* softened its position somewhat, holding that the program could provide a good start if its administrator was truly concerned with the welfare of the workers and not a "Washington crackpot." From experience the editors knew this to be "silly optimism," but they wrote that hope sprang eternal within them.[17] A *Sign* contributor carried this skepticism further, expressing admiration for the ideals which motivated the legislation but challenging "the undemocratic and immoral belief that the social progress of the human race can be speeded up by writing ideals into laws." [18]

In the early 1930's papers like *America* and the *Tablet* had combined constitutional conservatism with vigorous opposition to the individualism of the old order and to the business community in general. Later this antibusiness feeling faded as both papers expressed sympathy with businessmen laboring under the burden of government interference. *America* stated that business feared further assaults by the government and needed to be left alone. "It is time to formulate a program of cooperation between the Government and organized industry," the editors wrote. "Legislation predicated on the theory that the two are irreconcilable enemies will turn this depression into utter ruin." [19] Even the renewal of hard times in 1938 failed to check this

trend. Conservative editors severely criticized excessive government spending and borrowing, while Patrick Scanlan found in
the recession proof that "the poor we will always have with us."

Others, however, found evidence that business leadership had
not learned its lesson and continued to restrict purchasing power
by low wages, opposition to unions, and resistance to reform.[20]
Favorable comparisons of the President's policies and papal principles continued to appear as many Catholics defended Roosevelt
against attacks from their fellow churchmen. The *Catholic Charities Review* belittled fears of bureaucracy, and *Commonweal*
continued to provide reasonable if not enthusiastic support to
the administration. Father John A. O'Brien of Notre Dame
went further, praising Roosevelt, "who has fought with such
intelligence, ability, and courage to translate into the social and
economic order of our day the ideals of social justice and human
rights voiced so eloquently by Leo XIII and Pius XI." [21]
Nevertheless, as the reforming impulse of the administration
weakened and the President became more and more preoccupied
with foreign affairs, many Catholics normally sympathetic to his
programs sought other outlets for their energies and specifically
political matters drew less attention. Such a trend was evident in
the policy of the *Christian Front*. The editors saw in the events
of 1937 and 1938 the defeat of Roosevelt and the betrayal of his
program by the Supreme Court and Congress, all signaling the
"return of the Bourbons," the same men who had taken the
country to war and brought on the Depression. Like many other
Catholics they turned to organized labor as the only active and
promising force for reform, although the c.i.o. was not yet
"sufficiently radical nor sufficiently imbued with the wide vision
so necessary for radical social reconstruction." [22] Others looked to
agrarianism, to the integral Catholicism of the *Catholic Worker,*
or to the various movements for spiritual reform and renewal
within the Church.

The divisions within the Catholic community and the widespread hostility to the New Deal in the last years of the decade stood in sharp contrast to the enthusiasm which had greeted Roosevelt's first inaugural. The reasons for the change were varied, with foreign policy and the impact of events in Europe and Spain increasingly important. But domestic policy played a major part, with many Catholics fearful of increased centralization of government, supposed threats to constitutional liberties, and the rising tide of militant labor and of communism. As Father Francis Talbot, Wilfrid Parsons's successor at *America*, wrote in a thoughtfully critical account of the Roosevelt years, the New Deal had begun with an approach closely paralleling that of the encyclicals, but had ended with a "trend toward the left." In listing the characteristics of the "Roosevelt Revolution" he sounded the themes that marked Catholic suspicion of the New Deal as its domestic phase drew to a close.[23]

> In general it may be said that the Revolution affects the theory of the threefold powers of American democracy, strikes out for centralized control by the Chief Executive and his Administration, introduces a new type of paternalism as against the old-time rugged individualism, plunges directly toward Leftist Liberalism, so-called, batters down capitalism and a too-independent industry, favors the increase of power of the proletariat as against the barons and tycoons, bulwarks the labor union as against management, believes in vast expenditures of governmental wealth collected through taxation of those who can bear it.

Talbot found much in this to admire, but he deplored the leftist tendency and declared that the 1940 election would decide what direction the revolutionary forces in American society would take.

Talbot's outlook was shared by many Catholic leaders, but reformers could still point with pride not only to the achievements of the decade but to the increased acceptance by the hierarchy of the need for reform along the lines they had been preaching since the publication of *Quadragesimo Anno*. At the conclusion of the first National Catholic Social Action Conference in 1938 Bishops Edward F. O'Hara and Karl J. Alter issued a social manifesto which called for the extension of New Deal–style reforms.[24] More important, in 1940 the national hierarchy adopted a pastoral letter which called for wage increases, reduced profits, labor organization, and collective bargaining. Both documents stressed the immediate need to begin construction of occupational groups through which capital and labor could work cooperatively for the good of each industry and of society as a whole.[25] These pronouncements offered many proposals for the extension of labor and welfare reforms, but they seemed anticlimactic. By insisting that moral reform and spiritual renewal precede basic social reconstruction, the bishops pushed the immediately needed vocational groups into the unforeseeable future. They were no more successful in solving the other ambiguities of the encyclical and overcoming deepening Catholic divisions. Moreover, by 1940 few saw much hope of approaching the Christian social order through existing political arrangements, a feeling reflected in the bishops' warning against undue reliance on the State. Suspicious of the New Deal, fearful of communism and increasingly beset by a sense of isolation, Catholic writers and editors were likely to give these new episcopal pronouncements an even less enthusiastic reception than their more specific predecessors had received twenty-one years earlier.

New Deal domestic policy in the later thirties alienated much Catholic support, but Roosevelt's response to events abroad was increasingly important in shaping Catholic attitudes. Even in the early years many Catholics who sympathized wholeheartedly with the administration's domestic program were suspicious of its approach to foreign affairs. Recognition of Russia in 1933 not only went counter to Catholic opposition to Marxism but seemed to ignore Catholic sensibilities by refusing to recognize the legitimacy of their complaints about religious persecution. As early as 1930, *Commonweal* took notice of meetings to promote recognition and saw in them the efforts of the business community to open up Russian markets, aiming at profits regardless of the moral or political implications. The editors were unequivocally opposed, less for the ideological reasons than because they felt that it was useless to attempt to deal with a government that placed no stock in international law or morality. Father Edmund A. Walsh of Georgetown opposed recognition for the same reason, repudiating Al Smith's support of the move. Most active as usual on such issues, the *Tablet* organized mass meetings, petitions, and demonstrations against recognition.[26]

More important than the Russian question was that of the Mexican revolution, with its persecution of the Church and suppression of Catholic schools and religious foundations. Americans generally were apathetic, but prominent liberals publicly deprecated reports of persecution because of the Church's ties with the aristocracy and the counterrevolutionary classes. American Catholics just as naturally sympathized with their Mexican brethren and could not accept the argument that social change justified the murder of priests and nuns and the closing of churches. In particular they could not understand the failure of people who normally championed religious liberty to demonstrate some concern for its violation in a neighboring country. They were bound to see this situation as another expression of the bigotry they had experienced in 1928, a manifestation of their own second-class citizenship.

The *Tablet* described at length the treatment of the Church in Mexico and the friendly attitude of Ambassador Josephus Daniels to the revolutionary government. When President Roosevelt ignored a Knights of Columbus resolution for American action, the paper denounced him and warned of political retaliation. It wanted Daniels removed, the arms embargo lifted, and the nation left alone, in contrast with the administration's friendly actions, which were helping the revolutionary government to entrench itself. Father Gillis wrote in much the same vein, attacking the administration and secular newspapers and writers who either ignored or defended the Mexican situation. Other journals, including *America, Sign,* and *Commonweal* were, in varying degrees, upset by the President's refusal to act while the hierarchy quietly pressured the administration to speak out.[27]

Catholic demands for some form of intervention in Mexico contained more emotion than substance, for they were less interested in direct interference than in some symbolic verbal gesture by the President. In general, American Catholics remained staunchly isolationist, ready to criticize any effort to involve the United States in world affairs. Father Coughlin and the *Tablet,* for example, opposed American entry into the World Court and were joined by Father Gillis, who disliked all international co-operation involving sanctions that could draw the country into another war. Nevertheless, here as elsewhere Catholic opinion was not unanimous. Father McGowan was shocked at the "blatant nationalism" exhibited in the campaign against the World Court.[28] McGowan, Ryan, and Parker T. Moon had earlier formed the Catholic Association for International Peace, which demonstrated greater consciousness of international problems and responsibilities than most other organs of Catholic opinion. The c.a.i.p. and its leaders sought throughout the decade for international co-operation, reduced tariffs, scaled-down or eliminated war debts, a liberalized immigration policy, an international monetary agreement, and some form of international organization to supervise economic life.[29]

Such liberal approaches to foreign policy stumbled on the issue of communism, which, more than anything else, inhibited further progress in Catholic social thought after 1936. Just as the high water mark of the 1919 Bishops' Program preceded a decade of concern with Bolshevism, so the enthusiastic reform of the early 1930's was followed by increasing and sometimes paranoic concern with the Soviet menace, at home and abroad. Since the middle of the ninteenth century communism was regarded as the great enemy of Catholicism, the ultimate expression of modern man's revolt against God, the Church, and civilization. "Communism" became a slogan used to attack all policies seen as harmful to the Church and her teachings, from birth control to labor unions. Even the most socially conscious Catholics frequently defended their proposals as alternatives to communism, rather than as imperatives arising from Christian belief. Indeed, the entire Catholic social movement often appeared to be motivated less by genuine concern for the workers than by fear of social revolution.

This situation was compounded in the 1930's by the rise of fascism, which the Vatican apparently found preferable to communism. The concordats with Mussolini and Hitler, the support of the Church for the reactionary authoritarianism of Dollfuss and Salazar, its alignment with Franco, each was interpreted by many in the West as evidence of a Catholic alliance with fascist reaction. In 1937, as the democracies were awakening to the menace of Germany, Pius XI issued the strongest condemnation of communism to date, the encyclical *Divini Redemptoris*, setting clearly before the world the primacy of the red menace in the eyes of the Church.

The communist danger was nothing new to American Catholics who had always been vigilant against radical penetration in the United States. In 1930 Pius XI told a prominent American visitor to warn Catholics to beware of the spread of communism during the period of distress and unemployment, a problem which he feared Americans did not fully comprehend. Church leaders needed no such appeal from Rome. Cardinal O'Connell of Boston, Archbishop McNicholas of Cincinnati, and other prelates, time and again spoke out against the decline of authority, the weakness of public and private morals, the spread of birth control, the disrespect of children for their parents and superiors, and the hostility of the poor toward the rich, all of which were interpreted as signs of increasing communist influence.[30]

Throughout the early thirties, however, anticommunist Catholics emphasized the need to institute social and economic reforms in order to remove the grievances which gave communism fruitful soil in which to grow. Father John LaFarge wrote that the protest against the injustices of industrial society was so powerful that only a concerted attack upon the abuses of industrial capitalism could offset it. Communist support for good causes confused the workers and only the emergence of a unified, dedicated Catholic social movement could save them for the Church and prevent either revolution or fascist repression. "It is well to fight the evil that is communism," *America* editorialized, "but it is even more necessary to fight for the good by demanding that governments do their part in establishing justice and charity for all." [31] The sole dissenter from this relatively positive approach was Patrick Scanlan of the *Tablet*, who denied that communism grew from injustice and argued that it was "directly brought" to the United States, "mostly by Russian aliens." If they were deported and communist propaganda suppressed, Scanlan believed, "the 'red peril' would seldom be heard of." [32]

Scanlan, Father Coughlin, and Father Gillis raised the communist issue in the campaign of 1936 and thereafter it was an important factor in Catholic opinion. The old habit of labeling social legislation, union militancy, government action, and secularism as socialistic and communistic, revived under the impact of New Deal centralization, the rise of the c.i.o., and the intensification of Catholic minority consciousness. Spurred on by *Divini Redemptoris*, the hierarchy in 1938 expressed its concern over "the spread of subversive teachings and . . . the audacity of subversive action" in the United States. To counter this development the bishops inaugurated the "Crusade for Christian Democracy" aimed at instilling civic and social virtues in the young. The hierarchy linked the fight against communism with a call for social reform along the lines of *Quadragesimo Anno*, whose scheme of vocational groups provided the only possible middle ground between the abuses of liberal capitalism and the irreligious tyranny of red revolution.[33] Nevertheless, many Catholics appeared to ignore the bishops' often ambiguous demands for reform to concentrate on the clearly defined issue of anticommunism.

The spread of militant opposition to all that smacked of communism was intimately related to developments abroad. The resurgence of Nazi Germany and the outbreak of the Spanish Civil War raised important problems for American Catholics. Although most of their vigilance was directed toward communism and Soviet Russia, the increasing threat of Germany and her allies to democratic values was of even greater concern to many other Americans. The resulting division in American opinion greatly concerned Catholic leaders who feared that the nation would be led into a war against Germany in alliance with communist Russia. "There has been such a vigorous campaign against Fascism in the American press and furthered by numerous organizations of men and women," Bishop Noll of Fort Wayne warned, "that the attention of the people has been at least temporarily withdrawn from the even greater evil of communism." [34]

Like the bishop, most Catholics professed to dislike both fascism and communism but felt compelled to state their preference for fascism if forced to choose. Father Coughlin's argument that it was a "defense mechanism" against communism, which could be avoided only by the defeat of the reds, was popular with Catholic publicists.[35] Father John LaFarge of *America* attacked the problem more carefully. He held that communism was both the parent and the heir of fascism, which was the last resort of those whose unjust practices created unrest. Fascism was necessarily transitionary because its violence merely increased resentment. Communism remained the supreme enemy of peace. It could be defeated only by a basic and constructive program of social reform.[36]

Commonweal held that the choice of communism or fascism as alternatives was a false one, but it admitted that the Church, which was unswerving in its condemnation of communism, was able to live with fascism because the latter had not yet tried to enforce its final conclusions: it allowed the Church to exist as a corporate teaching body. If the choice of evils must come, the editors stated at an early stage of the Spanish Civil War, "most western peoples" would probably choose "the conservative reaction" rather than communism. But it argued that the true fight was between democracy and totalitarianism, and the Church stood foursquare with the former. The fact that its dislike of communism exceeded that of fascism did not mean that the Church had any admiration for the latter, and *Commonweal* denounced anti-Catholic liberals for spreading this falsehood.[37]

Similarly Father Wilfrid Parsons, retired editor of *America*, lamented the polarization of European politics around communism and fascism. He feared that this same pattern would reach America and that anticommunists would be forced into the fascist camp. Still, he argued that because communism was exportable and because it was not only a form of social organization but a philosophy of life, it was the greater evil. The Church, he said, opposed fascism on political and economic grounds in the name of democracy, but it opposed communism on religious grounds in the name of God. He urged Catholics to convince their fellow citizens that communism was undemocratic and that antifascist propaganda was often aimed at involving the United States in a war that could benefit only the Communists.[38]

The most outspoken anti-Nazi Catholic journal was *Commonweal*, whose editor, George Shuster, traveled widely in Europe and wrote two volumes denouncing the Hitler regime. When Pius XI signed a concordat with Germany in 1933, most Catholic papers went to great lengths to justify the action. Shuster was not unequivocally opposed to the treaty, which he felt gave the Church some real benefits and represented a gamble that it could help soften the Nazis. Yet he pointed out what other Catholics continued to deny: that the Pope's "marked personal opposition" to the spread of bolshevism made him welcome the emergence of a strong anticommunist movement in Germany.[39] Editorially the *Commonweal* reacted cautiously to the concordat and warned against Nazi racism. It noted with concern that the day the agreement was signed Father Stratman, the head of the German Catholic peace movement had been arrested. Pointing out the alternatives, none of which were attractive, the editor hoped that the new treaty would give the Church a strong basis for the defense of its rights.[40]

The Spanish Civil War was a critical experience for Catholics, as it was for so many other groups in America. To American liberals and most Protestants the war was a clear-cut case of democracy versus reaction and fascism; to the leaders of American Catholicism it was an equally clear confrontation of Christianity and civilization with communism and barbarism. Almost to a man the hierarchy and the American Catholic press supported the Franco side, insisting that the loyalist government was communist dominated, did not represent the will of the Spanish people and was bent upon destruction of the Church in Spain. Further discussion only solidified this position; reason was abandoned in a war of propaganda as one side tried to awaken the country to the menace of Nazism and fascism while Catholics fought to keep America neutral and to rebut arguments that placed them in the fascist camp.

Catholics, with some exceptions, did not attempt to justify their position on the basis of Church teachings. For the most part their arguments consisted of "a denunciation of 'communism' and, surprisingly, an affirmation of General Franco's *Movemiento Nacional* as liberal, democratic, and in the tradition of the American Revolution." While many European Catholics attacked the republic for its liberalism and democracy, Catholics in America defended Franco on the same basis.[41] They professed to see in Franco the George Washington of Spain; the *Tablet* compared the rebels to "our Patriots of 1776." [42] Few took notice of the program for postwar Spain, instead attacking the undemocratic and illiberal nature of the communist-dominated Republican regime, which had usurped power and attempted to destroy the historic religion of the Spanish people. This defense of Franco in terms of liberal democratic as opposed to Catholic values reflected Catholic fears about their own Americanism. If the argument that the Franco movement was anti-democratic was admitted, then the old question of the compatibility of Catholicism and American institutions would reappear with redoubled force. The election of 1928 and the controversy over the Mexican situation had kept alive Catholic sensitivity to their minority status and to the continued suspicion of their loyalty to American ideals and institutions. When these questions were again raised over the Spanish war, the leaders of the Catholic community sought for a rationale which would remove the question, rather than face the possibility of a conflict between Catholic thought and American practices. As the historian of the matter concludes: "The clergy's efforts to gloss over the situation and explain it away seems not so much an effort to deceive the Protestant opposition (or the Catholic laity) as to persuade *itself* of the compatibility of the two worlds." [43]

Whatever doubts may have entered the minds of the majority, they kept their attention focused on the communist issue. Father Gillis recognized that the Franco forces had committed some atrocities but held that the destruction of the Church in Spain and the restoration of religious freedom remained the crucial issues. *America* refused to associate itself with any program for postwar Spain, arguing that "whatever the nature and the policies of the government that would be established after the victory of the Rebel army, they could not possibly lead to greater disasters than those already perpetrated by the Red government now in control." [44]

America editor Francis Talbot was, like many others, incensed at attacks on the Church. He stated that the nation's liberals had always been "Catholic-baiters" and now sought to divide American Catholics.[45] Division was greatly feared as tensions increased and, when *Commonweal* announced its neutrality, *America* lamented that the liberals, Protestants, and Communists would rejoice. Father LaFarge accused George Shuster of betraying the Church, standing by neutral while Catholicism in Spain was destroyed.[46]

Led by Shuster, *Commonweal* abandoned its pro-Franco stand in April 1937 and soon lost one-quarter of its circulation.[47] Too many European Catholics saw injustice and atrocities on both sides, Shuster argued, and the Church could not allow recourse to immoral means, no matter how exalted the objective. In addition, the Church was weak in Spain, had ignored many opportunities to practice social justice, and promised nothing better under Franco than under a red republic. To argue that fascism was preferable to communism was to ignore the fact that it necessarily involved the use of violence and terror and did not eliminate the abuses which gave rise to communism. The question of why so many Spaniards hated the Church, Shuster felt, "lays bare what we modern men have done in nearly every country of Europe to the poor and to their love of our holy Church." He warned that "every effort to uphold Christian ethics by upholding an anti-Christian social order is bound to fail." [48] Finally Shuster argued that the Catholic position failed to account for the presence of Mussolini and Hitler in the struggle and wrongly accused all Loyalists of being Bolsheviks. *Commonweal* concluded that the war was a struggle between fascism and communism in which Christians should remain neutral, a position which the paper's founder, Michael Williams, strongly opposed on the basis of the pro-Franco pastoral of the Spanish bishops, which he thought should be definitive in the midst of so much conflicting propaganda.[49]

A second neutral publication, the *Catholic Worker*, followed the pacifist position of nonresistance to evil and refused to pray for either side; it would pray only for the Spanish people.[50] Cardinal Mundelein's diocesan weekly, the Chicago *New World*, also urged reservation of judgment. The *New World* attacked the Catholic press which, it felt, had been at least as zealous as the liberals in broadcasting propaganda. "American Catholics have no business in taking sides in Spain," the paper editorialized, "more especially as time begins to prove how Franco's sympathizers have tried to dupe us and are still trying." [51] Polls taken in the period showed that despite the outspoken support of the hierarchy and the press for Franco, Catholics were divided, with large minorities taking the loyalist side or remaining neutral. Some were scandalized at this evidence of Catholic disunity and urged various methods of building a unified national Catholic opinion.[52]

Non-Catholic hostility to the Church increased greatly in the later thirties because of its apparent support of fascist positions and the continued agitation of Father Coughlin and his supporters. Catholics reacted defensively, charging their critics with bigotry, denouncing intellectuals and teachers who manned the numerous antifascist and communist-front organizations as "parlor Bolshevists" and the "pink intelligentsia." Many felt that the liberals were in fact intolerant, that they "hated the Church just as bitterly, just as ignorantly and just as unfairly as any Klansman," a fact proved by their sympathy with the enemies of the Church in Russia, Mexico, and Spain.[53]

George Shuster struggled valiantly to keep the lines between liberals and Catholics open. He defended the Church against charges of fascism by citing numerous cases of German Catholic resistance and the many Catholics in Europe who opposed

Franco. He pointed out that American Catholics felt that what concerned their brethren in other nations was ignored by their fellow Americans. "Prior to 1928," he wrote, "there was abroad among American Catholics a constructive spirit which found partial expression in the episcopal statement on social reorganization in 1919. Afterwards a great change set in, which the observer could almost chart from month to month. Bound up with this disillusionment—the result not of a lost election but of triumphant bigotry—is the history of the Mexican question." Americans generally greeted the death of each nun in silence; her loss may not have meant much to Mexico but it meant a good deal to American Catholics. In addition, Shuster contended, the liberal community adopted a voguish attitude toward Russia, thereby insulting religious opinion. The result was a reservoir of bitterness that erupted when the Spanish war broke out. In their resentment of ingrained non-Catholic instincts, Catholics themselves fell into "minority-itis worse than at any other time in American history." Shuster's attempted explanation drew the fire of the *Tablet*, which accused him of disloyalty, but it was well received by liberals, who offered one dissent: they could not refrain from criticism merely because it offended Catholic sensitivities.[54]

As the threat of general war in Europe became more menacing, American Catholics lined up with those opposed to American involvement. Disillusionment with the last war, dislike of foreign adventures and the security in isolation felt by all Americans were shared by Catholics, who had additional reason for avoiding a war which might involve alliance with Russia.[55] *America* devoted the most space to the issue, condemning racism and tyranny but pointing out that there was much to be done to combat these evils at home before embarking on world crusades. Its contributors argued that American intervention could do nothing to save Europe from destruction, while its neutrality would preserve a basis from which civilization could be rebuilt.[56] When the war broke out the paper professed its sympathy with the allies but its friendship for all nations; it rejected isolation as an "unChristian" solution but nevertheless emphasized the welfare and interests of the United States.[57]

America endorsed the Ludlow amendment for a national referendum on a declaration of war, warned against allowing the President to control foreign policy and urged Congress to go into permanent session. Father Blakely defended a legitimate nationalism which recognized government's primary responsibility for the welfare of its own people. Father LaFarge held that a strict pacifist position was indefensible and that the best contribution Americans could make to their European brethren was to keep America strong, prosperous, and at peace.[58] A poll of its readers showed an overwhelming preponderance of opinion against American intervention and a great willingness to be conscientious objectors. A similar poll of Catholic college students, however, showed less certainty that American intervention could not help lead to a stable peace and a markedly decreased inclination to refuse military service.[59]

The *Catholic World* was suspicious of European diplomacy throughout the thirties. Father Gillis asked, "What business have we rough, stupid frontiersmen from the American backwoods among 'city-slickers' from the European capitals? They can fool us and laugh at us." Gillis urged his readers to recognize that they could not have both peace and prosperity and they must be ready to sacrifice the one to preserve the other—to endure heavy taxes, a slump in production, and violations of neutral rights if they wished to avoid war. He traced the cause of the war to the Versailles treaty, although holding Germany immediately responsible for defying law and unleashing aggression. Still he believed that if England had been willing to abandon her imperial ambitions and Germany had refused a fair accommodation, there would be grounds for American involvement. Given a choice of German totalitarianism and British imperialism,

however, he saw no alternative to neutrality. He strongly disliked Roosevelt's foreign policy and suspected him of desiring to
involve the United States in the war.[60]

The *Christian Front* also denounced conscription and urged
enactment of the referendum proposal. But the journal went
further, taking a pacifist stand and arguing that no modern war
could fulfill the conditions of justice traditionally taught by the
Church.[61] Father Gillis of the *Catholic World* was sympathetic to such arguments, which were also used by Archbishop
McNicholas in urging the formation of a league of Catholic
conscientious objectors. McNicholas charged that conscription
marked the "serious beginning of a totalitarian form of government." Although pacifists like Dorothy Day welcomed such
support they recognized that much of this zeal was based not on
Christian nonresistance to evil but on opposition to communism
and fear that Russia would be aided by an anti-Nazi war.[62]

There were some Catholics who dissented from the general
position. Monsignor Ryan was an early opponent of fascism and
defender of the administration's foreign policy. Bishop Robert
Lucey publicly condemned isolationism and the attempt to remain neutral in the face of international crime. *Commonweal*
stressed the necessity for a strong defense posture and international co-operation. Ryan, Lucey, Michael Williams, and several
other prominent laymen joined the Committee To Defend
America by Aiding the Allies. The Catholic Association for
International Peace adopted a program of education regarding
"the threat of Nazi-Communism," and stressed the need for the
United States to "join in building a just and peaceful world." In
1936, Roosevelt sent a personal representative, Myron C. Taylor,
to the Vatican and Catholics were gratified, but hostility to the
drift of foreign policy was not significantly lessened.[63]

George Shuster again attacked the basic premise of Catholic
attitudes, the preference for fascism over communism because
the former allowed the Church to exist. He described the situa-

tion in Germany where all possible centers of resistance were intimidated and only the churches remained outside; the regime, by its very nature, was engaged in an intensified campaign to bring the churches under its power, a campaign in which it had to succeed and in which it would use any method. In any case, the incorporation of all the nation's power centers into the regime made Hitler a much more powerful threat than Stalin, whose strength was lessened by the suppression of opposition at home.[64]

Despite the increasing obsession with communism in the Catholic community, many continued to take a constructive approach to the problem. "The only effective warfare against it," wrote Father John A. O'Brien, restating the sentiments common in the early Depression years, "will be waged by sanitizing our social and industrial order, making it conformable to the laws of . . . justice, and sensitizing the consciences of the rich, wealthy, and powerful to the rights of the poor and downtrodden." Virgil Michel protested the "imbecilities" of much Catholic anticommunism, citing a high school text which found nothing wrong with America.[65] The Association of Catholic Trade Unionists and other groups called upon Catholics to join organizations striving for legitimate reforms. Communist infiltration of such movements could be prevented only from within, after giving evidence of good intention by supporting justice and attacking reaction.[66]

Catholic personalists urged a warfare against communism with spiritual weapons of prayer and personal sacrifice for the poor. Michel, Paul Hanley Furfey, and others contended that Christians would never use "iron hand methods" but must rely upon charity, nonresistance to evil, and the power of divine grace to overcome communism or any other social evil.[67] One writer, J. F. T. Prince, urged Catholics to draw upon their religious heritage for a social program that would have far greater appeal than communism and would preserve the dignity of the person.

Such a program, he believed, was inherent in Christian teachings, was wholly opposed to capitalism and wholly devoted to equality, justice, and fellowship. This abhorrence of violence and repression, coupled with respect for the freedom and dignity of man, was typical of the Christian humanism of the personalist approach to problems, an approach that brought a new spirit and a new creativity to one section of the American Church.[68]

Throughout the 1930's events abroad greatly influenced the response of American Catholics to domestic issues and, by 1940, such considerations dominated the thinking of a broad section of the leadership of the American Church. When the editor of the labor-oriented journal, *Christian Social Action* (formerly the *Christian Front*), Richard Deverall, declared that the choice in 1940 between Roosevelt and Republican Wendell Willkie was one between "tweedledum and tweedledee," John A. Ryan angrily canceled his subscription. Deverall argued that, while he "bitterly opposed" the Republican candidate on domestic issues, he regarded "even more bitterly the imperialistic policy of the New Deal and its obvious attempt to thrust militarism upon the United States." Ryan and former *Commonweal* editor Michael Williams could dismiss Deverall's views as "detestable tripe" but they could not change the fact that probably a majority of journalists and prelates who declared themselves publicly regarded the administration's foreign policy with suspicion if not outright hostility.[69]

For Deverall and others associated with the Catholic Worker movement, opposition to Roosevelt's foreign policy was the logical outgrowth of a sincere, if often doctrinaire, pacifism. Many others, however, derived similar conclusions from premises that were, in the first instance, anticommunist, and were closely related to the social status of American Catholics. As the gulf between Catholics and other Americans widened over the issues of fascism, communism, and war, anticommunism provided a device which could ease Catholic insecurity and allow for the simultaneous assertion of loyalty to Church and nation. In fighting communism the Catholic was abiding by the most authoritative pronouncements of his Church. Although the Pope emphasized the need to work for social justice he was unable to provide a systematic program for its attainment, and the suggested modes of action raised serious problems for American Catholics bent upon achieving a secure place in their society. Moral reform and spiritual renewal appeared most difficult in an environment they had always regarded as Protestant and secular. State action and union organization, in their American forms, often seemed to threaten traditional American notions of politics and economic life, which Catholics had accepted, and sometimes appeared to conflict as well with other elements in Catholic teachings. Corporate reform, finally, challenged the individualism of American society, which had penetrated the Catholic community as well. All these methods involved a basic confrontation between the American Catholic and his society and would undoubtedly revive charges of disloyalty to American values. Not only would they arouse the opposition of many non-Catholic Americans, but they would precipitate a crisis for the Catholic himself, for he had long ago accepted as his own many of the practices and principles that Catholic teachings called into question.

Anticommunism, however, presented few such difficulties. The entire voice of authority in the Church from Pope to parish priest emphasized the evil of communism and the need to oppose its spread with a clarity lacking in the social encyclicals. Catholics had no choice but to oppose communism, and such activity could be seen as a most worthy form of Catholic social action. Most important the ideal of anticommunism raised no problems for the Catholic as American. As nothing was more Catholic than anticommunism, so there was nothing more fully American. Catholics learned from their religious teachers and from the most respectable elements in non-Catholic life that communism threatened the nation's most cherished ideals. They had always distrusted the liberal intellectuals who were the only prominent group seemingly attracted to communism. In fighting the red peril the Catholic could dedicate himself to action which was both Catholic and American. Few would disagree that he was proving his worth as an American and demonstrating the compatibility of faith and patriotism. Indeed, he could honestly believe that he was showing that the Church was a necessary ally and valuable asset to America, the strongest supporter of her ideals and institutions. Thus would the objective of a reconciliation of the nation and the Church and the attainment of a truly American Catholicism be realized at last.

V

Catholics and Organized Labor

Several recent commentators have argued that trade unionism has been the major form of social action which has interested American Catholics.[1] While this historical generalization undoubtedly needs qualification, there can be little doubt that Catholics, heavily represented in the working classes and as a minority fearful of State action on socio-economic matters, were attracted to the labor movement. Certainly in the decade of the 1930's, marked as it was by severe unemployment, crippling strikes, and militant unionism, Catholic social action leaders were preoccupied with labor problems. Interest was intensified by the feeling that unionization was necessary to fulfill the recovery program of President Roosevelt and to begin construction of the new social order described by Pius XI. Throughout the decade Catholic spokesmen denounced the injustices of the industrial order and supported the principle of free, independent labor organization. Catholics differed sharply, however, in their assessment of the methods and objectives of existing unions. They differed as well in their interpretation of the role of labor in papal teachings and the relative weight that should be assigned to collective bargaining in the general reform of society. The rise of the c.i.o. forced these divisions into the open, provoked bitter controversy within the Church, hampered efforts at social

97

justice, and challenged the widespread belief that the encyclicals provided clear answers to America's social and economic difficulties.

Prior to 1930, the efforts of James Cardinal Gibbons, Father John A. Ryan, Father Peter Dietz, and a handful of labor priests, had earned the Catholic Church a reputation as a friend of the American labor movement, although Catholic unionists remained generally indifferent to Catholic social teachings. Gibbons's intervention had prevented Vatican condemnation of the Knights of Labor in 1886. Later, bishops and priests generally refused to sanction antilabor campaigns and placed no unnecessary barriers in the way of Catholic participation in trade unions. The Social Action Department, established in 1919, was directed by men sympathetic to labor's cause who helped give a progressive tone to episcopal pronouncements and who used the educational facilities at their disposal to propagate a progressive social program. Other agencies of Catholic social action and many influential periodicals strongly defended the right of workingmen to organize and bargain collectively, to secure a living wage, and to participate effectively in industrial decisions relating to their welfare.[2]

On the other hand, Catholic support for organized labor was qualified by defense of private property, condemnation of violence, and hostility toward radicalism and strikes. Moreover, Church leaders were motivated by institutional and pastoral considerations as well as by an awareness of injustice. Cardinal Gibbons believed in the principle of free association but also feared that condemnation of the Knights of Labor might ignite anti-Catholic passions and alienate working-class Catholics from the Church. On a local level, priests sometimes took an active role in advising workers and supporting union activities, but on the whole indifference rather than support or hostility was the dominant Catholic reaction to the American Federation of Labor before World War I. Father Peter Dietz's attempt to organize

Catholic members of the federation received only slight support from the hierarchy and ended in frustration and disappointment.[3] Even the best-known Catholic defender of the rights of labor, Father John A. Ryan, was no unqualified friend of existing American unions. Like other pioneers of American social Catholicism Ryan regarded co-operatives and voluntary stock and profit-sharing programs as more promising avenues to social justice than trade unions.

The ambivalent labor attitudes of even the most progressive Catholic leaders was derived in part from the social doctrines of the Church which they were attempting to interpret and apply. In *Rerum Novarum* Leo XIII had clearly upheld the right of the worker to receive a living wage and to associate with his fellows for legitimate common purposes. Leo's powerful condemnation of individualism and his equally powerful defense of workers' association stimulated the growth of a Catholic labor movement and Catholic participation in nondenominational unions in nations where religiously based bodies were impractical. Yet the Pope also urged the formation of some form of joint association embracing both employers and workers as indispensable supplements to class organization. Leo, desiring to center attention on immediate problems rather than on long-range objectives, did not develop this proposal, but the direction was clear. Only organization based on the principles of mutual charity and universal dedication to the common good could overcome economic and social disorder, alleviate class hostility and conflict, and restore a harmonious social order.

Forty years later Pope Pius XI reviewed Leo's teachings and developed them into a program for the reconstruction of society. In *Quadragesimo Anno* the Pope argued that the living-wage concept demanded wage levels high enough to enable a worker and his family to live in decency and own some productive property and at the same time provide the widest possible employment. This in turn required a system of economic plan-

ning, one that could check the anarchy of individualism by
asserting the primacy of the common good and the supremacy
of the moral law. The Christian social order proposed by Pius
XI was based on a structure of vocational or occupational
groups through which capital and labor could jointly determine
wage standards and working conditions, ending ruthless competition and replacing it with social justice.

Quadragesimo Anno and *Rerum Novarum* provided Catholics
with an authoritative basis for analysis and action but by no
means led to uniform opinion or united action. American Catholic social thought in the 1930's was characterized by unanimous
acceptance of official Church teachings and wide and often
bitter disagreement as to their meaning and application. In particular Catholics differed sharply in their assessment of the
means by which the "Christian social order" outlined by Pius XI
could be brought into being. Some concentrated on political
action, some on labor unionization, some on moral reform and
social education. Others chose to emphasize more negative but
more clearly defined aspects of papal thought, such as anticommunism, resistance of undue increases in government power,
opposition to labor violence, and defense of private property.

All Catholics who thought about such matters in the 1930's
accepted the vocational group system as a goal for reform, often
utilizing it as a "yardstick" for evaluating current practices and
reform proposals. They argued that the papal plan provided the
only middle ground between individualism and socialism. At that
point agreement ended. *Quadragesimo Anno* left open many
questions regarding the character of the Christian social order,
the role of the State within it, and the means by which it might
be brought into existence. Nevertheless, acceptance of the papal
plan made all economic and social questions inseparable from the
more general problem of reconstructing the social order. In particular, the encyclical made it clear that social justice required
labor, like other groups, to look beyond its own interests to the

welfare of each industry and of society as a whole, to aim, in other words, at the establishment of a vocational group system.

Influential Catholic spokesmen on social issues like Ryan and his assistant, Father Raymond McGowan, argued that the Christian social order would emerge gradually as a natural reaction to concentrated economic power. Increased organization would lead to collective bargaining and this in turn to the formation of joint committees charged with industry-wide planning and control. Ryan, acutely aware of the power of large corporations and the tenacious hold of the individualistic ethic, looked primarily to the State as the only agency of reform sufficiently powerful to alter the structure of American economic life. While many of his fellow Catholics feared that increased federal power would provide their religious enemies with potential weapons against Catholic liberties and parochial schools, Ryan's pragmatic application of the principle of subsidiarity led him to regard the federal government as "by far the most important agent and instrument of social justice." [4]

Father McGowan accepted the evolutionary approach to the occupational group system but was unwilling to rely on the government. Although he supported legislation designed to protect unions and encourage collective bargaining, he feared State domination and insisted that the establishment of voluntary labor unions and trade associations was a prerequisite for the building of the Christian social order. These bodies, while free and independent, would have to look beyond their own interests to the welfare of industry and of society. They must aim to be not "only collective bargainers [but] also cooperators in the administration of industry." [5] This required a whole system of economic self-government, ranging from shop committees through industry councils to a national economic planning board drawn from the various industries and professions, an economic government within the political State, controlling its own affairs with only the most limited government supervision. [6]

Most Catholic writers agreed with McGowan's emphasis on private, voluntary organization rather than with Ryan's "Statism," particularly as they became disenchanted with the New Deal. Like McGowan, Father Wilfrid Parsons of *America* was suspicious of State power and emphasized that the new social order involved "the widest possible extension of the system of trade unions on the one hand, and on the other the complete organization of employers in trade associations," preserving a large measure of individual initiative, private enterprise, and price competition.[7] Others active in the labor movement and regarding it as the dynamic social force in American life, believed that the occupational group system meant the extension of collective bargaining into a "real partnership of capital and labor," an "industrial democracy" in which labor would share in "ownership, control, and profits." The State was merely to provide a "framework of liberty and order within which capital and labor could run their own house and cooperate in furthering the public welfare." [8]

The papal instructions seemed to most Catholics to call for union organization and collective bargaining as preliminary steps in the gradual formation of a Christian social order. Nevertheless, some rejected the evolutionary approach altogether, preferring to work for moral and spiritual renewal, which they regarded as a necessary condition for economic and institutional reorganization. Father Paul Hanley Furfey, Father Virgil Michel, and Peter Maurin and many of his followers in the Catholic Worker movement, all in one way or another rejected the reformist school because of its implicit compromise with the basic spirit of the present unjust social order. Distributists and agrarians likewise argued that Christianity was incompatible with an urbanized industrial order and attracted many to schemes for co-operation, rural settlement, and communitarian organization.

Still other Catholics rejected the gradual approach because of its concentration on class organization. Edward Koch, editor of the *Guildsman*, believed that the Pope's plan presupposed the elimination of class consciousness and reorganization along functional lines. Unions and trade associations were merely collections of individuals pursuing their own interests, a "multiplied egoism" as morally objectionable as the old rugged individualism. Emphasis on unionization, Koch argued, "militates against the formation of vocational groups, insofar as it emphasizes divergent interests of capital and labor and tends to maintain and increase hostility between them." Instead, all must come to recognize industry as a common undertaking and attempt "to unify, to make one unit of the entire industry." Believing that the Pope had supplied a complete scheme of Catholic social reform, Koch urged Catholics to repudiate nonsectarian organizations and to form distinctively Catholic associations aimed at the establishment of the vocational group system.[9]

Few were prepared to go this far, but many shared the *Guildsman*'s dislike of the "multiplied egoism" of existing unions and urged the far from militant A.F. of L. to adopt a more co-operative attitude. William Cardinal O'Connell of Boston told Catholic delegates to the 1931 convention of the federation that labor must recognize that its greatest gains would come from co-operation, not from competition, with capital and that, in the Depression crisis, only such co-operation could avert disaster. Cleveland's Bishop Joseph Schrembs stated his support for unions and his dislike of the open shop, but he called for the formation of joint bodies of capital and labor to settle industrial disputes and achieve justice for the worker.[10] In the early years of the Depression the Catholic press continually insisted that labor and management recognize their mutual interest in industrial and national welfare. While the refusal of business to allow labor to organize and negotiate was frequently and heatedly denounced, few viewed that refusal as a justification for labor's one-sided concentration on its rights and its interests.

Emphasis on the need for co-operation, however, in no way diminished the vigor of Catholic demands for justice for the worker. In 1931 the American bishops described the objective of Catholic social action as "an equitable distribution of the income and wealth of the country and the world." More specifically they outlined the goals of reform: "We ask a living wage for the family; a proper proportion between the wages of the different kinds of workers; an ample sufficiency for all. We ask for wages that will provide employment to the greatest extent possible, and for an equitable sharing of the goods produced by industry." [11]

The living-wage idea stressed by the bishops underwent something of a revival in the United States during the decade. Father Ignatius Cox, Father Arthur Gleason, and a number of others, wrote powerful statements of the "absolute right" of laborers to "a use in sufficiency of the material goods of this world." Increased wages had to come from the profits and not from higher prices, they insisted, rejecting arguments based on the inability of small businessmen to pay decent wages. In such cases the State must act to provide conditions in which the primary right to a living wage could be realized. If legal limitations on competition were not sufficient, then inefficient firms would have to close their doors.[12]

Wage problems were of particular interest because many Catholics joined John A. Ryan in blaming the Depression on faulty distribution of wealth and income. For Catholic moralists who adopted Ryan's underconsumption interpretation, economic factors as well as ethical principles supported their plea for higher wages. Many laid the blame for low wages and the lack of consumer purchasing power on the antiunion activities of corporations and the do-nothing policies of the A.F. of L. Father Francis Haas stated that, if 70 per cent of the nation's workers had been organized in strong unions in 1929, income would have been more equitably distributed and the Depression moderated, if not avoided. He argued that the necessary redistribution of purchasing power would not come about through voluntary action; both legislation and union pressure were imperative. The ultimate goal, the Christian social order, would "rest on the union contract as on a foundation." Intelligently led, enthusiastically supported, and honestly recognized, the unions would provide "the necessary basis of our future industrial society." [13]

While many shared these views and agreed with *Commonweal* that collective bargaining provided "the best solution for the problems of industry," few could see much promise in the American Federation of Labor.[14] The federation's restriction of organization to a minority of skilled workers, its opposition to social legislation, and its limited social philosophy, were frequently criticized in the Catholic press. *America* felt that existing unions offered workers little protection against technological unemployment or the contingencies of sickness, accident, or old age. The editors condemned the A.F. of L.'s lack of militancy and its failure to organize in the mass production industries and in the south. They even charged President William Green with using the principle of union federalism as an excuse to tolerate the presence of racketeers in labor's ranks.[15]

Faced with business resistance and union apathy, many Catholic spokesmen felt compelled to look to the federal government to relieve the ills of the Depression and initiate reform. Amid a deepening sense of crisis they enthusiastically welcomed the advent of the New Deal. Yet Catholic reformers retained their interest in organized labor and even the most unqualified supporters of the Roosevelt administration urged more vigorous enforcement of the labor provisions of the recovery program and the extension of labor participation in the administration of the NRA. On the other hand, they recognized the need to expand union membership if labor was to take full advantage of the new legislation. Father Francis Haas, who served in a number of labor posts with recovery agencies, led the way in calling for organizing drives, arguing that it was the "sacred obligation" of all workers to join a union, for only "complete unionization" could compel the shorter hours and higher wages needed for recovery.[16] Others agreed on the duty of workers to join unions, but some warned that the country's nonsectarian unions were far below the standard set by the Pope.[17]

When the A.F. of L. insisted on retaining its craft structure and hesitated to take advantage of the new opportunities, it drew the wrath of Catholic journals. Similar criticism was directed at business resistance to independent organization and at company unions, which deprived workers of the solidarity and power needed for collective bargaining. *America* editorially reaffirmed the right of the government to see that private property was not used contrary to the public welfare as it was by those steel companies that defied public opinion by crushing attempts at independent labor organization.[18] When the Wagner Labor Relations Act was before Congress, the administrative committee of the NCWC filed a strong statement of support with the Education and Labor Committee. "The worker's right to form labor unions and to bargain collectively," the bishops argued, "is as much his right as is his right to participate through delegated representatives in the making of laws which regulate his civic conduct. Both are inherent rights." Only through union action could the worker order his life and secure equality of contractual power; interference with his right was unjust both to labor and to the general public.[19]

One of *America*'s contributors defended the company union, but the editors and most others disagreed. They strongly supported the Wagner Act, although they had doubts as to the constitutional right of Congress to erect an agency which could go into the states and compel recognition of the rights of labor.[20] In later years, although there was some disappointment at the operation of the National Labor Relations Board, Catholic spokesmen generally approved its objectives of insuring the rights of labor and the public and assisting in the settlement of disputes. There were a number of proposals to strengthen the mechanism for settling strikes and many priests served as mediators and arbiters, but there was almost no consistent support for compulsory arbitration during the decade.[21]

While labor questions were widely discussed in the Catholic press during the early years of the New Deal, few constructive suggestions were offered for overcoming the conservative stance of the A.F. of L. This neglect was surprising, for Catholic spokesmen again and again criticized the NRA's failure to give labor an equal voice in policy determination and they urged complete unionization with eloquence and conviction. Ryan, McGowan, Haas, and many others believed that collective bargaining was essential both for economic recovery and for Christian social reconstruction. Complete organization would give labor the power to redress the imbalance of purchasing power which lay at the heart of the Depression, while its effective participation in NRA would make that program almost completely coincide with the papal plan. Until labor was organized the nation would face the twin dangers of class strife and government domination.[22]

The formation of the Committee for Industrial Organization in 1935 promised to be an important step toward that complete organization of labor desired by Catholic leaders. During the long fight within the ranks of the A.F. of L., Catholic opinion had been solidly on the side of the proponents of industrial unionism in the mass-production industries. Catholic writers noted the desire of the unskilled for unionization and their hostility toward the craft form of organization, and they urged the federation to open its doors to both vertical and horizontal unions.[23] Despite this predisposition to favor industrial unionism a number of disturbing factors prevented unanimous Catholic approval of the C.I.O. The split in labor's ranks was regarded suspiciously by Catholic friends of the labor movement who shared its traditional hatred of dual unionism. At first Catholic commentators blamed the split on the A.F. of L. and urged quick reconciliation.

Father Paul Blakely of *America,* later a critic of the c.i.o., defended the new organization, despite its "growing pains," because its formation was a reaction to the false and unrealistic policies of the a.f. of l. The *Christian Front* blamed the split on the "stupid" policies of the a.f. of l. The editors were consistent supporters of the c.i.o., but, like all their fellow social Catholics, they deplored the split and urged labor leaders to sacrifice personal feelings to work for reunification.[24]

There were other, more serious, sources of concern. The rash of strikes, the fiery temperament of John L. Lewis, the presence of Communists within the new unions, and the generally militant and politically conscious stance of the c.i.o. worried many Catholic observers. These doubts and fears came into the open during the sit-down strikes of 1937. Expressing shock and outrage, many Catholics regarded that episode as a confirmation of their suspicions. The Brooklyn *Tablet* charged that the strikes were led by "a radical, disturbing element with a definite link to communism," while Father Edmund A. Walsh referred to the sit-down as "an alien importation" borrowed from the Communists. Father Blakely regarded the strikers' objectives as just but condemned the sit-down technique as illegal, immoral, and foolish. Father Joseph Fichter believed that the workers would be most unwise to jeopardize public support at a time when they were close to realizing their traditional objectives of union recognition and improved conditions. Even John A. Ryan stated that the sit-down tactic was at least morally questionable, was extremely difficult to control, and should be rejected by organized labor.[25]

Others regarded the strikes more sympathetically. The *Christian Front* defended the sit-down as a defensive technique aimed at preventing further incursion on the workers' rights. A *Commonweal* contributor praised the strikers for asserting the solidarity and dignity of labor. Until management regarded the workers as persons rather than commodities he thought such

tactics inevitable. Virgil Michel, the Benedictine liturgical reformer, commented suggestively that the job itself might be a
functional form of property and the laborers might have rights
to their jobs comparable to other property rights. Michel concluded that, if a strike was justified, the sit-down was a morally
legitimate weapon. This position received detailed support from
Father Jerome D. Hannan, writing in the *Ecclesiastical Review*,
a monthly publication for clergymen. Hannan believed that
there was no inherent evil in trespass, for it was not in itself an
act of violence. If the majority of workers favored a strike, if no
innocent third parties were substantially injured, and if the conditions that normally justified a strike were present, he could see
no reason why the workers could not sit down as "a protective
expedient" to prevent the use of the plant to break union
morale.[26]

Strikes, violence, and communism in the c.i.o. disturbed all
Catholics, but the emphasis on them by some Catholic critics
tended to discredit the organization as a whole. Father Coughlin
sharply disagreed with other socially minded Catholics on labor
questions. In the early stages of his career he defended labor's
right to organize but denied the right to strike. He applied the
papal vocational group idea to the union alone and then held that
it was the government's responsibility to "advise" labor, to protect its rights, and to arbitrate disputes. In 1936, while he attacked some c.i.o. leaders as communist sympathizers, he temporarily endorsed industrial unionism, advocated a voice for labor
in the making of industrial decisions, and even supported the
right to strike in certain restricted cases. Nevertheless, until 1937
labor matters were of secondary interest to the radio orator; the
basic problems of the nation were financial, not industrial. Once
released from the yoke of the "money changers" labor would be
able, with government assistance, to secure an annual living wage
and an equitable share in the abundance of the nation.[27]

After 1936 Coughlin devoted more attention to labor, bitterly denouncing the c.i.o. and John L. Lewis, whom he regarded as an "ally of the reds." The priest believed that, because the Church opposed class war and collaboration with Communists, Catholics were forbidden to join c.i.o. unions. Coughlin even organized an independent auto union in 1938 in an attempt to draw Catholics from the ranks of the c.i.o.[28] When Edward Mooney became archbishop of Detroit in 1937 he stated that there was no reason why Catholics could not join the c.i.o. Coughlin could not agree and shortly afterward left the air in circumstances that led his followers to believe he had been silenced because of his position on the union issue. During the period of maneuvering which followed, Coughlin's paper, *Social Justice*, denounced the c.i.o. as communistic in "conception . . . methods . . . and personnel." It called for the priest's return, professing shock that an anticommunist like Coughlin was silenced, while Monsignor Ryan, a critic of Coughlin and a friend of the c.i.o., was allowed to continue giving "pro-leftist" speeches.[29]

Coughlin's labor program always had authoritarian implications, and they became increasingly clear. He believed the government should limit profits and output and guarantee employment, while the Department of Labor should "counsel and guide" workers in their negotiations with capital. Strikes and lockouts were "absolutely unnecessary" and should be replaced by compulsory arbitration. He interpreted *Quadragesimo Anno* as calling for a "Corporative State" which would be democratic but stripped of political parties. All citizens would be organized into vocational or trade bodies chartered by the government. The members of the national House of Representatives would be elected from these new bodies and the House in turn would elect the President. The Senate would be composed of one representative of labor and one of capital from each state. The government would tax incomes, regulate supply and demand, and settle labor disputes.[30]

While few prominent Catholics agreed with Coughlin's reading of the encyclicals, many echoed his opinion of the c.i.o. and its leadership. A number of articles appeared in the Catholic press attacking the c.i.o., the principle of industrial organization, and even the closed shop. Pointing to broken contracts, strike violence, and communist influence, the editors of *America* described John L. Lewis's leadership as "weak and impotent." Lewis, they believed, was dominated by an insatiable greed for power and publicity and was "an unsafe leader" for American labor, an opinion shared by other Catholic journals.[31]

Father James Gillis of the *Catholic World* was appalled by the increasing number of strikes, which he believed the Wagner Act should have made unnecessary. Coupled with evidence of communist penetration of the unions, they led Gillis to fear that Lewis might be "our Lenin." One contributor lashed out at Lewis's "mad leadership" of "an utterly unthinking, passion dominated, fanatic army of labor [who had] no legitimate grievances in the majority of cases." [32] Less heated but equally firm rejection of the c.i.o. came from Edward Koch, who still believed that the unions merely perpetuated class division and intensified class strife. He and many other Catholics accepted the judgment of a speaker at the second National Catholic Social Action Conference in 1939 that, while the labor movement contained many good men, it had "the red blood of communism in its veins." [33]

Another important critic of the c.i.o. was Bishop John F. Noll of Fort Wayne, editor of the widely circulated *Our Sunday Visitor*. Noll believed that the new unions were under the strong influence of Communists, and his paper went so far as to charge that c.i.o. leader John Brophy was not only not a Catholic but was at least a sympathizer of the communist cause. The accusation was picked up by other papers and Brophy, his wife, and friends, including Father Ryan and the editor of the *Pittsburgh Catholic*, were forced to respond vigorously. *Our Sunday*

Visitor withdrew its charge, although Bishop Noll insisted that Brophy had been a Socialist and did not understand the importance of the communist danger. Noll wrote the union leader that he found it "difficult to believe that you have the mind of the Church, which is certainly opposed to cooperation with communists." Brophy himself gave a number of speeches before Catholic audiences, defending himself and explaining the C.I.O.'s policy toward communism, but Noll was not alone in finding his arguments unconvincing.[34]

During these years of controversy no collective assessment of the new unionism came from the American hierarchy. In 1937 the bishops warned labor against the use of violence, coercion, and intimidation, but they continued to endorse unionization and collective bargaining generally while urging the formation of joint bodies—occupational groups—to settle labor-management disputes and pave the way for a just co-operative social order.[35] A common view was expressed by Bishop Karl J. Alter of Toledo, who feared that the old danger of rugged individualism was being replaced by a new threat of labor irresponsibility. Alter warned against violence and mass picketing, he defended the right of the public to assert its paramount interest in labor disputes, and he regarded the right to work to be equally sacred as the right to strike. On the other hand, Alter joined with Bishop Edwin O'Hara of Kansas City to issue a statement of social principles that endorsed labor organization, free collective bargaining, and the participation of workers in profits and management.[36]

Although national pronouncements and social manifestos were confined to general statements of principle and although many bishops remained neutral in labor disputes, the C.I.O. had important, highly placed defenders. In Chicago, where George Cardinal Mundelein set a progressive tone on social questions, Monsignor Reynold Hillenbrand trained a generation of seminarians in the responsibilities of the social apostolate and communi-

cated a highly positive view of trade unionism. Auxiliary Bishop
Bernard Sheil publicly insisted on the duty of Catholics to join
labor unions. Sheil supported the c.i.o.'s organizing drive among
the heavily Catholic packinghouse workers, and he openly
backed a c.i.o. strike against the Hearst newspapers.[37]

Detroit's Archbishop Mooney not only denied Coughlin's contention that Catholics could not join the c.i.o. but supported
groups working to encourage Catholic participation. "Let there
be no doubt about it," Mooney told a meeting of Catholic businessmen, "labor organization, sound and responsible organization
on democratic principles, is not merely something which the
Church accepts as an inevitable development of our industrial
society, it is something which she wholeheartedly approves."
Every worker had a responsibility to join and take an active
interest in his union, Mooney insisted, and any priest who urged
them to stay aloof was derelict in his duty.[38]

Archbishop Robert Lucey of San Antonio was another outspoken supporter of the c.i.o. Lucey insisted that organization
was a precondition for social reconstruction and he criticized
those who suggested that reform must await spiritual and moral
change. With all the money and power on the side of capital,
Lucey argued that workers had "a duty to join a labor union
for their own good, the welfare of their families, and the peace
and security of human society." [39] Noting that Catholics who
thought themselves loyal to papal teachings and compassionate
toward the poor often ended in alliance with reactionary opponents of reform and unionization, Lucey rebuked Catholics who
professed friendship for labor and criticized the unions at the
same time. "Devotion to the laboring classes," he insisted, "automatically includes the union." [40] The bishop told John L. Lewis
that the encyclicals endorsed industrial unionism but that the
Pope wished labor to go further, to join in the management of
industry. As for the communist issue, Lucey believed that
charges of communism leveled at the c.i.o., which was "a

messiah to millions," amounted to a slander of the working class. Depressed by the alacrity with which his fellow Catholics responded to anticommunist crusades, Lucey hoped that education in Catholic social teachings would enable them eventually to take a more constructive role in the nation's life.[41]

Outside the hierarchy the c.i.o.'s defenders were as numerous as its critics. John Ryan was personally friendly with several c.i.o. leaders, defending them against charges of communism and refuting Catholic attacks on the new unions. Nevertheless Ryan continued to regard unionism as inadequate; while urging labor to develop a broader social program, he concentrated his attention on government action as the only adequate method of weakening the power of business and initiating significant structural changes. Father McGowan was more enthusiastic. Pointing out that most of the strikes of the period were aimed at recognition of the union as a bargaining agent, he urged Catholics to support such recognition because collective bargaining remained a necessary basis for the future industrial democracy.[42]

The *Christian Front* defended Lewis against Catholic attacks and printed an article on industrial unionism by the embattled leader. The paper tried to divorce the union from the question of communism, arguing that its objectives were good in themselves and in full accord with the encyclicals. According to editor Richard Deverall, Lewis and his colleagues were attempting to break through the opportunistic traditions of the a.f. of l. and to establish a progressive, socially conscious unionism. Opposition to Lewis in 1937, Deverall believed, was tantamount to opposition to labor and to social justice.[43] The paper answered charges of communism by pointing to the conditions that made labor single-minded in its drive for recognition and improved conditions. The Communists were able to offer a program and were the most selfless and dedicated organizers and workers for the unions. The Christian task, the editors believed, was to regard the religiously neutral unions as fields for apostolic endeavor and to train and inspire Catholic workingmen with the social outlook and philosophy of the Church. This task was to be carried on within the c.i.o., and the Church should support its legitimate objectives, attempt to offset communist influence and broaden the organization's program to include a system of vocational groups as a long-range objective. The insistence of the *Christian Front* that the Catholic worker had an obligation to join the unions and work within them to counter communist influence and demonstrate that the Church was the friend of labor was echoed throughout important segments of the Catholic press.[44]

To further this end a group of workingmen connected with the New York Catholic Worker House of Hospitality formed the Association of Catholic Trade Unionists, the a.c.t.u., in 1937. The purpose of the new society was to promote unionization and the attainment of legitimate union objectives while educating Catholic members in the social program of the Church. Catholic unionists would thereby "gain the confidence and following, or at least the respect of their non-Catholic fellows by their zeal and by their self-sacrifice for the common good." In doing so they would "raise the level of the union's policy closer to a Christian plane." [45] The new organization was not a divisive faction seeking to "get control" of the unions, as Bishop Noll had urged. Instead, Catholic unionists attempted to break down Catholic clannishness by insisting upon the responsibility of Catholics to co-operate with others for the attainment of legitimate common objectives.[46]

The a.c.t.u. was forced to defend itself on two sides. Not only did conservative Catholics oppose its work within the c.i.o., but some of its friends in the Catholic Worker movement were upset by the a.c.t.u.'s acceptance of an urbanized industrial order.[47] In reply John Cort, one of the founders of the new organization, defended the conception of the Christian social order as a society in which industry and agriculture were organized on the basis of co-operation between capital and labor. Cort believed that the best hope of achieving the new order lay in developing effective labor participation in industry. Something like Michel's notion of property rights to the job was needed because the right to work could not long be maintained without actual rights in the means of production. Specifically the A.C.T.U. upheld the right of the worker to earn a living wage on an annual basis, to work decent hours under decent working conditions, to strike and to picket, and to share in profits after a just return to capital and management.[48] The organization consistently emphasized labor's duty to join and support the unions, to fulfill contracts, to refrain from violence, to strike only for a just cause after exhausting other means of solution, to conduct the unions democratically, and to join with employers who respected the rights of labor in order to end industrial warfare through a system of industrial self-government.[49]

The A.C.T.U. conducted labor schools and supported those established by individual bishops; it published several labor papers, investigated and supported strikes, attempted to interest priests in labor affairs, and provided legal assistance for rank-and-file efforts to overthrow racketeering and communist leadership. Pledging itself against dual unionism, the A.C.T.U rested upon faith in the power of Christianity to attract workingmen and make American labor a partner with capital in a new era of industrial democracy.[50]

The Pittsburgh chapter of the A.C.T.U. was among the most militant. An outgrowth of the local Catholic Worker House of Hospitality, the Catholic Radical Alliance, as the group called itself, was led by two priests, Fathers Charles Owen Rice and Carl P. Hensler. Both participated in the organizational drives of the C.I.O. among steel and textile workers. Attempting to offset antiunion propaganda they defended the C.I.O. and told Catholic workers they had a duty to join the union. Hensler warned steel workers that they faced a "hard bitter fight" against the industry's "vested interests." The employer who fought the union and spoke of his own benevolence toward his employees could be "trusted to sell his workers down the river whenever it is to his advantage," Hensler said. Recognizing the eventual need for an occupational group system, Rice, Hensler, and other "labor priests" concentrated on the minimum requirements of organization and recognition, without which all talk of a Christian social order was naïve utopianism.[51]

The *Christian Front* and the A.C.T.U. both manifested the influence on numerous young Catholics of the Catholic Worker movement, founded in 1933 by Peter Maurin and Dorothy Day. Maurin deplored labor unions because they compromised with the prostitution of human labor inherent in the wage system. Labor, he believed, was not a commodity to be bought and sold but "a means of self-expression, the worker's gift to the common good, which should not be sold for wages." [52] Although Dorothy Day dedicated herself to Maurin's program, her socialist background and her personal compassion drew her to the labor movement. Through the penny newspaper, the *Catholic Worker*, she pledged her support to the workingmen while she sought to indoctrinate them with Maurin's ideas of basic social reconstruction. Unions, while imperfect, were for Dorothy the "only weapons which Christian workers have to defend their rights as individuals and Christians against a system which makes the Christ-life impossible to large numbers of workers." [53] Accordingly she visited the sit-down strikers and defended their cause. When dock workers in New York struck, she published a special edition of the paper and set up a soup line for strikers. The *Catholic Worker* supported the C.I.O. because it offered workers a chance to reassert their dignity; it urged all unions to use "pure means," and it refuted Catholics who attempted to pin a communist label on the new unions and their leaders, assisted in all this work by the groups it fostered, the A.C.T.U. and the Catholic Radical Alliance.[54]

On labor questions, as on so many other issues, the American Catholic community was seriously divided in the 1930's. Despite the strong endorsement of unions by the modern popes, Catholics were able to disagree over the character and methods of existing labor organizations. Almost all spokesmen agreed that specifically Catholic unions were impractical in the United States, but many nevertheless criticized secular unions for not acting in accord with Catholic teachings. Too often Catholic critics appeared to expect the unions, organized for specific economic purposes, to act as though their objectives were religious. More realistic observers like Father Haas recognized that the immediate problem was one of power. The workers must organize and act to secure a minimum of justice in the face of the ruthless opposition of industry. Hopefully this would lead to the establishment of a balanced economy, which might serve as a basis for the construction of a Christian social order. In any case it would provide a more fruitful ground for the dissemination of the Christian message of love and charity than the old order of rugged individualism.[55]

All Catholics interpreted *Quadragesimo Anno* as calling for restructuring of the economic life of the nation. Those concerned with labor problems habitually placed the union within a broader program aimed at eventual co-operation between labor and management with some degree of labor participation in the new government of industry. Such a program sounded radical, but in a society where capital did not acknowledge the right of organized labor to exist, the workers themselves might not always manifest a delicate concern for the rights of property or the demands of the common good. Labor might, on the contrary, betray a militant self-consciousness and a narrow preoccupation with its rights rather than its responsibilities. In such a context emphasis upon the need for a broad social vision, for a charitable outlook, and for labor-management co-operation could eventuate in criticism of the unions and de facto alliance with the industrial paternalism of the old order.

In addition, Catholics had difficulty relating the goal of the Christian social order to the means at hand. The editors of *America* desired labor organization and collective bargaining, but they criticized the A.F. of L. for its lack of militancy and the C.I.O. for its class-consciousness. Unable to discover how their goals could be achieved without disorder and even violence they, and many of their contemporaries, could only fall back on moral reform, the change of heart which must precede the change of institutions. Such an attitude could be supported by Pius XI's insistence that "the first and most necessary remedy is a reform of morals," but it could easily hamper effective participation in a mass reform movement.

The more militant supporters of the C.I.O. recognized the tremendous obstacles to the construction of a new order. They chose the activist course, reasoning that the attainment of justice was a prerequisite not only of the new order but of moral change as well, for men would not think of their salvation, or of the common good, while they lacked the means of a decent livelihood and were treated with indignity in their work. The labor priests and their journalistic counterparts were unable to see the route by which the militant C.I.O. would become an instrument for establishing a co-operative social order, but they tried to clear the way for that order by joining the workers in their struggle as Leo XIII had urged. Some feared the communist alternative, but many were more concerned with the reactionary and ruthless activities of industry. They failed in one sense, for Catholic thought in the long run exerted little influence on labor's development. Once they attained organization and recognition, the workers did not move on to industrial self-government but settled comfortably into the middle class. Yet the new situation of an affluent America after the war was vastly more just than the industrial life of the thirties, and in contributing to that change Catholics fulfilled the mission of Christian social action in what was perhaps the most effective way possible during that decade.

VI

John A. Ryan and the
Social Action Department

After the establishment of the National Catholic Welfare Conference following World War I American Catholicism possessed an agency for co-ordinated national action. With headquarters in Washington, the NCWC kept in close touch with national affairs, informing interested Church leaders, Catholic organizations, and the Catholic press of developments effecting Church interests and acting as a spokesman, even a lobby, for the Church before congressional committees and executive departments. The scope of this activity was suggested by William Montavon, legal director of the NCWC, in his semi-annual report of April 1933. Montavon estimated that five thousand bills had been introduced in the Congress then sitting, of which about one-third demanded his department's attention, requiring at the time "daily contact" with thirty-six committees of the House and Senate. Items of particular interest to the Church, like Mexican policy, relief programs, and medical care, necessitated active intervention by one or more departments of the NCWC as well as the occasional assistance of the executive secretary or the administrative committee of bishops.[1]

The NCWC's involvement in legislative matters, inevitable given the wide-ranging social and charitable activities of the Church, remained but one aspect of its work. The departments for press, lay organization, and education, concentrated their attention on providing information and co-ordinating organized action, with varying degrees of success. Despite the apparent power of the NCWC, it remained essentially a voluntary educational body providing assistance to those who requested it and serving as a forum for the hierarchy when the bishops desired to use it. Nevertheless, while the actions of the departmental staffs could not bind bishops, religious orders, or Catholic agencies, the leaders of the NCWC were left relatively free to work for the spread and adoption of the positions they supported, and the prestige of their posts gave their work a sanction that was often invaluable.

This was clearly true of the Social Action Department. Its director from 1919 to 1944 was John A. Ryan, American Catholicism's foremost social reformer. The post gave Ryan great influence in the Catholic community: he conducted educational programs to familiarize Americans with the papal encyclicals, he offered his interpretation of papal thought and guided statements of the hierarchy, which were usually drafted in his office. On the other hand his position gave his work an official character that could improve the image of the Church in the eyes of non-Catholic Americans. Ryan, indeed, became the link between American Catholics and liberal, progressive groups, interpreting them to each other and helping lead his fellow Catholics to a more complete awareness not only of the Church's social teaching but of the necessity for reform in order to realize the ideals of their dual American and Catholic heritage.

Ryan's career extended back to the early years of the century when he had begun examining the moral side of economic questions in the Catholic press. With the publication of *A Living Wage* in 1906 he became the most prominent Catholic cleric interested in social problems. A leading progressive, active in the Consumers League, the Public Ownership League, the National Conference of Charities and Correction, and numerous other reform organizations, Ryan headed the fight for minimum-wage legislation in several states. Raised in rural Minnesota in the late nineteenth century, Ryan as a young man read Henry George and thrilled to the oratory of neighbor Ignatius Donnely and other populists in the state legislature. In 1894 he read *Rerum Novarum*, noted Leo XIII's call to the clergy to interest themselves in the social problem, and decided to devote his life to "the social gospel" of Christ. "It seemed to me," he wrote years later, "that the salvation of millions of souls depended largely upon the economic opportunity to live decently, to live as human beings made in the image and likeness of God." [2] The "pitiably small" number of bishops and priests engaged in such work distressed Ryan, as did the negative, antisocialist interpretation of *Rerum Novarum* current in the United States. He attributed these problems primarily to the material difficulties involved in caring for poor immigrant congregations, but he placed some of the blame on weak seminary training, which included nothing of Catholic social thought, nothing of social science, only an overly abstract moral theology, and which resulted in a large measure of ignorance among the Catholic clergy of the suffering and injustice present in their society. Even his great superior, Archbishop Ireland, who could not believe that the wealthy and good men who were his friends would stoop to economic oppression, had been "mistaken," Ryan believed, "because he was not in possession of the relevant facts." [3]

Ryan's own awareness of the problems of the agrarian west helped him reject the negative interpretation of the encyclical, while his independent study of economics and his training in new methods of moral theology assisted him in finding a more constructive application of papal teachings to American society. Ryan's knowledge of economics distinguished him from most other American Catholic reformers. From his reading of English economist John A. Hobson in particular, Ryan derived an economic basis for his own moral rejection of economic liberalism. Hobson's argument that maldistribution of wealth and income could impede production and stagnate the entire economic system became a mainstay of Ryan's thought. In the twilight of his life Ryan acknowledged that he had "embraced Hobson's underconsumption and oversaving theory" as soon as he had "a sufficient understanding of it" and that he still regarded the theory as the most satisfactory explanation of the economic developments of his lifetime.[4]

Ryan's was the reformer's approach to economics, beginning with the assumption that the economy was not autonomous but subordinate to morality and capable of serving distinctive human purposes. American Protestants had been preaching such a doctrine for twenty years before Ryan arrived on the scene. Many of the men who founded the American Economics Association were seeking to bring social science into accord with the ideals of the Protestant social gospel. Most prominent in this work was Richard T. Ely who, like his friend Ryan, upheld the primacy of morals over economics, rejected classical assumptions, and believed that the State should actively promote objectives of human welfare.[5] Ryan brought to American Catholicism the same religious zeal and social concern which characterized the social gospel, but he had a distinct advantage over his Protestant friends because of the social tradition of his Church, reawakened by Pope Leo XIII. Whereas Washington Gladden and Walter Rauschenbusch had to contend with an individualistic, even libertarian, Protestantism, Ryan could draw on the authority of Catholic philosophy and papal pronouncements in his advocacy of Catholic social reform.

Although Ryan's interest in economics for reform required a strong ethical background, he showed little interest in moral philosophy or theology until he went to study at Catholic University after his ordination. Father William Kerby, his professor

of moral theology, was a leader in the formation of the National
Conference of Catholic Charities and a pioneer in American
social Catholicism. He awakened in his students a concern with
social problems and an awareness of the difficulty of applying
traditional moral principles in changing historical situations.
Similarly, Thomas Bouquillon in moral philosophy had little
patience with abstract and a priori moral judgments, rendered
without regard to the social, political, and economic forces
at work on the individual. Bouquillon drew students away
from exclusive concern with the learning of moral principles
and directed their attention to the context of decision making.

Ryan's pragmatic temperament and progressive sympathies
made him particularly receptive to such an approach, which also
blended well with his concern about the clergy's lack of factual
information. On the other hand the accumulation of data was
only half of Ryan's methodology. Whatever the necessity for
correct information, Ryan still relied on moral principles derived
from natural law to interpret facts and suggest reforms. In attacking his clerical contemporaries for overemphasizing abstract
principles, he was not questioning the principles themselves
but only the failure to apply them realistically and effectively.
In moral philosophy per se Ryan was always a traditionalist.
One of his students wrote that in the application of papal teaching Ryan made "complete and unfettered use of his vigorous
intellect" but that his reliance on the principles of the encyclicals
was "truly childlike." [6] Reasoning from fixed first principles
Ryan arrived at moral judgments and only then, by a pragmatic method, sought to apply the results to contemporary
problems. Primarily a reformer, his major work was in this area
of application. In the early years of his career, when his aims
corresponded so well with the dominant reform mood, he
himself probably did not realize how great a gap separated him
from many of his liberal colleagues. Framing his arguments in

pragmatic terms and utilizing a semi-populist rhetoric that was second nature since his youth, he always sounded like a typical American progressive.

This combination of orthodoxy and reform characterized Ryan's early writings in which he drew heavily on the philosophical tradition of the Church, centering his attention on individual rights rather than the functional social organization that preoccupied many of his European contemporaries. For example, he defined society as "an organism whose purpose is to safeguard the rights and promote to a reasonable degree the welfare of every one of its members," but he warned that "its members do not exist and function for its welfare, they possess intrinsic worth and sacredness." The proximate end of society was the good life for the individual, the development of all his faculties "with greatest stress upon those that are most important for the individual's ultimate end," salvation.[7] Because the natural order was created by God, man's proximate and ultimate ends had to be in harmony. Accordingly Ryan believed that the advancement of the general welfare necessarily aided the attainment of individual salvation. Time and again he insisted that "in the long run genuine expediency is identical with right and truth." [8] On such a basis Catholics could co-operate with non-Catholics to obtain temporal objectives confident that necessary and just reforms would by definition not only bring about right social order but also establish conditions most conducive to proper Christian life.

Thus the conflict between the individual and society which so disturbed American reformers presented little problem for Ryan. Conflicts between personal liberty and the common good were mediated by the principle of subsidiarity: "The end of the state is to promote the common good only to the extent that this object cannot be obtained by the family and by voluntary associations." [9] The subsidiarity principle, often used by American Catholics in doctrinaire fashion to oppose federal action on social questions, in the hands of Ryan became a powerful support for governmental intervention when serious needs existed which could be dealt with in no other manner. A good deal of Ryan's energies were directed to showing the national character of social and economic problems and the inadequacy of private, local, and state action in solving them.

Ryan's pragmatic application of traditional principles to new problems challenged many of the economic and social assumptions of his day. *A Living Wage*, with its plea for legislated minimum-wage standards, established Ryan's reputation in progressive circles. Ryan's thesis manifested his emphasis on the primacy of the individual:[10]

> The laborer's claim to a Living Wage is of the nature of a *right*. This right is personal, not merely social: that is to say, it belongs to the individual as individual, and not as a member of society; it is the laborer's personal prerogative, not his share of the social good; and its primary end is the welfare of the laborer, not that of society.

In the modern world the right to sustain life required the payment of decent wages. The duty of providing them fell on employers, whose control of the means of producing goods should not be used to prevent others from making a living. In addition, consumers were bound to pay fair prices, sufficient to allow the payment of fair wages, while workers had a responsibility to organize for the purpose of improving wage levels. The State, by its very nature the guardian of natural rights, was bound to help by establishing conditions conducive to the practice of justice, in this case by the passage and enforcement of minimum-wage laws.

Uniquely, Ryan put his economic training to work to quantify the living-wage idea for the United States. Consideration had to be taken of "the material requisites for decent living," food, clothing, and shelter for the worker and his family. In addition provision had to be made for sickness, accident, and old age and for the satisfaction of mental and spiritual needs such as amusement, recreation, education, membership in literary, benefit, and labor organizations, and contributions to churches and charities. In 1906, he set $600 as a minimum figure in the South with more needed in the North; in 1920, he revised his figure to one of $1600.[11] The majority of workers did not meet either standard.

The preoccupation with justice in his first study was symptomatic of Ryan's general concern. Unlike other Catholic thinkers, he devoted little effort to consideration of the virtue of charity, to which justice is subordinate in Catholic thought. In his second major work, *Distributive Justice*, he carried his treatment of justice beyond wage policy to consideration of the economy as a whole. Nowhere was the potential flexibility and practicality of Catholic social thought more clearly demonstrated than in Ryan's repeated arguments of social utility. He upheld the right of private property in land on the pragmatic grounds that "in present conditions the institution is necessary for individual and social welfare." On the other hand Capitalists had no intrinsic right to interest on investments; the question was solely one of whether sufficient capital would be forthcoming without the interest incentive. Ryan argued that after the vital needs of all participants in industry had been met, further distribution of profits should be allocated to wages, higher profits, and lower prices on the basis of "maximum net result" in terms of productivity, talent, sacrifice, and, most important, the welfare of society as a whole.[12]

This emphasis on justice and welfare had important implications. The demands of justice are relatively clear and subject to legal enforcement; the function of the State, indeed, is to protect rights, to enforce justice, while safeguarding the general welfare. Concentration on justice, and use of welfare as a criterion for cases where no intrinsic right is involved, leads naturally to the State and, accordingly, reliance on public authority was a characteristic that distinguished Ryan's thought from that of many other progressives. In the early years of his career, Ryan's individualistic inheritance led him to place his hope in private, voluntary action, with the State establishing minimum standards and clearing the field of monopolies. As his awareness of the power and selfishness of business increased, he was prepared to endow the State with ever-greater responsibilities.

In some respects the early years of the century were Ryan's most successful. Prominent for his advocacy of the living wage, he was closely associated with the leading reformers of the day, sharing their Christian idealism and their concern for the fate of the individual in the emerging industrial order. Dealing like the others with the problems of a functioning and relatively prosperous society, Ryan's program was limited. He gave his greatest attention to wages because he believed that higher wages would make the worker capable of caring for himself without the aid of such temporary expedients as social insurance. Concerned with the status as well as the material sufficiency of the working class, Ryan took great interest in co-operatives, both of consumers and of producers, and was attracted to schemes for profit sharing and copartnership. In the 1920's, with the assistance of Father Raymond McGowan, Ryan developed these ideas into a general program of industrial democracy. Through a series of steps, including co-operative decision making on the plant level, profit sharing, and eventual sharing in ownership, the worker, though deprived of individual ownership of his tools, would become an integral part of the industrial system. By sharing in decision making, he would be able to exercise all of his faculties and gain a sense of responsibility for the welfare of his firm. Increased wage levels, profit sharing, and ownership of stock, would provide workers with security against contingencies, independence, and status.[13]

This development of a full-blown program for industrial democracy involved changes in Ryan's attitude toward labor unions. His first published articles had dealt with compulsory arbitration, an idea he did not abandon until well into the 1920's. His increasing awareness of the selfishness of the business community combined with his recognition of the value of the union for educating the worker in co-operation and group consciousness to bring some modification in his views. He still considered unions primarily self-interested organizations, and he urged them to acquire a wider social vision, looking toward a system akin to his own industrial program. He did not approve of the A.F. of L., for he had always thought the craft union form a selfish one, preferring industrial unions in which skilled workers joined with the unskilled in a common effort to raise wages and better conditions. His dislike of the A.F. of L. was sharpened by the federation's opposition to minimum-wage legislation, which Ryan took to indicate their acceptance of a pagan individualism.[14]

The Social Action Department's advocacy of industrial democracy implied its recognition of industrialism as a permanent phenomenon to be accepted and Christianized. Ryan's populist heritage might have led him to approve Hilaire Belloc's arguments against the possibility of Christian living in an urban industrial environment. Further, Father Edwin V. O'Hara's National Catholic Rural Life Conference was a mainstay of the department in the twenties, and this organization, dedicated to a realistic program of rural improvement, contained elements fundamentally hostile to the city and factory. Ryan was not immune to these feelings. Many times he stated his conviction that farm life was more conducive to the development of Christian character than life in the city. In 1920, he wrote that cities larger than 150,000 were, "on the whole, an evil rather than a blessing." [15] Like many of his fellow Catholics, he was concerned by statistics that purported to show that urban populations did not reproduce themselves, raising the fear that the Catholic Church would face ultimate extinction in the United States if more Catholics did not settle on the land. Fortunately, his economic training and pragmatic sense led Ryan to reject any long-range program based on a return to the land. The Depression, raising immediate problems of unemployment and human misery, forced his attention almost completely to industrial matters. Although he approved New Deal experiments in subsistence homesteads and continued to support the work of the Rural Life Conference, agriculture never drew his serious attention as a solution to economic or Christian problems.

During the twenties Ryan's new post made him a Catholic spokesman on issues like Prohibition and Church-State relations, distracting his attention from socio-economic problems, which were his primary concern. A member of the American Civil Liberties Union and a consistent defender of free speech, Ryan nevertheless engaged in a running battle with other liberals over such questions as birth control and religious persecution in Mexico.[16] Ryan frequently expressed his "disgust and disillusionment over the cowardice and illiberalism of most American liberals" who, by ignoring or defending curtailments of religious freedom in Mexico, Russia, and, later, Spain, were implicitly admitting that liberal principles were not of universal validity, as Ryan believed, but were limited by circumstances, a view Ryan branded as "Toryism." [17]

The presidential campaign of 1928 intensified Catholic minority sensitivity and one episode of that campaign sheds light on Ryan's beliefs. In 1924 he had published with Moorhouse F. X. Millar a collection of writings on Church and State. In his part of the book Ryan had set forth traditional Catholic teachings, even stating that in a Catholic country suppression of some of the religious liberty of minorities could be justified. Ryan added modifications, stating that such restrictions could not unduly violate civil order, and citing a German Jesuit to the effect that no modern nation could be called Catholic, and therefore, the doctrine was irrelevant. Smith's critics picked up the passage, naturally ignoring the modifications, and Ryan was forced to defend his writings during the campaign. The articles, arguing the good citizenship of Catholics and their acceptance of American separation of Church and State, were not particularly convincing and lacked the emotional appeal of Al Smith's own reply to Charles C. Marshall.[18] Ryan blamed Smith's defeat on anti-Catholic prejudice, and a rift opened with the Protestants similar to that which had developed with the liberals. Fortunately, Ryan did not allow his bitterness to interfere with continued interfaith co-operation for social reform.[19]

Ryan's problems in the twenties were not all with non-Catholics. Though his position in the NCWC had increased his stature in the Catholic world, he nevertheless had powerful critics. The Social Action Department supported the proposed child-labor amendment to the Constitution which the Catholic hierarchy and most of the Catholic press opposed, as it appeared to give undue control over education and family life to the federal government. Ryan was not always fair in such controversies and he frequently charged opponents with being apologists for big business. Cardinal O'Connell of Boston bombarded Archbishop Curley, Ryan's superior, with demands that he be removed from his post at Catholic University. Ryan could count on widespread support in the hierarchy and his position was never really in doubt, but the Boston archdiocese remained closed to him thereafter.[20]

The pervasiveness of business influence, the reactionary decisions of the Supreme Court, government's neglect of basic human needs, business's open shop campaign, these things made Ryan regard the twenties as an age of emerging "industrial feudalism." Ryan's Catholic philosophy, with its realism and long memory, strengthened him against the despair that gripped many of his fellow progressives. His political theory and his pragmatic application of the subsidiarity principle indicated that the federal government was the natural and necessary organ for the realization of justice and the common good. Accordingly, he concluded that only government supervision of the bituminous industry and actual operation of the anthracite industry could relieve chaotic conditions in the coal fields. Ryan also supported Senator Norris's campaign for public ownership of Muscle Shoals and devoted a good deal of time to the issue of utilities regulation, which he called "the most important political and economic question now before the American people." [21]

When the Depression arrived in 1929, Ryan possessed a tool for analyzing its causes and its cure in the theory of underconsumption drawn from his earlier reading of Hobson and he had already come to rely on federal action, a shift many progressives still had to make. What the experience of the Depression added to Ryan's writings was a new sense of urgency borne of the spectacle of want amidst plenty. His rationalism and moralism were equally offended; poverty in the United States was both unchristian and un-American. "If our economy were organized rationally and functioning rationally," he wrote, "no person nor any family would be compelled to live in poverty because of lack of income." The experience of depression clearly demonstrated the fallacy of the idea of a self-regulating economy; from now on the responsibility for establishing a just prosperity fell on the State: [22]

> In a country as rich as ours men have the moral right to something more than immunity from starvation. They have the right to decent maintenance and elementary comfort. The obligation of enabling them to enjoy this right falls upon the State. In our country the State, at least the federal government, is fully able to perform this obligation. If the President and Congress do not meet it, they are guilty of grave inhumanity to their fellow citizens. They are false to their public trust.

The emotions of the 1928 campaign perhaps were echoed in Ryan's vehement denunciation of President Hoover for his failure to act to relieve distress. Rejecting Hoover's contention that foreign influences on the economy caused the Depression, Ryan held that it was 90 per cent domestic in origin and cure. Unemployment was "due to the chronic capacity of our industries to produce more goods than can be sold," [23] and this in turn resulted from lack of consumer purchasing power: agriculture was depressed and at least one-third of American workers received less than a living wage. Solutions based on confidence, foreign trade, or currency manipulation all ignored this basic problem. In a mature economy unemployment and instability were inevitable as long as there was not sufficient demand to keep consumer-goods industries operating. Demand could not be sustained unless wages were sufficient to allow the public to purchase these goods. The economic, and moral, imperative was redistribution of income to allow all Americans to share in their nation's plenty. Here again was proof of Ryan's belief that good ethics was good economics.

To implement this theory Ryan had a program: stable and higher wages, shorter work week to distribute available jobs, lower interest rates to forestall excess profits, prevent further expansion of productive capacity, and absorb the cost of increased wages. Most important in the short run was a huge, $5 billion public works program. Only this large an expenditure, Ryan felt, could bring significant re-employment. The program would be financed by a bond issue bearing no interest, which would attract the huge amounts of idle capital. As public authority could not abide starvation, the only alternative Ryan foresaw was public operation of basic industries.[24]

Keeping one eye on the ever-rising unemployment statistics, Ryan castigated Hoover for "his lack of political ability, of intellectual honesty, of straight forwardness and of courage." Writing frequently of "our bankrupt leadership," Ryan came to see the President as the incarnation of economic liberalism, a man imprisoned by the a priori reasoning of the classical economists, willing to tolerate suffering in the naïve hope that the economy would somehow automatically right itself. He demonstrated, in

Ryan's view, his "incapacity to grapple with the problem of the depression." [25]

In this atmosphere Ryan received the second of the great social encyclicals, Pius XI's *Quadragesimo Anno*, published in May 1931. With some justice the encyclical was called a vindication of Ryan. This was especially true of the Pope's extension of the living-wage principle to include the maintenance of the worker's family, which Ryan had urged twenty-five years earlier. The endorsement of labor unions, the call for clerical action on social problems, and the recognition of the common interests of capital and labor, were frequent Ryan themes. Ryan accepted the occupational group system as the only possible middle ground between socialism and individualism. He professed to see in the system the reconciliation of capital and labor, of planning and democracy, of individual rights and dignity and the common good. Ryan's interpretation of the occupational-group idea differed little from his own program for industrial democracy. To the earlier scheme of profit sharing and copartnership he now added an additional stage, when all the factories of an industry would join together to set policy for the industry as a whole. Such a system, Ryan believed, would still be capitalistic, but stripped of its liberal philosophy. The new capitalism would make provision for the sufficiency and security of labor, which would share in responsibility, operation, and ownership of each firm. Monopoly would be checked by competition, or if necessary, by government ownership and price fixing. Some degree of competition would remain, and the profit system, limited by societal needs, would be retained.

Because Ryan devoted himself to explaining and defending the New Deal to American Catholics, his description of the occupational group system was less significant than his conviction that the Pope had placed primary responsibility for the establishment of social justice on public authority. This meant that not only should government take the initiative in establishing the occupational group system, but it must also accept responsibility for alleviating distress, stabilizing the economy, and providing work for all citizens. In particular, the new principle of social justice meant a call for class legislation, for action on behalf of groups too weak to obtain their rights in the private economic order.[26]

As *Quadragesimo Anno* appeared a vindication of John Ryan's efforts in the field of Catholic social action, so the administration of Franklin D. Roosevelt seemed to cap off his work as a progressive reformer. Although Ryan hoped Newton D. Baker would be the Democratic candidate in 1932, he soon recognized the similarity between his own ideas and those of Franklin D. Roosevelt, and he responded eagerly to the latter's invitation to serve as an advisor on policy. The objective of the new President was the same as Ryan's: the rational direction of the economy to attain moral ends. The New Deal would teach Americans, Ryan believed, "that economics is subject to ethics, that industrial activities are governed by the moral law." [27] In Pius XI's encyclical Ryan found a demand to use State power to check greed, assist weaker classes, and promote the general welfare; in his eyes the New Deal would do just these things.

In numerous articles and speeches Ryan applauded the long-sought expenditures for relief and public works and urged the spending of even more. An early advocate of the voluntary domestic allotment plan for dealing with agricultural surpluses, he welcomed the AAA and particularly defended its tax on food processors. Most important, the NRA, in reducing hours of work and establishing minimum-wage standards, followed a theory of the Depression similar to Ryan's and accepted his life-long goal of the living wage. The system of code authorities closely approximated the occupational group system, Ryan believed: "they could readily be developed into an industrial system which could be in complete accord with the social order proposed by the Holy Father." [28] For Ryan the New Deal legislation represented a "new industrial revolution [which] contradicts every element of the old economic liberalism." America, he told British readers, had been "the classic land of *laissez-faire* and of *almost* universal faith in the beneficent and automatic operation of a regime of practically unbridled individualism." If one did not look too deeply, the doctrine had appeared to be vindicated by the scope of the achievement. The Depression cleared the air of hypocrisy and laid bare the falseness of the prosperity which preceded it.[29] The New Deal abandoned the old philosophy and adopted something akin to the traditional Christian concept of the State, as expounded most recently by Pius XI. Ryan summed up his views of the New Deal, views which he never altered: [30]

> The general policy of greatly increased governmental regulation and assistance is constitutionally justifiable and morally right. The particular policies are on the whole ethically sound; they are morally right. . . . Never before in our history have the policies of the federal government embodied so much legislation that is of a highly ethical order. Never before in our history have government policies been so deliberately, formally and consciously based upon conceptions and convictions of moral right and social justice.

Ryan himself served the New Deal in a number of capacities, most notably as a member of the Industrial Appeals Board of NRA. He bitterly opposed the critical report of the board's majority (the so-called Darrow report), denying the existence of widespread price fixing and pointing out that the complaints of small businessmen were usually aimed at avoiding the wage and hour provisions of the codes. For his part, Ryan favored further reduction in hours, even if the resulting high costs drove small and inefficient firms out of business.[31]

His few criticisms of the New Deal were based upon his belief that Roosevelt did not go as far as the Pope. NRA lacked sufficient labor representation and its production controls often allowed business high profits. More money had to be spent on public works, and the unemployed had a right to an income of at least $50 a month, in contrast to the lower wages of WPA. In 1935 Ryan feared that the President was still operating under the "great illusion" that recovery would come from the private sector, and he welcomed the renewed legislative activity of the fall. He became increasingly critical of the business community, attributing the problems of NRA, the slowness of recovery, and the failure of labor organization to the "great majority" of businessmen who remained "as selfish, as credulous, and as greedy" as they had been in the 1920's. They were "like the Bourbons, those preposterous persons who have learned nothing and forgotten nothing." [32]

Ryan saw such men arrayed against the President in 1936. He dismissed the Liberty League's Americanism as pagan individualism. The Republican party's rejection of government action in favor of private enterprise was a call "to go back to the policies of Hoover," a path that would bring an even more serious economic crisis. Between such alternatives and the New Deal, the choice was clear and Ryan argued "no believer in social justice should hesitate for a second." In addition to attacking the "advocates and retainers of plutocracy," Ryan also struck out at impatient reformers who foolishly turned "their backs on the only existing social force that is likely to bring about any reforms." [33]

Ryan was convinced that the possible identification of the Church with opposition to the New Deal through the activities of Father Coughlin posed serious dangers for the country and for the Catholic population. He, therefore, abandoned his usual aloofness from partisan politics and, at great risk to his career, delivered a radio address sponsored by the Democratic National Committee. Ryan directed his attack at Catholic critics of the New Deal. Far from being communistic, as Coughlin and others were suggesting, the New Deal defended America against totalitarianism. All the measures passed since 1933 accorded fully with the principles of *Quadragesimo Anno;* in fact the Pope went much further in calling for change than did Roosevelt. Both the Church and the New Deal held to the middle ground between communism and individualism; both fought communism by attacking its causes. As for Father Coughlin, whose campaign threatened to split Catholic support from the New Deal, Ryan said that his "explanations of our economic maladies are at least fifty per cent wrong, and his monetary theories are at least ninety per cent wrong. . . . Moreover, Father Coughlin's monetary theories and proposals find no support in the encyclicals of either Pope Leo XIII or Pope Pius XI." [34] Ryan came under bitter attack for this speech, but he considered it "one of the most effective and beneficial acts that I have ever performed in the interest of my religion and my country." [35]

In the early thirties Ryan had been the unquestioned leader of American social Catholicism; his only challenger, Coughlin, then agreed with Ryan's support of the New Deal. But the unity of socially minded Catholics behind Roosevelt had begun to collapse, as the events of 1936 indicated. When Ryan's friend, Father James Gillis, editor of the *Catholic World*, broke with Roosevelt on the issues of centralization, spending, and constitutionality, Ryan replied that the constitutional issue was a false one and he challenged Gillis to show how federal spending could be cut even 5 per cent without serious harm to human welfare. The alternative, he warned, was the return of the "Bourbons" and their pagan attitude toward social justice.[36]

The constitutional issue would not go away so easily, and when Roosevelt presented his court plan in 1937, Ryan was one of his very few Catholic supporters. Since the decisions against the minimum-wage laws in the 1920's, Ryan had been calling for an amendment to empower the federal government to pass social legislation. In 1935, he wrote Roosevelt: "I do not think the New Deal can be completed without a constitutional amendment." [37] Though he would have preferred the slower amendment process, he recognized the necessity for action and warmly defended Roosevelt's 1937 proposal. This drew the wrath of many Catholic leaders and when Ryan unfairly implied that opposition to the plan hid reactionary motives even the diocesan organ of his old friend and defender Archbishop Curley accused Ryan of having a "Fascist, dictatorial mind." [38] Ryan was similarly isolated when he defended the appointment of his friend, Hugo Black, to the Supreme Court.

It was Ryan's preoccupation with the pervasive individualism of American society and his ever-increasing consciousness of the power of the business community that led him to deprecate the fears of his fellow Catholics concerning excessive government power. Catholic leaders were acutely aware of the Church's minority status and feared the development of a strong government in the hands of a hostile majority with constitutional safeguards removed. Ryan, too, was aware of being part of a minority, but his experience led him to see danger from another direction. He believed that only progressive measures, necessarily involving government action, could cure the nation's economic ills. If Catholics from fear of future persecution should assist in blocking such reforms, the resulting economic distress might combine with the anti-Catholic tendencies of American liberals to produce an even greater reaction.

Similar considerations were involved in his defense of the C.I.O. against the attack of fellow Catholics. Long a critic of the A.F. of L., Ryan welcomed the appearance of the new organization. Recognizing the existence of Communists in the C.I.O., Ryan urged Catholics to work within the new unions to influence them in a Christian direction. He was friendly with Catholics prominent in the labor movement and he had defended David Dubinsky and Sidney Hillman against charges of communism in his 1936 campaign address. Nevertheless, despite his general support of labor unions since his abandonment of compulsory arbitration in the twenties, Ryan was never excited by the labor movement as were many of his fellow Catholics. Recognizing the necessity for labor organization as a prerequisite for the occupational group system, he continued to urge labor to pursue wider social objectives than mere self-improvement. His awareness of the power of business led him to continue to rely on the State as the only institution with sufficient leverage to bring any basic changes in the social structure.[39]

In 1939 and 1940, the problems of the economy had not changed, but the necessity for solution was more intense. A decade of depression had proven to Ryan's satisfaction that the economy had reached maturity, and a declining population, which Ryan foresaw, meant that there was no necessity for further plant expansion. He blamed the 1938 recession on the cut in government spending and urged a Keynesian policy to "prime the pump." The problems of a mature economy could be solved only by conscious planning directed toward the redistribution of income. Labor organization would help, but higher minimum wages, reduced hours, more public works, a progressive tax policy aimed at taking money from the hands of savers and directing it into the hands of spenders, all these were even more important. To check the growth of monopoly and administered prices strong government action was needed. The planning necessary to solve these problems had to come from the State, but in the long run something akin to the occupational group system would be needed if democracy was to be preserved and regimentation avoided.[40]

In 1940 Ryan believed he saw the same reactionary forces he had been fighting throughout the decade lined up behind Republican presidential candidate Wendell Willkie. His private correspondence was filled with praise for the administration, criticism of its Republican opponents, and frequent denunciations of "Roosevelt-haters" within the Church, among whom Ryan grouped the editors of *America*, the *Catholic World* and the Brooklyn *Tablet*, and several prominent bishops. Yet publicly he remained silent during the campaign, despite frequent appeals for his active intervention to offset the efforts of other prominent Catholics. The administrative board of the NCWC had ordered its staff to avoid "any public part in politics," to remain "entirely free from political partisanship" and to join no organizations or sign any documents without permission. Ryan, who had been retired from his chair at Catholic University the previous year, was anxious to retain his post with the NCWC and he reluctantly accepted the directive and remained quietly on the sidelines. Nevertheless, he continued to give active support to the President's foreign policy, combatting Catholic isolationism and pacifism and urging resistance to Nazism through aid to the Allies.[41]

Until his death in 1945 John A. Ryan persevered in his liberalism while becoming increasingly apprehensive about the future. In his last public address he warned against the postwar return to power of "the authentic Bourbons of our time." "When I reflect upon the enormous and insidious power of the American plutocracy, and its retainers and satellites in politics, in journalism, and in the professions, I am inclined to be pessimistic," he told his audience. Only the extension of New Deal policies could provide jobs for returning servicemen and keep America economically and politically healthy.[42]

If any American Catholic could have supplied an intellectual basis for unified Catholic social action it was John A. Ryan. Strategically situated in the Social Action Department, supported in his work by a number of reform-minded bishops, thoroughly grounded in economics, and on intimate terms with non-Catholic reformers, Ryan appeared to combine the best features of the Catholic social tradition with the most valuable elements in American political life. His stature as the nation's leading Catholic spokesman on public issues was unquestioned. In 1939 a public celebration of his seventieth birthday was held in Washington and tributes came from the President, from Supreme Court justices, Cabinet members, Senators, Congressmen, and clergymen of every faith. Yet, at the same time, Ryan was coming under heavy, and even bitter, attack from his fellow Catholics. He appeared to many to have become a partisan whose efforts only served to divide the Catholic community and frustrate attempts to deal with the dangers of secularism, communism, and war.

In retrospect it might seem that Ryan's very success was his undoing. In 1930, few Catholics knew enough about the papal encyclicals to challenge his interpretation or question his leadership. By 1940 his own efforts, together with those of Father Coughlin, Dorothy Day, and many others had made Catholics aware of the existence of the papal program but had presented a multiplicity of interpretations, all of which made sense to some elements in the Catholic population. Many preferred to emphasize elements in Catholic thought that Ryan ignored. He was aware of their work, sometimes supported it, but ultimately did not consider it of great importance. In fact, he had a very self-centered view of the Catholic social movement in the United States. He wrote a friend in 1937: "It is not too much to say that the only adequate and effective leadership both in education and in social problems that exists in this country derives from the Catholic University"—that is, from Ryan and his disciples, such as Fathers Raymond McGowen and Francis Haas.[43]

Yet there were clear limitations to Ryan's understanding of the encyclicals. Many Catholics believed that before Pius XI's Christian social order could be established, there had to be a religious revival, which would make all men aware of the implications of their salvation in Christ. Only then would there be a basis suitable to build a Christian society on. Ryan, on the other hand, was preoccupied with immediate economic and political problems; he had always believed that the establishment of at least a minimum amount of justice was a necessary prerequisite to any genuine religious revival. Moreover, for all his allegiance to the occupational group system, Ryan never satisfactorily integrated this idea into his reform thought. He recognized that the new economic agencies would have to be endowed with coercive power if they were to fulfill their planning functions, yet he never spelled out the relationship which would exist between the State and the occupational groups. This question was of particular interest in the United States, where experience indicated that labor and capital, left free of legal control, might act without regard for the public interest. Furthermore, while Ryan presented the scheme as one which would improve the status and dignity of the worker, he never clarified how a system built on existing unions and trade associations would solve the problems of large scale industry and give the workers status and responsibility. In fact, Ryan never judged reform measures on the basis of their promotion of occupational groups. Rather his standard remained human needs and the general welfare. Writing in 1941, Ryan described the middle way between socialism and individualism as the "general welfare" theory: the government should try to establish conditions in which individual action would be possible and supplement such action by provision for those needs which individuals and groups could not provide for themselves. All State intervention necessary for the promotion of human welfare was justified—was, indeed, required. In effect, leaving the occupational group aside, Ryan combined economics, whose object is prosperity, and social justice, whose object is the common good, into a Catholic philosophy of the welfare State.[44] The danger that increasing State power offered to the individual and to those institutions which Ryan had called the "primary social objectives"—religion, family, and education—was resolved by reference to the papal program of social reconstruction, but Ryan failed to explain how pragmatic application of the welfare principle would necessarily lead to the establishment of occupational groups.

The weakness of Ryan's thought as the basis for unified

Catholic action was evident in the extent to which his ideas diverged from those of his assistant, Father Raymond McGowan. Ryan interpreted and defended American reform in terms of Catholic thought; McGowan reversed the process, rigorously measuring reform proposals against "the yardstick" of papal teachings and seeking to develop an independent Catholic program based on the occupational group idea. He was well aware of the difficulty of popularizing a corporate vision in the United States where traditional individualism underemphasized "interdependence, brotherhood, the unity of people, the society of men, the general welfare, the common good." The corporate nature of the papal program made it hard for Americans to grasp. "It is the idea of a living organism to fulfill continuous obligations," he wrote. "We have been so long accustomed to going it alone that the thought of going it together is hard to swallow." [45] This was a Catholic ideal, McGowan decided, and for its realization "a people that is Catholic minded seems necessary." For this reason McGowan devoted his efforts to educating American Catholics in "the yardstick" of papal teachings so that they would come to "think Catholic answers to every problem of their lives." [46]

While Ryan stressed the need for immediate legislative action to deal with the Depression and sometimes spoke of the occupational group system almost as an afterthought, McGowan focused on structural defects and advocated basic reorganization along the lines of *Quadragesimo Anno*. Fully accepting Ryan's underconsumption theory, he regarded faulty distribution of income as symptomatic of more basic moral and structural weaknesses. The Depression "is an inevitable consequence of our present way of producing and particularly our way of distributing goods and income," he wrote. "It cannot be understood and cured apart from understanding and curing the system itself, however much it might be reduced and tempered." [47]

The best cure was the system of occupational groups that

would provide a mechanism insuring the responsible use of property without endangering the power of the State. He hoped that the system would develop through voluntary efforts to establish rural co-operatives, trade associations, labor unions and, eventually, joint labor-management committees. The government had a responsibility to assist such efforts at economic self-regulation and control. Challenging Catholic fears of the State he turned to *Quadragesimo Anno* to justify government action in two directions: [48]

> The idea of the encyclical is indeed to have an active and vigilant government making both general laws and special laws in the interest of the people, but a government also that will help re-establish organized, associative, cooperative, autonomous economic life which then it will direct, stimulate and restrain as occasion requires.

He argued that the State could be trusted with great power if at the same time economic organization was developing that would eventually relieve the State of the administration of economic life. The only alternative, it seemed to McGowan, was business domination of an increasingly powerful government and eventual social upheaval.

However, the State was eventually to divest itself of power, and turn over the administration of economic matters to an "economic nation within a nation, our soverign economic state." Once each industry and profession had organized from local to national levels, a new council of all the "guilds," acting "with the help and under the sovereignty of government," would plan and direct a unified economic life for full production and equitable distribution. The center of gravity of the Christian social order would be the "cooperating, democratically organized industry and profession, ruling itself in alliance with other industries and professions [and] doing so with government help." [49]

On the basis of these principles McGowan was considerably more restrained than Ryan in his reaction to the National Industrial Recovery Act's system of industrial organization. While he felt it a great advance over previous American practice and the closest approach ever made to the papal system, he wrote that the "new regime . . . may become a worse regime" because it increased the power of business. The NRA, McGowan felt, organized "one class in each occupation, the employers alone, to control industry" and could therefore never bring about the redistribution of income necessary for recovery or the democratization of the economy needed for permanent reform.[50] Unionization and collective bargaining were basic needs, but alone they would lead only to class conflict and increased government control of the economy. Society must move beyond collective bargaining to joint organization and copartnership in industry. The lesson that America had to learn, McGowan believed, was that "if unions are only collective bargainers and not also cooperators in the administration of industries, then we do not establish justice nor do we promote domestic tranquillity." [51]

McGowan denied that the new order was utopian. He argued that it would emerge gradually through collective bargaining, through "legislation which increasingly relies on organization," through "farm organizations doing one thing and then another and then another," through doctors' and lawyers' guilds acting to put order and justice into their professions.[52] As much a gradualist as Ryan, McGowan more clearly focused on the long-range goal, which was to emerge from the partial measures that both supported. For example, while he welcomed the passage of the Wages and Hours Act in 1938, he still stressed that planning and organization remained essential if America was to have a balanced economy and full employment. Ryan's position, undoubtedly, was more practical and realistic given the potentialities of American reform, whereas McGowan's corporatism was, in the context of the American tradition, too radical and too closely linked to a European and Catholic theoretical foundation to be popular or effective. On the other hand McGowan's insight into the structural problems of American society and the need for integrating the workers into the decision-making process of industry was as well grounded as Ryan's emphasis on problems of income distribution. Both McGowan and Ryan glossed over apparent contradictions between the encyclicals and American traditions. The German-Americans were probably closer to the Pope's intent when they referred to the papal plan as the vocational group system, with the implication that all connected with an industry were to be joined together, conscious not of occupation, of being at a job, but of vocation, of being engaged with others in a common creative endeavor, an idea which they drew from the medieval guilds. It was inconceivable to this school that such a system could evolve from American unions of either the craft or industrial type. They realized that the establishment of such a system in the United States would require a fundamental ideological shift away from the traditional individualism, to a consciousness of being a member of a group and of society. Without such a shift, they argued, no artificially State-established system could succeed; on the contrary, establishment by the State would only lead to the political domination which the Pope wished to avoid.[53]

If all this were true, two alternatives remained open: to engage in a long-range process of education, the course chosen by the Germans, or to work for a religious revival, which would reawaken a spiritual consciousness of brotherhood. Those who chose the latter path usually sought to bring about such an awakening among Catholics, hoping that this would in turn affect the society as a whole. In the latter case religious reform in the supernatural order would have to precede material reform. This was the position of the Benedictine, Virgil Michel, and he accordingly regarded Ryan, with his stress on material reform, as superficial and shallow. Michel felt that Ryan saw structural social and economic reform as the only immediate need, disregarding the absolute need for moral reform. Ryan, of

course, paid lip service to the need for simultaneous moral reform to go along with the economic, but he admitted his lack of
interest in the former. "Of course I do not regard the supernatural order as kind of a second story, built as if by afterthought on
top of the natural order," he wrote a friend, "but I confess that
the assumption of no connection between the two except by
elevator has always seemed to me rather logical and involving
fewer difficulties than the opposite assumption." [54]

Lacking Michel's theological sophistication and the capacity
for compassion of Peter Maurin and Dorothy Day, Ryan did
possess what the others lacked: a sound knowledge of economics
and an awareness of the difficulty of moving society in a moral
direction. One reason for differences among reformers was that
different empirical judgments led to an emphasis on different
actions. Most responded to this by reference to theoretical ab-
stractions or slogans; Ryan's answer was to look at the facts. Although this method had its limitations, it injected some badly
needed realism into Catholic social thought in the United States.
Many awakened to social consciousness by the Catholic Worker
movement or the liturgical movement found in Ryan's writings
a detailed analysis of immediate problems missing from other
Catholic groups. More fully than the others Ryan was a part of
the American reform tradition, and because he shared in it, he
was able to interpret that tradition to American Catholics and
bring them to the side of reform.

As an American reformer Ryan was less important than as a
Catholic; even in the glory days of the thirties he was less a
"Catholic ambassador to the New Deal" than the New Deal's
"political legate to American Catholics." [55] Aside from his pioneering work for the minimum wage he contributed little that was
original to the reform movement, and specifically Catholic influence he exerted on the content of reform was imperceptible.
His function was rather that of a mediator. He helped break
down the traditional liberal image of the Church as reaction-

ary and tied to the political machine. More importantly he helped overcome Catholic fears and educated his fellow Catholics toward a positive sense of social responsibility. He helped overcome the inherent conservatism of the Catholic minority, fearful that in working for reform it might bring down on itself the wrath of the Protestant majority. Particularly, he overcame the traditional Catholic fear of the State; he demonstrated that government power could be used in co-operation with all men of good will to effect human goals without endangering the religious or personal liberties of minorities. When he died in 1945, he left behind a Catholic community more informed, confident, open minded, and socially concerned than the one he had found a half-century earlier. As his friend and colleague George Shuster wrote of Ryan recently: "the thing that really mattered was that he happened to be a good, square-shooting priest who helped turn the face of American Catholics toward the future." [56]

VII

Father Coughlin and
American Catholicism

The concern of the Catholic Church with the moral and spiritual aspects of social questions was expressed within a natural law frame of reference which lent itself more readily to negative than to positive pronouncements. While the Church did not hesitate to issue condemnations of specific movements seen as hostile to Catholic doctrine and dangerous to faith and morals, it was extremely cautious about endorsing programs and organizations claiming to represent Catholic teachings. This attitude was reflected in the United States in the New Deal years, accentuated by the traditional American suspicion of clerical interference in supposedly political affairs and the reluctance of the Catholic clergy to engage in activity which might divide their diverse congregations. In the 1930's, American priests vigorously denounced individualism and rejected the twin dogmas of laissez-faire and socialism. In doing so they at times appeared to be offering an apologetic for New Deal Policies, yet most disliked political association and consciously sought to avoid identification with any political party or secular movement. A notable exception to this rule, Monsignor John Ryan, had many companions in denouncing the evils of the old order, but very few in openly endorsing the Roosevelt administration in the campaign of 1936.

Even more than Ryan, the exception to the rule of noninvolvement was the radio priest of Royal Oak, Michigan, Father Charles E. Coughlin. While his clerical contemporaries for the most part hesitated to say anything that could be construed as a commitment on a controversial issue not directly associated with the interests of the Church or the faith of its members, Coughlin alternately praised and condemned men and measures in clear and forceful language. In 1936, he defied a strong American tradition by organizing and directing the presidential campaign of a major American third party. He was one of the decade's most colorful and controversial figures and the most famous of the American "social Catholics." [1]

Charles Edward Coughlin was born and raised in Hamilton, Ontario. At thirteen he entered the seminary of the Basilian fathers in Toronto, studying there and at St. Michael's College of the University of Toronto until his ordination in 1916. For seven years he taught at Assumption College in Sandwich, Ontario, occasionally crossing the river to assist in parishes of the Detroit diocese. In 1923, when the canonical status of the Basilians was changed, Coughlin decided to become a secular priest under the authority of the bishop of Detroit, Michael Gallagher. After a number of preliminary assignments he was chosen in May 1926 to construct a new parish in Royal Oak, a Detroit suburb and hotbed of Ku Klux Klan activity. A successful fund raiser, Coughlin built his church but the hostility of his neighbors persisted. After a Klan incident in October of 1926, he approached a Detroit radio station, WRJ, with the idea of a religious program designed to offset anti-Catholic prejudice. The program was accepted and was an immediate success. With a flowing melodious voice that had a remarkable effect on his audience, Coughlin was a natural for the radio. The talks themselves were devoted to religious themes, avoiding, in his words, "all prejudicial subjects and controversies, and especially all bigotry." [2] Three years later the program added outlets in Cincinnati and Chicago and the radio preacher's fame spread.

For reasons yet unexplained, Coughlin shifted the subject matter of his talks drastically in the fall of 1930.[3] He told his listeners that the Depression had aroused his concern for the unchristian character of the nation's economic and political life and that he wished to fulfill the Pope's directive that priests preach the social gospel of Christ, showing the poor the reasons for their plight and the Christian solution of their difficulties. He began by denouncing the economic philosophy of the twenties and the moral evils of the day and went on to castigate the policies of the Hoover administration, the work of the Reconstruction Finance Corporation, and the power of the "international bankers." Moving to a national network in 1931, his name became a household word and his voice familiar to millions of listeners. Before that year was out his audience was estimated at ten million, his mail was the heaviest in the nation, and his influence was a potent factor in the calculations of politicians and government officials. For the next four years he was generally acknowledged to be "the most persuasive voice in America." [4] From the beginning he was a "shepherd of discontent," putting into words the fears and frustrations of his listeners. In one of his first sermons he sounded the theme which was to dominate his subsequent career and account for much of his popularity, "want in the midst of plenty," the contrast between the widespread unemployment and poverty of the Depression and the inherent beneficence of America and the essential goodness of her people:

> In our country, with its lakes and rivers teeming with fish; its mines heavy with minerals; its banks teeming with money, there are approximately five million unemployed men walking aimlessly through the streets of our cities and the by-paths of our country sides, seeking not doles but labor.[5]

In early broadcasts he blamed the Depression on the American departure from the Constitution and from the religion of the Founding Fathers. What Coughlin described as the decay of democracy into "a form of plutocracy and gang rule" was due "not to the inherent weakness of the Constitution but to the godlessness and hypocrisy of the citizens who live under it." [6] Poverty itself was not a political but a moral issue, to which the competence of the clergy extended; it was "God's issue" and could be solved only by a return to Christ and his teachings. But this approach did not last; soon Coughlin was telling his listeners that the fault lay not in themselves but in a small group of men who, for their own selfish purposes, blocked the nation's emergence into the promised land of freedom from want which its abundant resources and the energy and ability of its people made possible.

Like his audience Coughlin wanted nothing to do with communism, but neither did he wish to defend traditional capitalism. He devoted a number of his early sermons to exposing the atheism, internationalism, and dictatorial methods of communism, but he described it as a reaction against capitalism and plutocracy, "a protest . . . an irrational attempt to escape from an irrational oppression." [7] Modern capitalism was plutocracy, with wealth and power in the hands of a few and the masses left to the mercy of the "money changers." "On the rotten carcass of modern capitalism," he said, "are bred the maggots of Russian communism." The "thoughtful American" was convinced that "the most dangerous communist is the wolf in sheep's clothing of conservatism who is bent upon preserving policies of greed and oppression, and of Christlessness." [8] Unless reforms were forthcoming, he warned, the people would rally to the banner of revolution.

In the election of 1932, the priest implicitly backed Franklin D. Roosevelt and subsequently became an enthusiastic exponent of the New Deal, with "Roosevelt or Ruin" as his slogan. The new President welcomed his advice and six senators and fifty-nine congressmen went on record supporting his appointment as an advisor to the American delegation to the London Economic Conference. When Al Smith belittled the New Deal's monetary policy Coughlin attacked him unmercifully and his popularity rose to new heights. In April 1934 he made his pledge: "I will never change my philosophy that the New Deal is Christ's Deal." [9] At Coughlin's call, letters flooded Congress and politicians feared that his idolatrous following could be translated into votes. For a time it appeared that he might bridge the gap between rural and urban America, between western farmers and urban laborers, a breach that had almost destroyed the Democratic party in the twenties and which Roosevelt had overcome only with difficulty.

Still, even in 1933, the radio priest identified himself more with the personality of the President than with the policies of his administration. From the beginning he disliked the agricultural policies of Henry Wallace and Rexford Tugwell. He regarded the National Industrial Recovery Act as inadequate, and he called for a thirty-hour week and eighty-cent minimum wage to replace its low rates. Most important his attention increasingly focused on monetary matters and here, after 1934, the New Deal continually disappointed him. Pushing strongly for an inflationary policy he regarded all other remedies as shortsighted and inadequate. He told his listeners that "before the labor problem, before the wage problem, before the social problem can be rectified, industry must issue its declaration of independence from the financialist." [10] When Treasury Secretary Morgenthau released a list of silver speculators that included the name of Coughlin's secretary, the priest denounced him as a tool of the international bankers. In addition, Roosevelt's foreign policy alienated Coughlin, especially his recognition of the Soviet Union and his support of the friendly attitude toward the revolutionary government of Mexico of Ambassador Josephus Daniels. Irritated by the President's supposed internationalism, Coughlin openly challenged the New Deal in 1935 by calling on his radio audience to protest American entry into the World Court. The dramatic response was a major factor in the defeat of that administration-sponsored measure.[11]

Emboldened by this success, Father Coughlin became increasingly outspoken in his denunciation of the Roosevelt program. Both the agricultural policy of crop destruction and the industrial policy of restricting production "out-Hoovered Hoover," he believed. Attacking from two sides, he found evidence of communist infiltration in the unlimited powers granted to various government agencies, while the refusal of Roosevelt to openly oppose the private banking system showed that he remained wedded to the prime error of plutocracy, the private control of money and credit. He concluded by condemning the New Deal on both counts: the administration "protects plutocrats and comforts communists," he charged. "While its golden head enunciates the splendid program of Christian justice, its feet of sordid clay are mired, one in the red mud of Soviet communism, the other in the stinking cesspool of pagan plutocracy." [12]

Consistency was Coughlin's weak point and he was slower to abandon the President, the "head," than the "feet" of New Deal policies. Instead he swung back and forth between support and opposition, apparently testing his support. He established the National Union for Social Justice in 1934 as a "people's lobby" to bring pressure to bear on politicians to pass measures in accord with social justice. The National Union platform consisted of sixteen points, with monetary issues receiving the most attention. In addition it called on government to recognize the right of labor to organize and offer its protection to the unions. It endorsed a "living annual wage" for labor and "the cost of production plus a fair profit" for the farmer, favored government ownership of natural monopolies and control of private property for the common good, and at the same time called for "simplified" government and decreased taxes.[13]

The new organization was presented as an instrument for overcoming the "sham battles" of politicians. More and more, Coughlin stressed the inability of the political parties to deal with the basic issue of monetary reform; both parties and their leaders were merely the puppets of the bankers. Not one politician could honestly accept the sixteen points, the priest believed, and local units were told to beware of infiltration by partisan politicians, "sly rats" who would only destroy the organization. Instead Coughlin hoped that by endorsing principles and candidates the National Union could use politicians to carry out its program. But these hopes were not realized, and in June 1936 Coughlin suddenly announced the formation of the Union party and its entry into the 1936 presidential election with William Lemke of North Dakota and Thomas C. O'Brien of Boston as its candidates. The immediate occasion of the announcement was the defeat of the inflationary Frazier-Lemke farm mortgage bill and the ignoring of the money issue by both parties. Convinced that the existing parties were essentially the same, irrevocably tied to banker control, Coughlin apologized for his earlier support of the New Deal and confidently promised to deliver nine million votes to the ticket or retire from the air.[14]

Coughlin regarded the choice between Roosevelt and Landon as one between "carbolic acid and rat poison," but he focused his attack on the Democratic party and candidate. He charged that the Communist party supported Roosevelt, that the Democrats used communist electors like David Dubinsky in New York, and that Wallace, Tugwell, Harry Hopkins, Felix Frankfurter, and John L. Lewis were friends and allies of the Communists. On the other hand, the New Deal borrowed from the bankers instead of revolutionizing the money system so that the potential wealth of American could be equitably distributed; it was merely "the old deal turned inside out." A "living annual wage" and production for profit for the farmer could easily be achieved once Congress had regained its constitutional control over the money and credit of the nation.[15] Lemke received less than nine hundred thousand votes and his overwhelming defeat made it obvious that the Coughlin movement had passed its peak. Fulfilling his promise to leave the air, Coughlin interpreted the election as a betrayal of himself and of Christian principles, but less than a year later he returned to the radio, denouncing the administration and the "anti-Christ of Communism," but never regaining his old popularity.

Father Coughlin later blamed his defeat on the infiltration of his party by professional politicians and he despaired of finding political solutions to the nation's problems. "I am morally certain that America has gone too far into the depths of depression to be rescued either by politicians or by political parties," he said. The country was experiencing a "bloodless revolution instigated and propagated by the powers of anti-Christianity [who] taking advantage of the mass ignorance of the people, accomplish their purpose under the cloak of humanitarianism and justice." [16] His confused and embittered anticommunism led Coughlin into increasingly controversial positions. In 1938, he embarked on a course of anti-Semitism; the Christian Front, which he inspired, became a focal point for Americans sympathetic to Nazi Germany. Archbishop Edward Mooney, who succeeded Gallagher in 1937, made things difficult for Coughlin but was outmaneuvered by his subordinate. Mooney refused to silence Coughlin, whose activities increasingly divided Catholics and irritated many of their fellow citizens. Eventually, after his work had greatly increased animosity against the Church, the Department of Justice intervened with the coming of World War II. Under the threat of government action Mooney in early 1942 forced Coughlin to abandon public life and return to his parish.[17] Coughlin submitted, his voice was silent, and his paper went out of business. Since then he has lived in relative obscurity, a quiet parish priest far removed from the turmoil of agitation and demagoguery.

One of the most popular interpretations of Father Coughlin and his movement has been to see him as a twentieth-century populist, echoing the traditional demands and panaceas of the western farmers. According to Charles and Mary Beard, Coughlin's program "stemmed largely from the creed of American populism with its attachment to the decent owners of small property and its enmity for high finance and large enterprise." [18] The association of Coughlin with populism is based particularly upon his monetary theories, which reflected the concerns of a debtor class, whose "cheap money dogmas . . . became an essential part of the traditions of the common people [in the United States] receding into the background in times of prosperity, but ready to reappear whenever economic plague descended upon the land." [19] In the 1930's such inflationary ideas were widespread beyond the confines of the western plains; Coughlin himself was introduced to the subject by easterners, Robert M. Harris of the New York Cotton Exchange and George LeBlanc, a Canadian gold trader. A speech delivered by Coughlin in November 1933 before a New York rally of monetary reform advocates from all over the nation "signalized, more than any one act, the popular revolt against monetary orthodoxy." Support for reform was overwhelming; Coughlin's function was to translate "biases into dogmas" more plausible to voters than academic discussions. He was "the most effective [of the numerous reformers] in arousing popular support for monetary action and in focusing pressure upon the national legislators." [20] He was unsystematic and often wrong, but the causes he espoused were not only popular but were addressed to questions which were of concern to all serious students of the economy in the early New Deal years.

To try to summarize Coughlin's monetary theories is to make

them appear far more consistent than they really were. He began by backing the New Deal's policy of revaluation, increasing the price of gold in order to raise commodity prices. Coughlin based his support on a comparison of the existing ratio of debts to gold of 117 to 1 with supposedly ideal ratios of 12 to 1 for debts and 2½ to 1 for currency. These were based in turn on the priest's conviction that all debts had to be repaid eventually in "real money," gold. Thus, when credit was overextended the bankers could, by recalling all loans, confiscate the property of the nation. In the vast overextension of credit the only alternatives were revaluation or repudiation and in Coughlin's eyes this was a choice between Christianity and bolshevism.

The problem of debts and low farm prices weighed heavily on Coughlin and led him to see the money question as crucial and all-embracing. Faced with the spectacle of want in the midst of plenty how could the sufferings of Americans, willing to work, with enormous productive facilities available, be explained? What was missing? The answer was simple and obvious: "Everything is plentiful except money!" [21] Once this answer was given the solution quickly followed: increase the supply of money on a stable basis, safe from the machinations of greedy men. Thus, revaluation, an end to interest-bearing government bonds, and the creation of a national banking system, were necessary but in themselves insufficient. There also had to be an increase in the supply of money sufficient to raise prices. Coughlin looked first to silver remonetization, which would increase the money supply and open oriental markets to American goods. Coinage of silver would be not inflationary but reflationary, aimed at curing the shortage of money, which the bankers, by overextending credit and cornering gold, had created. In September 1933 Coughlin explained his position to the President: if silver were monetized "we would speed up our factories, consume our surplus wheat, cotton, and pork and get rid of that asinine philosophy propagated by Henry Wallace." "My dear

Mr. President," he continued, "there is no superfluity of either cotton or wheat until every naked back has been clothed, until every empty stomach has been filled. There is a superfluity in the minds of those men who with their deflationary policies are opposed to accepting good silver money." [22]

Coughlin's espousal of silver marked his first break with the New Deal. He heartily approved the nationalization of gold, and then was appalled when the administration, instead of issuing greenback currency based on this gold, continued to borrow from the bankers, increasing the national debt and the control of the private financial oligarchy over the nation. The priest considered the Federal Reserve System to be the privately owned tool of the bankers, and he supported the nationalization of credit and the establishment of a government owned and operated central bank. When the New Deal tightened controls over the Federal Reserve without altering its fundamental character, Roosevelt was accused of compromising with the "old deal" and the financial community.

As the Depression deepened, Coughlin's faith in the 12 to 2½ to 1 formula faded, as did his reliance on a silver panacea, for both approaches appeared to limit the supply of currency to less than the country's needs. He found a new key to the mysteries of finance in the confusion of wealth and money: the country had great wealth in terms of resources and the products of labor, but less than sufficient currency. Again the solution was simple: divorce the money supply from a metallic base altogether and base it instead on the wealth of the nation, increasing the amount in circulation as the national wealth increased. Currency and credit must be nationalized and placed under the control of Congress, as the Constitution provided. Having visited the leaders of the Canadian social credit movement, Coughlin showed the influence of their ideas; money should be regarded as receipts for wealth, and credit should be available to workers and farmers as well as to entrepreneurs. This whole program was embodied in the so-called Prosperity Bill of 1935 (the Nye-Sweeney Bill) which Coughlin helped draw up in conference with other monetary reformers and which he supported vigorously over the air. By the provisions of the bill a national bank would be established under the supervision of a board of congressional control. The proposal was very vague; it assumed that the new organ could raise prices by merely scientifically examining the facts and acting honestly on the results. The problem, in Coughlin's eyes, was not one of ignorance but of will; the facts clearly pointed to the solution. In addition he advocated a $10 billion public works program to be financed by greenbacks supported by the national wealth and the Frazier-Lemke bill which provided for the refinancing of farms with currency issued on the farm values themselves.[23]

The problems that Coughlin dealt with were real: the unstable condition of the dollar, the lack of adequate control over the volume of currency, the burden of debt in a period of deflation. The *New Republic* estimated that two-thirds of American progressives desired some form of central monetary and banking authority. Devaluation and stabilization were proposed in varying forms by Professor Warren of Cornell and Sidney Fisher of Yale; Fisher, LeBlanc, Harris, and numerous others supported the Nye-Sweeney Bill; silver had its backers and many spokesmen called for the issuing of greenbacks. But the pressure for monetary and credit reform decreased as prosperity returned and particularly after passage of the Banking Act of 1935. Coughlin continued his agitation into the 1936 campaign but found that his emphasis on money no longer evoked much popular response.[24]

One distinctive element in Coughlin's presentation was his nationalism: from the beginning he denounced such traditional symbols of financial oppression as the international bankers and "the British propaganda of the Tory bankers of lower Manhattan." He hit at the export of gold and the financing of loans for foreign industry enabling it to compete with American; he urged his listeners and the government: "Keep American money for the American people." [25] The policy of the National Union for Social Justice was described as "America for the Americans" and America was identified with Christianity: "America was cradled in the spirit of Christ's doctrine." [26] The great creditor nation of the world, the United States had the power to end the world-wide reign of gold and the "tyranny which at one moment wears the painted mask of plutocratic domination and at another the sheep's clothing of wolfish communism." [27] Drawing on the same popular Christian symbols as the early populists, he spoke of the common people, who paid tribute in the form of compound interest to the bankers and were betrayed by their political representatives: "Today these same people are on Calvary's heights, crucified between the two thieves, symbolic of the two political parties. Their garments are diced for. Their thirst for the bountiful goodness which a generous God has supplied is quenched with the biting vinegar of want in the midst of plenty." [28]

He fit his ideas into a simple historical framework that supported popular attitudes toward past events and present realities. America, Coughlin repeatedly told his audience, had been able for the first time in history to solve the problem of production. The expansion that had preceded and accompanied World War I had made it possible for everyone to earn a decent livelihood. Realization of this potential was prevented by the bankers who had maneuvered the country into the war to protect their investments. After the war they encouraged the export of American money to rebuild foreign industry, depriving the nation of European outlets for manufactured goods, while English bankers destroyed the purchasing power of silver, thus closing off oriental markets. Under the influence of the sinister international bankers the same American government that refused to assist the poverty-stricken unemployed at home in the early thirties extended generous loans to European governments. The Treaty of Versailles with its broken promises to Germany eventually led to world-wide collapse. But this hurt not the bankers, whose investments were in the form of unreal credit money, but the small investors and depositors, farmers and laborers.[29]

The solution to all these problems lay with the people, their traditions, and their religious faith. The Constitution was sound, for it gave Congress the greatest power of any sovereign, the right to coin and regulate money, and it was the Constitution that pointed the way to solution of the Depression, the "money crisis." Until such unconstitutional laws as the Federal Reserve Act were repealed and control of the people's money returned to Congress, "democracy with us is little more than an ideal which has not been ordered to practice." [30] This could be done within the Constitution, with no additional delegation of power to the federal government and no increased government spending or bureaucratic paternalism. Popular control would destroy the domination of the few and solve the problem of poverty; in forming the National Union for Social Justice Coughlin told his listeners: "I believe that wealth . . . originates from natural resources and the labor which the children of God expend upon these resources. It is all ours except for the harsh, cruel and grasping ways of wicked men who first concentrated wealth in the hands of a few." [31] He believed, according to his biographer, that if the people but saw the truth, they would do the rest. Their eventual failure to do this he blamed on a political system that had been corrupted by the bankers and led him to reject political parties and flirt with other ways of implementing the will of God and the people.

As for the danger of communism, it was an extreme reaction to financial oppression which could be avoided only by removing its causes: the selfish policies of the bankers. Just as the Constitution and Christian principles pointed the way to a solution which preserved traditional forms, so they involved no natural class hostility. Instead the American ideal still held true: [32]

> The poor man of yesterday is the capitalist of tomorrow. The fertile fields, the almost infinite number of scientific secrets awaiting to be discovered, the native industry and thrift latent in every heart—these and many more items invite the laborer of today, if opportunity is presented, to rise as did the pioneers of old from the vallies of hardship and toil to the mountains of affluence and estate. Our democracy is identified with the concept. It justly opposes the insane levelling of classes. It condemns the agitator who sows seeds of dissension between employer and employee, between capitalist and laborer.

Thus Coughlin's policies, so radical at first glance, were in some ways very conservative. He strongly and consistently upheld the right of private property and the Christian character of a purified and reformed capitalism. He denounced the Hoover regime as spendthrift and paternalistic, denied any natural hostility of classes, and affirmed the need for more millionaires. He denounced the Roosevelt tax program of 1935 because he feared it would lead to the destruction of property. Americans, he believed, wished to produce more wealth, not redistribute present wealth or destroy all class distinctions. Inequality was natural; only the present concentration of so high a proportion of wealth and power in the hands of a few bankers and their satellites who had no patriotism and who perpetuated an unnecessary poverty was to be overthrown. Coughlin's utopia was the old American faith: "In this country there is ample room for everyone to profit according to his merit, provided he is willing to work." [33]

As an American radical Coughlin was an eclectic. A supreme egoist, Coughlin boasted that he knew "the pulse of the people" better than any newspaperman or industrialist. He sensed the discontent of his audience and he played upon it, using traditional American and Christian symbols that they understood. In addition, he recognized the weakness of a strictly agrarian-based movement and he broadened the older ideas sufficiently to attract small businessmen, merchants, small town professionals, and workers. He focused on a problem and developed a rhetoric and solution that would unite these groups. The problem was want in the midst of plenty, the amazement and shock of Americans that progress had been checked, that national abundance did not necessarily mean private prosperity, that personal virtue and hard work were not necessarily to be rewarded. Here the New Deal gave him openings by its policy of limiting agricultural production and acquiescing in restrictions on industrial output, thus apparently preferring destruction and stagnation to progress and the welfare of the consuming masses. The cause was greed and selfishness, not of all but of a few bankers and their servants, often foreign. Here all the discontent with the war, with big business, and with Wall Street could be summed up. The rhetoric was Christian—not denominational, but the vague kind of Christian imagery that could find a response among Methodist and Baptist farmers and Catholic immigrants and laborers. The solution was not the improvement of the individual or the manipulation and direction of the economy by the government. It consisted merely in removing the obstacles to progress, placing the control of money and credit under Congress. Then, the people would have the most powerful lobbies, government would be responsive to their needs and would insure everyone the decent livelihood that was his birthright as an American.

This approach had more in common with the thought of the early populists than with the later progressives. The stress on money and concern for the debtor, the suspicion of Europe and the loyalty to traditional American values, the faith in progress and the natural man, were all expressive of the populist spirit. Likewise the use of the conspiracy thesis, finding the source of trouble in a small, identifiable, and alien group, and the glorification of the humble producer, the farmer, laborer, and small busi-

nessman, were older radical themes.[34] But Coughlin's program
and rhetoric was never merely agrarian and the core of his support was always in the cities.[35] For a time in the early years it
appeared that the priest might be able to fulfill the dream of the
populist leaders of uniting under one banner all the producing
classes. He was able to approach this objective as a focus of discontent, but not as a popular political leader; his program was
too vague and indefinite, the discontent was not sufficiently
deep, and his personal position was too precarious. Midwestern
Protestants were not, after all, traditional admirers of the Catholic Church, while Coughlin's fellow Catholics were increasingly
uneasy at the sight of a priest engaged in politics.

In her biography of Father Coughlin his friend Ruth Mugglebee contended that the radio priest was an early and enthusiastic
exponent of the teachings of Leo XIII and that the Pope's call to
a social apostolate decisively influenced young Coughlin's vocation. Coughlin drew on Leo's injunction to priests to interest
themselves in the social question and fight for the rights of the
poor when defending himself against the criticism of Catholics
like Cardinal O'Connell.[36] To his radio audience Coughlin was a
"simple Catholic priest" shocked at the abuses of Christian teachings and fighting Christ's battle for social justice. The social
question was not a political issue and it had but one side: "It is
God's question and it is God's side," the priest cried. Coughlin's
organizations went on crusades, inspired by Scripture and
launched with divine support: "God wills it," he said of the
National Union for Social Justice and he asked his audience, "Do
you?" [37] In Coughlin's eyes there were no ambiguities; Christian teachings gave clear guidance as to right and wrong in society. Coughlin stood on the Christian side and, by definition,
whatever he espoused deserved Christian support. As Miss Mugglebee wrote, "Father Coughlin was no reformer. . . . He
merely considered himself an instrument of God, disseminator
of Christian principles, ordained to tear to shreds the veil behind

which America's leaders and America's failing social and economic system were playing hide and seek with truth." [38]

His favorite appeals were to popular Christian Scripture: "drive the money changers from the temple," "the laborer is worthy of his hire," "he who is not with me is against me." He appealed to the popes as well; Catholics expected this and needed it to overcome their doubts about a political priest. Protestants were considered, however, and appeals to the encyclicals were always simple, so that a Protestant listener would be pleased to hear that the Pope understood his difficulties and agreed with the popular solutions. For example, Coughlin said in citing Leo XIII: "Not since the Divine Master . . . has a voice been raised so clearly and fearlessly as was that of Leo XIII, who, like a divine prophet, pronounced the basic principle of Christian economy: 'Thou shalt love thy neighbor as thyself' and drew the conclusions which necessarily follow from this teaching." [39]

Another characteristic of Coughlin's appeal to the encyclicals was that they were often used as authority for positions independently arrived at. In this context Leo XIII and Pius XI served the same purposes as Jefferson and Lincoln; they were sources of support rather than teachers who were to be studied and applied. "Social justice" was not original with the popes; the term represented the traditional Christian approach to life, common to Catholics and Protestants and deeply rooted in America and its religious people. There could be "no lasting prosperity —no semblance of it—unless Christ and His principles are adopted," Coughlin told his audience. But this need only take the form, apparently, of a broad Christian consensus closely tied to American traditions.

Because Coughlin's use of the encyclicals was secondary rather than primary, because he was building a movement and not just inspiring Catholics, he offered no systematic analysis of the papal teachings. His allusions to them, however, and the interpretation applied, indicated that he was confused as to their meaning and application. This was least true in the early years when he was denouncing the evils of the old order; then he found support and probably inspiration in the writings of Leo XIII. As he moved on and began to search for solutions his interpretation of papal thought became more strained. His focus on the money question was peculiarly American; while other countries have had currency reformers, nowhere have they been as common and as influential as in America. The popes in their approach to modern problems have recognized the existence of an important financial problem, but on the whole, their emphasis has been on industrial matters. While Austrian social Catholicism may have had some influence on Coughlin's thought, that movement's dislike of interest was a function of its distaste for modern capitalism; it had none of the characteristics of agrarian natural values, xenophobia, or "poverty in the midst of plenty," which Coughlin espoused, especially before 1936.[40]

On the other hand there was a real distrust among European Catholics of the monopoly of credit, a distrust reflected in Pius XI's warning against the insidious dangers of centralized credit control. The passage became a key one for Coughlin, serving as his defense against Catholic critics, yet it was one thing to acknowledge the danger and another to attribute to those who actually possessed this power responsibility for the evils that plagued society. The Pope's attention was not fixed on men, or even on power, but on the philosophy of individualism which denied the obligations of justice, charity, and the common good. His solution was at least half moral, necessitating a change of heart on the part of all men, not just a few. As one prominent Catholic critic wrote: "We will be saved by no mechanical, automatic plan, but by a change of mind and soul. It seems a shame that Father Coughlin, with his power over the popular mind, has not restricted himself to the reformation of this mind, but has risked all on doubtful economic legislation." [41]

Among the many inconsistencies of Coughlin's thought was a

real confusion as to the role of the State. In the early years he cried, "uncurtailed mass production must go," and called on the government to guarantee jobs to all at a "fair, permanent and equitable, annual wage." [42] He further demanded that the price level be stabilized and that government exercise paternal functions toward labor. Yet he denounced the NRA for controlling private property and curtailing production, charging that it brought a communist-style control. Combining the ideas of Technocrats, Socialists, Capitalists, and popes, he called for "production for use at a profit" but never told how to bring it about.

Several observers saw Coughlin as an American Fascist. One wrote that his was the "most incisively Fascist voice in America." [43] Apart from their often ambiguous use of the term, these critics usually focused on Coughlin's sympathy with European Fascists rather than on his corporate ideas. In fact, despite his attempt to outline a nonpolitical "Corporative State," corporatism was a minor part of Coughlin's teachings when compared to his financial theories, his opposition to communism, his nationalism, or his anti-Semitism. His rhetoric and many of his ideas were thoroughly American and his attention in later years was centered on the preservation of American innocence and isolation. The thrust of his speeches was profoundly negative, striking out, often blindly, at foreign involvement and economic complexity. It was his dislikes and his scapegoats that accounted for his appeal, and it is here that the similarity to fascism must be found; in his nationalism, his intolerance, his baiting of the Jews, his hatred of political parties, his simplifications—in these things he had much in common with European fascist leaders.

Coughlin did not use the encyclicals as a starting point for an evaluation of American society. Catholic thought played a role but was eclectic, employing a papal condemnation here, an episcopal denunciation there. He can be classed in no school of thought because he was unsystematic and confused. He was, most likely, far more concerned with the immediate purpose, destroying the money power or heading off the Communists, than with developing a consistent program for the reform of society. Such reform was unnecessary when the enemy was not social organization or faulty ideas but the anti-Christ. For, if Coughlin belongs anywhere, it is among those who see life as a struggle of Christ and anti-Christ, of good and evil, and find these forces personified in people and institutions: Christianity and America versus communism, the bankers, and the Jews. Thus, at one time Coughlin espoused vocational groups modeled on the Mystical Body of Christ, requiring acceptance of Christianity for their foundation and implying clerical leadership. Yet even here the desire for power and influence destroyed consistency, and the categories broke down. Rather than Catholics it was Christians or just "religionists" and good Americans called to fight in the Coughlin crusade.

There is one further point which must be made about Coughlin as an interpreter of Catholic thought. Just as the sanction which Christianity lends to the individual and his rights can be a powerful revolutionary tool, so can its stress on order and authority serve to buoy up the status quo or justify reaction. Coughlin was able to find support for many of his positions in Catholic thought, although often at the price of consistency. The fact that he could do so, however, indicates the dangers inherent in attempting to translate the absolute categories of religion to society. Unless approached with humility and understanding such attempts can take on a conviction of truth tantamount to fanaticism. Untempered by charity these efforts at social improvement can easily lead to hatred and the destruction of the very institutions and values they are supposed to preserve.

In the later thirties Coughlin became increasingly outspoken in his denunciation of the administration, the plutocrats, and the Communists. Desperately he predicted the early advent of a communist society in the United States, the forerunners of which he saw in the support of the New Deal by Communists, the court-packing plan, the reorganization bill, and increased government spending. He declared that the nation had been tolerant so long that communism had become entrenched in the schools, politics, banking, labor, and industry. A newly explicit element now appeared in his thought, anti-Semitism, a device which conveniently linked the two great evils of plutocracy and communism. Most, though not all, of the financial oligarchy were Jewish, Coughlin argued; the instigators of the Russian Revolution and many of the world's leading Communists were also Jews. They controlled the press and propagandized against Christians, most notably during the Spanish Civil War. Nazism, like fascism before it, was a "defense mechanism" against communism; to prevent a red take-over, Hitler, Mussolini, and Franco acted "as patriots rising to a challenge." Fascism, he contended, "was and is Europe's answer to Russian communism's threat of world revolution and it is the bulwark against long active agencies of destruction." [44] Jews were persecuted because of their association with communism and their lack of patriotism. For the same reason, Jews would eventually face persecution in the United States, Coughlin believed, particularly if they continued to denounce Nazism while ignoring the threat of communism and the plight of Christians under persecution in Russia, Mexico, and Spain. He reminded them that to destroy Nazism it was first necessary to destroy its cause, Russian communism. He denied that he was anti-Semitic; for him it was "not a question of anti-Semitism; it is a question of anti-Communism." [45]

He saw his task as saving the Jews from themselves. "Anti-Semitism is spreading in America," he wrote, "because the people sense a closely interwoven relationship between communism and Jewry. . . . It is the *duty* of American Christians to aid their Jewish fellow citizens in shaking off communism before it is too late." [46] He claimed that he was not opposed to religious

Jews but only to those who supported communism. Yet he printed the spurious *Protocols of Zion,* invited contributions from Nazi sympathizer George Sylvester Viereck, attributed the disasters of modern history to Jewish influence, and, in sum, conformed to the popular image of the anti-Semite. He became the central figure and rallying point for pro-Nazi and anti-Semitic groups while denying he had any particular dislike for the Jews or admiration for the Nazis.[47]

Anti-Semitism could find support in the Church's history and among numerous European Catholic groups. Edward Koch, editor of the corporatist magazine *The Guildsman,* in Germantown, Illinois, faithfully reflected the views of one wing of Central European social Catholicism. He was even more explicit in his defense of the Nazis and his dislike of the Jews than was Coughlin. Koch was vigorously anticapitalist and regularly attacked Catholics who supported labor unions or social legislation, which he feared would only perpetuate the immoral liberal capitalism of modern times. He defended dictatorship as a method of overcoming private interests and introducing a corporate social system and he was vigorous in his support of Franco and his denunciation of antifascist activity. He admired the economic and diplomatic accomplishments of Nazi Germany and praised Hitler's *Mein Kampf* for its devotion to German greatness and its concern for the welfare of the common people. He professed to find a strong Catholic influence on Hitler's writings. Koch drew on German and Austrian sources to excuse the persecution of the Jews, who "reject and disapprove of everything Christian," who controlled the anti-Christian socialist movement, and who "to a great extent represent the money power." He argued that all the supporters of the present unjust social order opposed Hitler and used the defense of democracy as a shield for capitalism. In 1941, he declared that if Mussolini and Hitler were successful in the war, they would "initiate a new Christian social order." [48]

Coughlin himself drew more heavily in the later years on specifically Catholic sources. His favorite appeal was to the writings of the Irish priest, Denis Fahey, who in turn relied heavily on British and French Catholic anti-Semitic groups. In his books Fahey described the existence of a "mystical body of Satan" paralleling that of Christ, embodied in human institutions and seeking constantly to deceive and defeat Christians. The presence of this enemy could be seen in almost every person and policy which opposed the Church.[49] Coughlin shied away from identification only with the Church rather than with the broad Christian consensus, but this view of good and evil using the world as a battleground was present in most of Coughlin's work. Again and again, when distinguishing his policy from that of his enemies, he utilized the imagery of the Crucifixion and challenged his listeners to choose their side, that of Christ or "his enemy who goeth about like a roaring lion . . . roaring in the press, roaring on the radio, roaring on the silver screen." [50] Thus, whether the issue was revaluation of gold, the New Deal, the c.i.o., or the Spanish Civil War, the choice was always "Civilization or Communism: Christ or Chaos." [51]

Coughlin's anti-Semitic activity was a source of division within the American Catholic community. *Commonweal*, whose editors Coughlin and the *Tablet* denounced as traitors because of their opposition to Franco, repeatedly attacked Coughlin and his Christian Front supporters. The *Catholic Worker* always opposed the radio priest and took the lead in fighting anti-Semitism. John Ryan and George Shuster refuted Coughlin's slanders against the Jews while Father Joseph N. Moody, at the request of Cardinal Hayes, published a pamphlet exposing all the old canards of Jewish power and radicalism.[52] A group of Catholics formed an organization to combat anti-Semitism and published a journal, *The Voice*, which sought to offset Coughlin's influence. Cardinal Mundelein publicly stated that the priest was not authorized to speak for Catholics and his views did not rep-

resent "the doctrines and sentiments of the Church." Milwaukee's Archbishop Stritch denounced Coughlin while numerous
others, including Archbishop Mooney, spoke out vigorously
against anti-Semitism.[53]

Many of Coughlin's American Catholic colleagues, who would
have nothing to do with anti-Semitism, nevertheless agreed with
his premise that communism was a far greater threat than fascism and they found support for this position in the policies of
the Vatican. In addition, many were hurt and puzzled by the
failure of other Americans to share their view of events in
Mexico, Russia, and Spain. Father Gillis of the *Catholic World*, a
long and consistent opponent of anti-Semitism, deplored the fact
that Catholics suffering under persecution did not receive the
same sympathy from Americans as did the Jews. *America* too
deplored anti-Semitism, but shared a widely held belief that the
Jews had brought their problems on themselves by ignoring the
threat of communism and accusing anti-red Christians of being
anti-Semitic.[54] The Brooklyn *Tablet*, Coughlin's major supporter in the East, was especially outspoken in denouncing
American Jews and liberals for failing to speak out against
communism and anti-Catholic persecution. Similar attitudes appeared in other Catholic journals, including the *Ave Maria*.[55]
Coughlin played skillfully on these fears and frustrations, urging
the "spineless Christians of America" to demand "the same
protection . . . sympathy . . . and comfort" for their "co-
religionists" as the Jews demanded for their German "co-
nationals." [56]

Catholics who saw communism as a greater threat than fascism, a position contrary to that of the majority of Americans,
often felt isolated and mistreated. In this situation the presence
of Coughlin and his work was a further irritant in their relations
with non-Catholics, who suspected the Church of an accommodation with fascism. These fears were not without foundation
and the refusal of the Church to silence the radio priest seemed

to give the argument weight. Archbishop Mooney perhaps feared a scandalous fight, a possibility which *Social Justice* raised. Others like the editors of *America* and staunch anticommunist prelates like Bishop Noll of Fort Wayne, undoubtedly welcomed Coughlin's powerful asistance against communism and against American involvement in war with Germany. Whatever the motives involved, Coughlin's activity and his popularity in some heavily Catholic areas of the country were evidence of the failures of the American Church and constituted a standing rebuke to the Catholic professions of loyalty to Christian ideals and democratic values.

In the early years Coughlin's radio audience was national, reaching into most sections and classes. His program and rhetoric were aimed at all the distressed and discontented, regardless of creed. Still, he was a Catholic priest, he did refer to Christian and Catholic teachings, and he received wide support within the Catholic community. The few attempts that have been made to determine the nature of Coughlin's support indicate that it was heavily Catholic, the proportion increasing through the decade. By 1936, his educated, middle-class, small-business supporters appear to have fallen away, leaving a remnant of the truly poor, the despairing sections of the population, without hope and totally alienated. Those who wrote bitter letters to Monsignor Ryan after his anti-Coughlin radio address were for the most part Irish and German Catholics, as were the Union party's main bloc of supporters in the election. The letters to Ryan indicated that the hard core Coughlinites were filled with hatred of Roosevelt, the New Deal, and even of the Church and its leaders. Father Parsons of *America*, like Ryan, received a flood of abusive and anticlerical letters after writing a series of articles moderately critical of the radio priest. The historian of Coughlin's political activities concluded that "the Coughlinite movement represented a potential break from hierarchical authority." [57]

Coughlin himself did not hesitate to play on this resentment of the poor against the clergy and hierarchy. He denounced Cardinal O'Connell, his most prominent Catholic critic in the early years, as a tool of the plutocrats. The priest criticized "prominent midwestern ecclesiastics," probably with Cardinal Mundelein in mind, who maintained that the Church had no preference for any political party. Coughlin said that this view was typical of the "apathy and clumsy thinking which is in vogue in too many pulpits." [58] When Coughlin temporarily left the air after a disagreement with Archbishop Mooney over the c.i.o. in late 1937 his paper, *Social Justice*, launched a vigorous campaign against his Catholic opponents. Mooney was linked with Ryan and the latter denounced. Ryan's associates John Lapp and John Haggerty of the Catholic Association for International Peace were accused of having "aided Communists and Communism for years." John Brophy, a Catholic prominent in the c.i.o. was denounced as the "Church's leftist Number One." Bishop Boyle of Pittsburgh was attacked for allowing priests of his diocese to assist the c.i.o. The *Catholic Worker* was accused of teaching communist doctrines, and of supporting birth control and the Spanish Communists. The paper concluded that the Catholic press was smearing Coughlin, who was being silenced not by the powers of Christianity "but by deaf, dumb and blind Churchianity." [59]

Yet many of those whom Coughlin later denounced had warmly approved his work in the early years. Little progress had been made in popularizing *Rerum Novarum* and Coughlin, by use of the radio, was able to reach more Catholics than any other Catholic leader. He appeared on the scene at an opportune time. With Al Smith becoming more conservative and Roosevelt not yet a rallying point for reformers, Coughlin in 1931 and 1932 provided an outlet for the discontent and disillusionment of American Catholics. Moreover, he helped lead them from a minimalist view of the state to belief in active, positive government.[60] Ryan, Parsons, and many others recognized Coughlin's power and appreciated his contribution so long as he remained within the traditional boundaries.[61] But a number of factors created divisions. One was the priest's intolerance of criticism; when he responded to mild rebuffs with bitter attack, Catholic editors began to be suspicious of his assumption of infallibility and the hysterical character of his speeches and his movement. A second factor was the priest's entry into politics. Church leaders and Catholic journals almost universally deplored the use of political means; they feared that Catholic social teachings would be discredited and the dignity and influence of the clergy permanently damaged. Coughlin himself acknowledged the strength of this bias against clerical political activity. He attributed the weakness of religion in America in the twenties to the involvement of the clergy with politics and Prohibition. In 1936, he denounced politicians and parties and urged Ryan to "give up his political work and become once more the genuine scholar and exemplary priest whom all could admire." [62] Apparently he never regarded himself as a politician but as a spokesman for Christian principles and the common people.

The traditional reverence of American Catholics for the clergy was based upon an image of dignity and aloofness far removed from the behavior of Coughlin in the campaign of 1936. Associated with a bigot like Gerald L. K. Smith, denouncing the President as "that great liar and betrayer" and "anti-God," Coughlin's methods did not attract Catholics fearful about their status and acceptance in American society. Coughlin's early fame, his association with the Democratic party and the President and his importance in American political life, attracted status-conscious Catholics; his later activities drove them away. When he broke with the New Deal he challenged the traditional loyalty of many of his followers to the Democratic party, a loyalty intensified by the material benefits received at the hands of the New Deal and the political "recognition" that the Roosevelt administration had given to Catholics. Like so many others in the lower middle class, Catholics wished to be conservative and respectable, if events would allow. Coughlin attracted them because he represented protest within the confines of religious allegiance and political loyalty. When he challenged the leaders of the Church, the Democratic party, and the new unions, which claimed another share of the allegiance of many Catholics, the strain was too great.[63]

After 1936, Coughlin's popularity among all sections of the population declined sharply, but the remainder of his followers were more disproportionately Catholic than earlier.[64] His nationalism and desire to avoid war were attractive and his campaign against neutrality revision and lifting of the embargo attracted wide support. Most important was his opposition to communism, which offered a chance for alliance with earlier opponents. Cardinal O'Connell had early denounced Coughlin for setting class against class; later Coughlin denounced the c.i.o. for the same reason. In 1935, Congressman John J. O'Connor of New York had threatened to kick Father Coughlin from the Capitol to the White House; three years later the two were anti-New Deal allies. Bishop Noll of Fort Wayne denied he was a Coughlin supporter in 1936, but in 1938 he endorsed the call for an anticommunist Christian Front and was found with Coughlin on the same side on most issues.[65]

Fears of communism, a sense of isolation from general American opinion, and the lifting of the sense of economic crisis led some Catholics to welcome Coughlin's leadership against communism. A transition from "interest" to "status" politics may have been present, as there was a clear following of interest lines among Catholics in the years of serious depression, while Mexico and the Spanish Civil War reawakened older concerns of status. But the two coexisted; economic reformers looked at the New Deal for evidence of Catholic inspiration while anticommunists coupled their opposition to the "Reds" with support of a Catholic reform program, however vague. The Brooklyn *Tablet* was, from the beginning, both antibusiness and nationalistic and, unlike Father Coughlin, it was always anxious about Catholic prestige.

In Brooklyn, in fact, status played a special role. It was there that the Christian Front, the anti-Semitic organization inspired by Coughlin, had its greatest strength and engaged in numerous physical attacks on Jews. The Irish in Brooklyn rose slowly on the social scale. Although they attained lower-middle-class rank early, they tended to remain at that level. The Jews, who arrived in Brooklyn much later, soon attained economic and social positions comparable to those of the Irish. The resulting tensions were felt for years and were brought to the level of action by the events of the thirties. Patrick Scanlon of the *Tablet* asked the editors of *The Voice*, a Catholic publication, to combat anti-Semitism, if they were interested in the question of racism, "why do they not assail the discrimination against the Germans, Italians, Irish and other races of New York who are fast being reduced to the most inconspicuous places?" It was within this context that the incendiary writings of Coughlin were received and acted upon. Although Coughlin denied being an anti-Semite, his views were sure to be taken seriously in an area predisposed to view the Jews with dislike and suspicion.[66]

Coughlin's significance for American Catholicism was considerable, but more as a symbol than for any real contribution he made toward solving the peculiar problems of the Church in America. Just as he reflected in the early years the distress that affected a wide segment of the population, so many of his later crusades mirrored the tensions at work within the Catholic community. For a time he was in tune with that community, helping its members to relate their economic and social problems to their faith. In that period he made constructive contributions, opening the minds of his listeners to the possibility of an active and dynamic government seeking to realize the ideals of justice and

equality. Even more than Ryan he succeeded in communicating
to his listeners the basic immorality of the old order's concentration of wealth, low wages, and social insecurity.

But he lacked the stability to stay within the boundaries of
moral advice and economic explanation. Instead, he drove for
power with a dogmatic and inadequate monetary scheme, and this
was bound to separate him from the bulk of American and
Catholic opinion. In later years he utilized portions of Catholic
teachings to supply socially insecure Catholics with rationaliza-
tions for their personal and group fears and prejudices. In this
period he was a positive obstacle to the maturity of American
Catholics, helping to keep alive the ghetto mentality and a
narrow vision of Christian social action rather than assisting
Catholics to surmount their limitations by an awareness of the
richness, humanity, and universality of the faith.

He drew on little that was constructive and much that was
harmful in both Catholic and American thought. To the limitations of Catholic minority consciousness he added the teachings
of some of the most backward and exclusivist European Catholics and supported both by appeal to isolated and ambiguous
segments of papal teachings. From the American radical tradition he extracted the most negative elements, perverting the
populist dream into a program of hatred and fear. Both Catholic
and American traditions contained ideas which could be utilized
to support authoritarianism, reaction, even race hatred. Coughlin's attempt to draw the two streams together ended by concen-
trating on the worst elements of both.

If Coughlin's ideas had represented the dominant strain of
American Catholicism, the weight of non-Catholic resentment
might have brought disaster to the Church and country. Fortunately, in the 1930's an increasingly large number of priests and
laymen were attempting with some success to make their religion relevant to their lives as Americans and were bringing
much that was admirable in America to bear on their interpreta-

tion of Catholic thought and the meaning of the Christian heritage for the problems of their society. One of these young Catholics who matured in the Depression years was Richard Deverall, a protégé of Dorothy Day and founder of a "radical" Catholic journal, the *Christian Front*. He recalls the impact of Coughlin's words in the depths of the Depression awakening him and his fellows to a concern with social problems and the surprising discovery that the Church had a social message of its own. Subsequent events led him through the Catholic Worker movement and into the c.i.o. In the later thirties he found himself with other Catholics forced to form an organization to combat the anti-Semitism of the priest who had been their early inspiration.[67] In such a sequence of events lies the tragedy of Father Coughlin and of a whole segment of American Catholics who would go on to fight communism while ignoring the social problems around them. In the same story lay the hope of the American Church. Unafraid of controversy and little concerned with the institutional interests or public recognition of the Church, men like Deverall were finding in their religious faith the inspiration and strength to undertake social and political action aimed at making America not necessarily Catholic, but a just and humane society in which men could live in dignity and attempt to work out their salvation in freedom, unrestrained by economic privation, political domination, or social insecurity.

VIII

The Catholic Worker Movement

Monsignor Ryan and Father Coughlin differed on most political and social issues after the latter's break with the New Deal, yet each claimed to be basing his position on the teachings of Pius XI. Disagreement over the correct interpretation and application of the encyclicals in the United States was symptomatic of the dilemma of modern social Catholicism. All Catholics agreed that justice and charity formed the basis of Christian social order, and they developed a consensus against certain unchristian principles and programs. But they were unable to translate their acceptance of revelation, natural law, and the teaching authority of the Church into a concrete program for society. Even the system of *ordines* suggested by Pius XI, although accepted by most Catholics as an objective for social reconstruction, contained in itself no directives as to the means of bringing it about in any particular historical context. Disagreement arose over the nature of the new order and of its constituent groups as well as over the means of approaching its realization. *Quadragesimo Anno* endorsed labor unions but might have meant only Catholic unions; it upheld the duties of the State to promote the common good, yet called for a decrease in its administrative burdens; it suggested that the State had a key role to play in bringing about the new social order, then limited it by the principle of subsidiarity, which presupposed an already organized autonomous social life. Finally the encyclical called for State action, independent organization, and moral reform as means of bringing the new order into being, but assigned the latter primary importance. The encyclical, in fact, offered no firm basis for constructing a unified program of Catholic social action. All could justify their approach on the basis of the encyclicals: those who looked to the State as the primary instrument of reform, those who were attracted to the dynamism of the labor movement as the best hope for establishing a just social order, those who rejected both as permeated by a false liberalism and a selfish individualism, and those who concentrated on individual spiritual perfection and the practice of works of charity.

For many American Catholics such division was a source of scandal and disappointment. They had hoped that the Catholic minority, organized into "a united front" on economic and social matters, could turn the institutions of American life into Christian channels.[1] Many of these had been attracted to the program of "Catholic Action" called for by the Pope. Catholic Action, defined as "the participation of the laity in the apostolate of the hierarchy," was designed to return society, threatened by "pagan forces," to its Christian foundations.[2] Because the bishops and clergy were no longer able to exert leadership in secular affairs, the Church could bring influence to bear only by organizing, training, and directing the laity. First, laymen were to be made aware of the Church's teachings as interpreted by the bishops. Then they were to be mobilized under episcopal direction to bring these teachings into practice. In the words of Father Raymond J. Campion, once "the Catholic body is conscious of its powers and zealous in explaining its program [it could become a] well-nigh irresistible force for good in the community."[3] Although everyone emphasized that Catholic Action was nonpolitical, the metaphor used to describe it was frequently that of an army, with bishops as officers, clergy as

noncommissioned officers, and laity as a disciplined body, an
imagery that naturally excited the hostility of totalitarian governments in Europe and the suspicion of liberals and Protestants
in the United States. This was true of the foremost example of
official Catholic Action in America, the Legion of Decency,
which was heavily praised by Rome and which succeeded in
preventing the production of morally objectionable films. Many
non-Catholics felt that the pressures exerted by the Legion restricted freedom of expression and prevented the development
of serious, creative work. Later many Catholics would agree, but
in the thirties the Legion of Decency drew unanimous applause
from all sectors of the Catholic community.[4]

In contrast to the emphasis on episcopal direction in official
guides to Catholic Action, the leaders of the NCWC Social Action
Department argued that, while the Church should strive to make
the laity more aware of its teachings, it should leave the application of principles to individual laymen. As one editor expressed
this view: "The work of Christianizing temporal affairs is one
for the individual Christian in contact with them."[5] This stress
on education and independent action appeared to cross the
boundaries of Catholic Action as defined by Rome but was far
more suited to the situation in the United States than the clericalism and authoritarianism implicit in the hierarchical approach.
It was particularly attractive to an increasing number of laymen
distressed by the poverty and injustice of their society and
anxious to involve themselves in its alleviation. The Depression
made clearer than ever the persistent conflict between Christian
ideals and social practices and institutions, while the presence of
the Catholic laity in a society that emphasized freedom and initiative was bound to lead to a rejection of clerical domination.
Led by the proponents of Christian personalism and inspired by
the liturgical movement and the *Catholic Worker*, a significant
minority of lay people refused to rely on clerical leadership or
await hierarchical direction. Instead they sought to make their

personal Christian commitment meaningful, to realize in practice the implications of their faith.

Personalism in America was activist. It emphasized the responsibility of each individual Christian to live his faith by assisting his neighbor at a personal sacrifice. It stressed personal sanctity and holiness, a strong grounding in the liturgy, and an apostolic desire to improve the lot of mankind. Perfectionist and unsystematic, focusing on the giver rather than the recipient, on the action itself rather than the social change that such action might bring about, personalism sought to realize love of neighbor through personal commitment and voluntary action. While others directed attention to legislation, organization, and institutional reconstruction, personalists concentrated on reforming themselves and changing society by the example of Christian love. Their actions were self-consciously Catholic; they were vividly aware of the gap that separated them from other social reformers, and they stressed the superiority of the Christian way. But their exclusiveness was different from the self-righteousness of the ghetto for they went out to others, attempting to see in each man the image of his Maker, to regard each individual regardless of creed or lack of it as "another Christ" of inherent and absolute dignity and worth. American personalism received its strongest support from sociologist Paul Hanley Furfey, liturgist Virgil Michel, and the founders of the Catholic Worker movement.[6]

Furfey's sociology was a self-conscious tool for a Christian reform that was more radical than anything advocated by his Catholic University colleague, John A. Ryan. Furfey charged that exponents of moderation in Catholic social action bargained and compromised with the world, overlooked the need for fundamental change, and acquiesced in materialism, racial discrimination, and injustice. In return they were allowed to sit on the boards of community chests, their charities received large grants from millionaires, their schools were objects of philanthropic favor, and their religious liberty was respected. Furfey regarded himself as an extremist, who interpreted Gospel teachings literally. He purposely set impossibly high standards that he knew could not be reached without God's help; he relied on grace and example rather than politics as methods of reform, and he regarded social work as a "poor substitute for charity." Extremists should love poverty, glory in the world's hatred, and denounce injustice clearly and forcefully. They should refuse to compromise, instead stressing the truths they knew from faith, including the concepts of sin and damnation anathema to their time. They should proclaim without modification that men are bound to assist their neighbors, to identify with the poor and the oppressed or risk eternal punishment. Furfey despised arguments from prudence that would neglect the Negro in order to avoid hurting the Church in the South, or that would teach business courses in Catholic colleges in order to prepare young Catholics to compete successfully in an unjust society.[7]

A Christian society, according to Furfey, was one in which the "citizens edify one another by the practice of supernatural virtues, in a word, a society where man is aided socially to his supernatural end." It could be established only with the aid of divine grace, which in turn demanded the practice of personal acts of charity and sacrifice. It was not enough to strive to remove social abuses; Catholics had also to attempt "to reproduce in their common living the unearthly beauty of the Mystical Body of Christ." [8] Accordingly, Furfey held that the basis of social action was supernatural, the practice of the works of mercy in imitation of the life of Christ: feeding the poor, clothing the naked, providing shelter for those without, visiting the sick and imprisoned, instructing the ignorant—in general attempting to assist one's neighbor both materially and spiritually but always from a supernatural motivation, the desire to fulfill the love of neighbor that had to follow from love of God. Ordinary social reform was inadequate because it dealt only with the material side of life and did not assist in the construction of a Christian society. Social work, while good as an instrument, was too often permeated by a coldness, a lack of respect for the dignity of the client, far removed from the warmth and selflessness of true charity. It could materially assist the poor but could not achieve true reform, which was regeneration through grace.

Furfey stressed voluntary poverty as the foremost virtue and primary technique. He rejected the argument that one could be detached, "poor in spirit," in the midst of worldly possessions and held that "poverty of spirit is genuine only when it is accompanied by the maximum of actual poverty possible under the circumstances." Voluntary poverty followed from the logic of Christianity: "If we really love the poor," Furfey wrote, "we shall be forced . . . to share our goods with them until we ourselves have become poor." A life of voluntary poverty was a prerequisite for true freedom, he contended, for it released men from avarice, convention, and competition, leaving them at liberty to practice the supernatural virtues, which were not conformable to life in a materialistic world. Poverty was not destitution, but a dignified, simple, and obscure condition comparable to that of Christ. Once one attained this level he was to strive to assist others in reaching it rather than pushing on for more for himself. On this basis, for example, he severely condemned the policy of organizing craft unions of skilled workers.[9]

Furfey believed that civilization was at a point of crisis. Christians should support all measures of legislation that would bring just social reform and join organizations that would further these ends. But they should never forget that "the prime Christian method of social reform is through the works of mercy." If these were practiced, the power of example would bring fundamental social revolution, just as the lives of the early Christians had won over the pagans of their day.[10]

Furfey deplored the efforts of some Catholics "to solve social problems by purely human methods without reference to the

supernatural truths of faith." On the contrary, these truths had
to be the starting point for the Christian sincere in his belief, in
contrast to the dominant tendency to stress scientific and philosophical sociology, where the only contribution the Catholic had
to make was the negative check of dogma, leading to the rejection of some schemes but the construction of no distinctive
Catholic program. Insisting that Catholics recognize that true
social reform depended upon acceptance of Christian faith as
taught by the Church, Furfey attempted to develop a "theological sociology" which would apply directly the principles of revealed religion to social problems. "Let us do away with all false
over-emphasis on purely natural reason as an instrument of
social thought," he lectured Catholics. "Let us set Catholic sociology before the modern world in its true light—as a branch of
knowledge dependent on Divine Revelation." [11] Finding support
in the encyclicals he stressed the need for moral reform, not
only of those outside the Church but of Catholics as well, so that
all would be inspired and animated by Christian love. Personal
commitment to Christian ideals and the voluntary practice of the
virtues consequent on that commitment were more important
than the "reform of institutions." Both were necessary but
"personalist action can function without organized action, while
the reverse is not the case." [12]

Many disagreed with Furfey's emphasis on moral reform. All
Catholics recognized the need for men to recognize and accept
their social responsibilities; it was a commonplace that legislation
or organization could not alone bring the Christian social order
into existence. Nevertheless, many felt that immediate problems
were so great that they deserved the bulk of attention. As one
writer put it: "It is useless today to talk of reform in the social,
political, or perhaps even the religious life of men unless a radical change can be effected in the economic sphere, whence most
of our present day disorders originate." [13] Furfey often seemed
to confuse the natural and supernatural levels, holding that soci-

ety and its institutions had to serve only the supernatural end of man. They did this best by providing for the real material needs of men, thereby creating the necessary framework for men to work out their salvation in freedom.

Furfey's conception of a society based upon common faith did not necessarily imply coercion or restrictions on human dignity and freedom. He insisted on voluntarism and respect for the inherent value of the human personality, but these concepts were difficult to reconcile with a theological sociology which sought to establish institutions which would consciously assist men to the practice of Christian virtue and to salvation. What Catholics had to realize was that political parties, the State, labor unions, and other social institutions were "not eligible for Baptism." [14] They could not be Christian without being dominated by the clergy, involving the Church in temporal affairs, restricting freedom, and violating human dignity. But institutions could be human, they could be made to serve distinctively human ends through the organized efforts of all men who valued liberty and the dignity of the individual. The specifically Catholic contribution lay elsewhere, in inspiring men to seek to realize their love of God both through the humanization of institutions and through the Christianization of their own lives.

Closely allied with the personal approach to reform was the liturgy, or public worship of the Church. If the basis of Christian society was essentially religious, then one way to prepare for the advent of that society was to concentrate on the development of spiritual life based on the liturgy. "The Liturgy is the perfect expression of the new social Catholicism," wrote Father Furfey. "The new movement is founded upon faith and the Liturgy is the public expression of our faith." [15] The liturgical revival in the United States had a strong social cast. It flourished first in the areas where the Catholic Worker movement was most active and its foremost exponent, the Benedictine Virgil Michel, was also a leading interpreter of the social encyclicals.

Michel, in fact, possessed a deep vision of the needs of his society and of his fellow Catholics and, unlike his European counterparts in liturgical reform, he attempted to clarify the relationship between the liturgy and social life.

Michel recognized that the spirit of individualism that dominated the modern era had even penetrated the Church and its worship. He agreed with Furfey that the primary change had to be moral and spiritual. Recognition that all men are saved through Christ, that they share a common nature, destiny, and end, was imperative if the Christian was to see God in every man, to see the image of Christ in the face of the poor. The object of liturgical reform was to awaken Christians to an awareness of their fellowship in the Mystical Body of Christ. Once awakened they no longer would be able to conceive of salvation in isolation: only in and through the fellowship of the Mystical Body could men be saved. In the performance of spiritual duties one contributed to the spiritual welfare of the fellowship, while a failure to live the Christian life was an injury to the whole body. Such a vision of the solidarity of mankind and the effect of all actions on one's fellows was, for Michel, a solid foundation for the corporate and co-operative spirit of the Christian social order.

Michel feared that American Catholics had become too American, too immersed in an individualistic and materialistic culture. "As long as the Christian is in the habit of viewing his religious life from the subjectivist and individualist standpoint," Michel wrote, "he will be able to live his daily life in terms of the prudent individualism and subjectivism without any qualms of conscience." [16] The liturgy hopefully could open the eyes of the American Catholic to Christian culture, a culture built upon mutual concern, respect, and love growing out of the recognition of fellowship. While, unlike Father Furfey, Michel denied that Christianity offered a "detailed scheme of social reconstruction, or anything of the kind," the liturgy did supply a model of society, the Mystical Body, and it put the concept into action by inspiring and strengthening the laity "to live it out in everyday life." [17]

The liturgical movement gave new meaning to the life of the laity. Bringing them back into participation in the liturgy and emphasizing their responsibilities for the spiritual welfare of the Mystical Body were important steps in overcoming the strictly juridical view of the Church, which had been dominant since the Reformation and had reduced the laity to a passive role in Catholic life. The liturgical movement stressed the responsibility of the laity to live Christian lives in the world and to attempt to Christianize the milieu that surrounded them. True appreciation of the liturgy, Michel was convinced, would bring a sense of solidarity and love, which could not but effect the layman's view of the social order. "Not paper programs, not highsounding unfulfilled resolutions once renewed the world," Michel wrote, "but new and living men born out of the depths of Christianity." [18] For this reason Michel, while admiring the social action of others, regarded the liturgical movement as the primary apostolate.

While others located the enemy in communism, the State, or immoral social practices, Michel saw that it was closer to home. Men like Father Coughlin and Monsignor Fulton Sheen often spoke of a struggle between the Mystical Body of Christ and the anti-Christ, sketching a picture of the world as divided between the forces of good and evil, with the Church and Catholics aligned on "God's side." [19] What Michel saw was that the greater evil was the permeation of the Church and its members by bourgeois values of materialism and individualism. Irresponsibility toward their fellow men and apathy in the face of social injustice were greater enemies than communism, and these had to be combated by a heroic perfectionism of sacrifice, simplicity, and poverty.

Michel stressed the solidarity of men in the Mystical Body of

Christ, and yet he was a personalist. The solidarity was one of free men, raised to a supernatural dignity by the Incarnation and possessing ultimate value. For this reason the depersonalization of life, the infringement of personal dignity by war, destitution, and tyranny were abhorrent to the Christian. What was needed was a social order that would allow men to live and think and worship freely and creatively. He drew no sketch of the Christian order, but emphasized that the important element was a spirit of love and mutual sacrifice. Economic and political structures would grow naturally from this spirit and could not be predetermined without violating the freedom and voluntarism that followed from recognition of the personal dignity of man.[20]

The most significant practical expression of the integral Catholicism and personalism taught by Furfey and Michel was the Catholic Worker movement. Founded by two of American Catholicism's most unusual personalities, the Catholic Worker was, and remains, a movement, not an organization or a paper or a series of settlement houses, but a collection of diverse ideals, crusades, and people. Whether the Catholic Workers were distributing their newspaper, picketing a Christian Front meeting, feeding Bowery derelicts, or engaging in civil disobedience, they were doing so on their own, each individually trying to realize an ideal of Christian responsibility and yet, in the absence of formal organization, joined together by the strength of their common religious convictions and their love of their "Brothers in Christ." Most of all they were bound together by Dorothy Day, a woman who failed to carry out the program of her teacher, Peter Maurin, but who exerted a tremendous influence on the maturing Catholic community. Dorothy Day and the Catholic Workers followed few of the rules of social action, yet they were able to do something that their fellow Catholic social actionists were never able to accomplish: they dramatized and manifested the inherent conflict between Christian ideals and social realities. By doing so, they assisted American Catholics to understand their heritage as Catholics and challenged them to live Christian lives in a society that was often unchristian.

The story of the Catholic Worker in the 1930's is the story of Peter Maurin and Dorothy Day. Maurin was a poor itinerant French philosopher who was truly beloved by all who came in contact with him.[21] Born in France in 1877, Maurin was educated by the Christian Brothers and took preliminary vows in the order. After teaching for a number of years he abandoned the religious life to devote himself to the Sillon, the mystical and democratic Catholic movement that swept France in the early years of the century. Some time later he grew disillusioned with the Sillon and, to avoid military service, he left France for Canada. From that point little is known of him other than that he held a number of jobs, and crossed the Continent in search of work, finally turning up in New York in the late twenties, offering language lessons and preaching a doctrine of Christian poverty and service. He refused fees and lived in the Bowery, occasionally leaving the city to work on the farm of a priest friend, and he talked ceaselessly of Christian reform. In 1933, he visited George Shuster of the *Commonweal*, who listened attentively to Maurin's program of social reconstruction. Shuster sent the French reformer to see a young convert, Dorothy Day, a free lance writer who was at the time in Washington on an assignment for *America* and *Commonweal*.

Dorothy Day was born in Illinois but lived in a number of cities around the country.[22] Although her family was not religious, Dorothy, a reflective and sensitive child, was early attracted by the religious practices of her friends and joined the Episcopal Church at a young age. Warm and affectionate, she had a deep love of nature and of people and her compassion accounted in part for her becoming a socialist while at the University of Illinois. Forced to leave school for lack of money, she went to New York where she worked on the staff of the radical paper, *The Masses*, and mingled freely with the political and cultural Left Wing. She later said she had been a Communist, though not a party member, but her attraction to the Left was always more romantic than ideological. When she was expecting a child by her common law husband her thoughts returned to the religious experiences of her youth. Her exact contact with Catholicism is unclear but the child was baptized in the Church, and the mother followed a year later. Dorothy's conversion was a religious, even a mystical act, and had nothing to do with her social concerns. Indeed, her fear that she was abandoning social action was one of the biggest obstacles to her conversion. To support herself and her daughter she wrote articles for the Catholic press describing the religious practices and customs of Mexico and other areas that she visited.

Her desire to serve the poor remained strong, however, and was intensified by the Depression. She had a deep understanding of and sympathy for human suffering, a sympathy that was all-embracing. Catholic "to her finger tips," she lacked great powers of constructive thought or precise analysis, but her zeal, selflessness, and dedication were near universal. When she returned from Washington in 1933, Peter Maurin was waiting with a program which would consume her efforts for the rest of her life. Of Maurin she wrote: "He was my master and I was his disciple." [23]

Maurin began by introducing Dorothy to the social and intellectual tradition of the Church, matters that she was wholly ignorant of. He disliked writing and preferred to talk in a simple and rhythmic style, reducing complex ideas to a single, simple phrase. When he did write he set down the phrases as he would speak them, in a kind of free verse which became known as "Easy Essays." This style was part of his concept of his vocation as an agitator and propagandist of Christian ideas, attempting to carry them to the workers who had the power to put them into effect. His objective was to influence public opinion by reaching those who formed it, "the thinking people who know how to transmit their thinking to the unthinking people." He contended that all ideas had to be rewritten in the vernacular of "the man in the street," particularly the unemployed, who supplied a ready field for indoctrination.[24]

Maurin's great concern was secularism, the separation of the spiritual from the material, of the Church from political, economic, and social life. Society, he felt, by definition required a "unity of thought," a common belief in what underlay its life. He aimed at a new synthesis, a restoration of unity to the chaotic modern world by means of an integral Catholicism. The size, complexity, and impersonality of modern life preoccupied Maurin, particularly mass production, which brutalized man. The conditions of modern society destroyed what he regarded as the heart of Christianity, personal responsibility, the need to recognize in every man the image of God and to treat him accordingly. This could not be done by the State or by social workers but only by Christians whose faith allowed them to see in the most oppressed of men the image of Christ. To inspire men to regard each other, and treat each other, in this way, was the objective of Maurin's life. The Catholic Worker's importance derived from its attempt at a Christian synthesis based upon the knowledge that all men are created by God and redeemed by Christ and therefore possess inherent dignity and worth. Everything the Catholic Worker movement did was inspired by this vision and was directed toward making men aware of this fundamental truth and creating a society where their dignity could be protected and fulfilled.[25]

These concerns Maurin embodied in a threefold program which he presented to Dorothy Day. First, he called for roundtable discussion through which workers and intellectuals would be brought together, keeping the intellectuals in touch with the real and showing the workers how things should be. The latter function would also be carried out by means of a labor paper. Second, Maurin wanted Dorothy to visit the bishops and urge them to establish houses of hospitality, where Catholics could fulfill their personal responsibility to the poor by practicing the works of mercy. Finally, he wanted to establish farming communes where groups of Catholic workers and students could learn to provide for themselves and build the cells of a future Christian social order.

His program differed markedly from the usual Catholic social outline. Although believing strongly in the dignity of labor, Maurin had little use for unions, since in selling their labor, workers were equally guilty with capitalists of treating it as a commodity. Maurin feared that as long as men accepted the assembly line and the abundance of the factory system, they would not think in terms of personality or community. The commune proposal was an expression of this. Influenced by the distributists, Maurin called for decentralization, voluntary co-operation, mutual aid, and rural handicrafts, free from State control, centralized power, and commercialization.[26]

He saw no hope of achieving these objectives through politics because politicans were forced to follow rather than form public opinion. Of the New Deal he wrote: "When people stand back of the President and the President stands back of the people, the people and the President go around in a circle, getting no-where." [27] Furthermore, he rejected organized action as an eva-sion of personal responsibility. Reform began with the individ-ual's acceptance of solidarity with the poor and personal responsibility for the reconstruction of his own life and the life of society. The personalist ideal could unite "humanists, theists, Protestants and Catholics" in a "Pluralist State," where govern-ment would refrain from interfering with all movements based on personal responsibility and would "not try to solve the social problem by passing laws and creating bureaus." [28]

Maurin's interpretation of papal social teachings was unique. He believed that Leo XIII's *Rerum Novarum* was a departure from an ideal of personal, charitable social action. Leo was say-ing, in effect, that as men would not reform personally, they must be coerced by organization and State action; Maurin preferred to stick to the ideal. Thus he regarded unions as weak expedients, rejected the wage contract, and opposed all increases in State power. Although the *Catholic Worker* admitted the necessity for government to deal with problems that could "in no other way be dealt with," it strongly emphasized the qualification.[29]

Maurin and Dorothy Day were quite different, and their disagreement was evident in the history of the Worker. Peter came from an agrarian peasant background and deplored industrial civilization. Dorothy, while agreeing with much of Peter's criticism, had experienced the class war as a Socialist and it continued to absorb her interest. In addition, she was a journalist and found the idea of a labor paper with a Catholic slant most attractive. On May Day 1933 the *Catholic Worker* appeared in Union Square. Issued throughout the decade at monthly intervals, and priced at a penny a copy, the paper achieved a circulation of over 100,000. In its pages Maurin offered his "Easy Essays," but the paper pledged itself to represent no one Catholic social program. The writings of the most advanced European Catholic writers: Maritain, Berdyaev, Eric Gill, and others occupied a prominent place. News of the houses of hospitality was also published. But from the start the *Catholic Worker* was a labor paper stamped with Dorothy Day's love of the poor and downtrodden.

The paper featured extensive descriptions of unjust labor conditions in all areas of the country; it covered strikes, reported the grievances of the workers, and assisted their cause where possible. When a dock strike hit New York City the Catholic Workers published a special edition of the paper and set up a soup line for the strikers. They applauded the advent of the c.i.o. and considered the question of communism less important than the hopes the new union aroused and the chance it offered workers to reassert their dignity. The work of labor education went beyond the paper. Weekly lectures and study sessions were held to acquaint workers with their rights, with the social doctrine of the Church, and the program of Peter Maurin. A group of Catholic Workers led by John Cort established the Association of Catholic Trade Unionists to support unionization and strikes and indoctrinate Catholic laborers in the Church's social teachings.

The second portion of Maurin's program was the establishment of houses of hospitality where Catholics, practicing voluntary poverty, could assist the poor. Maurin stressed the need to see the poor as the image of Christ and at all times to treat them as guests whose dignity was to be respected, who were not to be patronized or proselytized. No attempt was made to convert, discipline, or train those who came to the house that Dorothy founded in New York or to the other houses that sprung up around the country. Voluntary poverty was a technique which they felt would free them from the burdens of the world and assist in carrying out their program. By practicing detachment from worldly goods and asserting human and spiritual values, they hoped, with God's help, to influence others to follow their example. "It has always been through the performance of the works of mercy, that love is expressed, that people are converted, that the masses are reached," wrote Dorothy.[30]

The houses of hospitality became centers for apostolic, dedicated, and socially conscious young Catholics. They read and debated the writings of the new generation of European Catholics and discussed various programs of Catholic reform. John Ryan, Virgil Michel, and Paul Hanley Furfey were frequent visitors to the New York house. Groups broke off to engage in work of their own. Rural life, co-operatives, labor, or the liturgical movement drew them, as did such new areas for social action as the interracial apostolate. As war became an immediate possibility the paper and many of the Catholic Workers became pacifists and conscientious objectors. The *Catholic Worker* took the lead in fighting anti-Semitism. Dorothy was a vocal supporter of Tom Mooney, the imprisoned West Coast labor leader.

Many of Dorothy Day's followers were irritated at the passive role of the laity in the Church and were anxious to live their faith in a manner beyond what was possible in the parish or in a job. They were often accused of anticlericalism, but they merely refused to await clerical leadership and urged the laity to accept personal and immediate social responsibility. At the request of the New York archdiocese the house accepted a chaplain, who stayed in the background and seldom interfered. Despite criticism, most informed Catholic leaders admitted that Dorothy Day never refused to follow the directions of her superiors in the Church.

In 1936, a farming commune was finally established near Easton, Pennsylvania, designed to be "an essentially Catholic community, living a truly Catholic culture." If the group was to have a "common culture, different from that of the rest of the world," they felt it could be brought about only on the land. Maurin, drawing on such diverse sources as Gandhi, Eric Gill, and Kropotkin, believed that the long-run solution to unemployment lay with common ownership and mutual help on the land. There the unemployed could get the food, shelter, skills, training, and spiritual guidance that they needed. Dorothy agreed that the commune could assist in the rehabilitation of some men and provide an opportunity for the Catholic Workers themselves to strengthen their dedication by sharing ideas, work, and food in common. Most important, she felt that the paper should not teach something that they were not practicing. Because they preached the importance of the land, because they preached charity, mutual assistance, and communitarianism, Dorothy felt they must exemplify these virtues and ideals in communal life.[31]

Peter had hoped that the commune would be an example of "a new society within the shell of the old with the philosophy of the new," and the experiment did draw wide attention. Father Furfey was critical of some of the "romantic and utopian agrarianism" which appeared in the movement and urged them to be realistic and realize that essentially the same problems had to be faced on the land as in the city. Father John Hugo answered Furfey, stating that life on the land was normal and that industrialization had brought decay. He charged that the refusal of Catholics to specify the objective of reform, which should be rural and anti-industrial, had assisted the increase of government power which was leading all into "slavery." Others went all the way, rejecting technology and insisting on the use of only those tools that were the extension of the hand.[32]

But whether they rejected technology or not, the Catholic Workers would have nothing to do with the values and institutions of bourgeois society. They sought to construct, in the houses and on the farms, places where "Catholic thought can flourish in a pure environment, untainted by the materialist jungle without." They wanted to develop an integral Catholicism, asserting Christian spiritual values over modern material values; this in turn "ultimately depends upon spiritual individuals. Personal sanctity is a prerequisite of any lasting, effective social reform." The young were urged to abandon the middle-class values and the search for security they had learned, sometimes in Catholic schools, in exchange for a heroic sanctity. "If they sell their labor," the paper editorialized, "they are prostituting the talents God gave them. . . . What right has any one of us to have security when God's poor are suffering?"[33]

By means of voluntary poverty the Catholic Workers stood as witnesses against greed, avarice, and display. Stressing the solidarity and unity of men in Christ, they thought it hypocritical to hold superfluous goods when others were in need. Seeking to assist the worker's quest for justice while avoiding class struggle, they preached and lived the idea that true reform must be animated by charity, not greed or hatred. Instead of compromising they practiced the counsels of perfection, including nonresistance to evil. The *Catholic Worker* declared itself a *"pacifist paper"* opposed equally to class war and imperialist war. In the houses of hospitality themselves they attempted to work out a "gentle personalism," which would lead men to love one another by the force of example. The *Worker* insisted that the use of impure means would corrupt a good end, that violence to attain social justice would still leave society without a true Christian alternative. "Unless we preach love for our brother, a love as strong as death," the paper stated, "there will be class war and hatred." [34]

Solidarity, spiritual fellowship, and community, along with personalism provided the foundation of the Catholic Worker movement. Its "wisdom" was described as the "brotherhood of man and the Fatherhood of God." To live in accord with this belief in the Mystical Body of Christ was "to live as though we really believed that we are all members one of another." [35] Dorothy's conviction of solidarity went back to her radical days—her involvement with the Industrial Workers of the World and with the suffragettes, and her hatred of poverty, prisons, and war. She wrote of her feeling for the imprisoned: "We all formed part of one body, a social body and how could any limb of that body commit a crime alone?" [36] Her fears at her conversion that she had abandoned the poor were answered by the idea of the Mystical Body, which appeared to offer a "third way," the way of "the communitarian approach with emphasis on personal freedom and personal responsibility, all organizations decentralized so far as possible." [37]

It was this devotion to the principle of solidarity that underlay her sympathy for the workers and her strong support of their struggles during the decade, despite the paper's theoretical deprecation of unions. She visited the sit-down strikers and strongly supported their actions. She recognized that the concrete merit of the workers' immediate demands was frequently not the most important element in determining the justice of a strike. Rather they were often following a "good impulse . . . to uphold their right to be treated not as slaves but as free men." The paper pledged itself to their support, promising to seek at the same time to indoctrinate them in the need for a basic reconstruction of the social order. Dorothy rejected violence and supported the back to the land movement, but the Catholic Workers would not leave the city to the Communists.

The Catholic Worker movement had arisen in part to help offset Communist influence among the unemployed. Yet its founders deplored redbaiting, urging Christian action to overcome the hostility of the workers and restore their confidence in the Church. Until Christians accepted their personal responsibility for injustice and recognized their solidarity with the poor and the workers, the latter would be attracted by Marxism. Communists were not the anti-Christ; like all actual or potential members of the Mystical Body they had to be treated with fairness and respect. The *Worker* rejected the nationalistic anticommunism of the *Tablet*. When the workers "see red," Peter wrote, "it is useless to present the red, white and blue." Dorothy was convinced from her early experience "that often the Communist more truly loves his brother, the poor and oppressed, than many so-called Christians." [38] She was sure that the radicals who gave up the good things of life to devote themselves to the cause of the working class with no hope of eternal reward, were beloved by God.

One area where few Catholics had been active was in dealing with the problems of the Negro. The *Catholic Worker* featured a white and Negro worker arm in arm with Christ on its masthead and showed an early interest in interracial work. A house of hospitality was established in Harlem in the first year, and several of the houses around the country were situated in Negro areas and dealt with racial problems. The paper printed many articles on the plight of Negro laborers and continually reported discrimination against Negroes in the administration of government policies. Similarly, it denounced anti-Semitism and fought vigorously against Father Coughlin and the Christian Front.

The paper's positions on foreign policy and war involved it in difficulties. The *Worker* opposed recognition of Russia in 1933 and held the general Catholic position on Mexico, but it maintained a firm attitude of neutrality on the Spanish Civil War. The war was seen as tragic, with great evil on both sides. Maintaining its pacifist position it urged Spanish Catholics to defend their priests with their lives if necessary "but not by taking up the sword." [39] It reprinted articles from neutral and pro-loyalist European Catholics and resented efforts to describe Franco as a zealous anticommunist.

Similarly it consistently resisted efforts to involve the United States in war, denounced Roosevelt's foreign policy, and firmly opposed preparedness measures. Workers were urged not to manufacture munitions. The *Catholic Worker* led in organizing Christian pacifist groups and pledged itself to resist conscription and war. The paper firmly rejected the idea that any modern war could be just because of the massive involvement of civilian populations. When the world war came, the *Worker* refused to abandon its position of conscientious objector and lost many of its followers. The seven years of growth of the thirties were followed by seven years of decline, suspicion, and hatred.

The *Catholic Worker*, despite its lack of faith in the efficacy of State action, was generally sympathetic to the policies of the New Deal. Unlike Maurin it welcomed the NRA enthusiastically as the first concrete attempt of the government to support the cause of the workers. Later it urged the improvement of NRA along the lines suggested by McGowan and Ryan, but in practice it feared that the program was leading to capitalist control of labor in near fascist style. Still it felt that the program was, in conception, an attempt to release workers from their slavery to industry and to publicize conditions that would arouse sympathy with the workers' plight. It was infuriated when the Supreme Court defeated the New Deal's "wholehearted attempt to benefit the working masses of the country and to curb the greed and speculation of capital." [40] Maurin, however, had little sympathy with the administration's attempt to reform "through a hit and miss policy, through a policy of experiment, through a policy of muddling through." [41]

Unlike most American Catholics, Dorothy Day, perhaps because she was a convert, was far more conscious of her Catholicism than of her Americanism. While most Catholics concentrated on winning a secure place for themselves within American society, the *Catholic Worker* pointed to the unchristian character of much of American life. It was shocked at the extent to which Catholics had been "Americanized" and had accepted "the standard of the bank account." The American industrial system was "as truly materialistic and hence atheistic as Marxism." Even reformers accepted social planning, which led to regimentation, and emphasized legislation, which could not create a "social order in which the way of life will help man to save his soul." [42] Maurin deplored the tendency of Catholics to imitate their non-Catholic neighbors, to overlook or fail to apply the principles of their faith. Like Father Furfey the leaders of the Catholic Worker movement feared that the Church too often upheld minimum standards of behavior and underemphasized the heroic standard of the gospels.[43] As Maurin put it, Christians relied on the State to fulfill their responsibilities, so that men said of them not "see how they love one another" but "see how they pass the buck." [44] Part of the blame rested with the clergy. Dorothy reported:

> I loved the Church for Christ made visible. Not for itself, because it was so often a scandal to me. . . . The scandal of businesslike priests, of collective wealth, the lack of a sense of responsibility for the poor, the worker, the Negro, the Mexican, the Filipino, and even the oppression of these, and

the consenting to the oppression of these by our industrial capitalist order—these made me feel that priests were more like Cain than Abel.[45]

Dorothy's feelings at the time of her conversion were revised after her contact with many socially active priests, but the movement continued to contain an implicit criticism of the apathy of many of the clergy.

The Catholic Worker movement received overwhelming support from the Catholic press and leading Catholic prelates in its early days, but its later radical stands on labor, Spain, and war caused a decline of enthusiasm. Monsignor Ryan was a friend of the movement until its pacifism conflicted with his own support of Roosevelt's attempts at collective security and aid to the Allies. Father John LaFarge of *America* gave powerful assistance to the interracial work and admired the movement's work of charity and labor education, which he felt did more to express Catholic teachings of social justice than all the writings in the Catholic press. However, he doubted the efficacy of voluntary poverty as an instrument for large scale reform because of the difficulty of maintaining it outside the religious life. He also doubted the wisdom of Maurin's attachment to handicrafts. Machine production was here to stay, he warned: "Like a big dog, it can be trained to obey man's personality." Further he felt that the Catholic Worker movement had to be ready to render a stricter accounting when it attempted to broaden its program into one of complete integral Catholicism, embracing not only charity, but international relations. He hoped that the teachings could be separated from the work, so that the former could be debated without appearing to censure the movement's practice of the works of mercy.[46] Others, too, disliked one or another of the movement's stands, while professing the greatest admiration for the intentions and the works of charity of the Catholic Workers themselves.[47]

The *Catholic Worker*'s neutrality on the Spanish Civil War

drew the heaviest criticism. Patrick Scanlan accused its leaders of "disloyalty" to the Catholic cause and Father Coughlin attacked their failure to fight communism. Coughlin and his ally Father Edward Lodge Curran of Brooklyn attacked the Catholic Worker movement and the Association of Catholic Trade Unionists for their co-operation with the c.i.o.; Curran warned against "collaboration with Communists" and told them they must work in Catholic groups to attain social justice.[48] The editors replied by attacking Curran's brand of anticommunism and continued to hold that "Christian love, being addressed to all men, is the worst adversary of Communism." They urged Catholics to "forget the negative ideal of fighting Communism and concentrate on building up the Mystical Body of Christ." [49]

The *Tablet* had a more general criticism of the *Catholic Worker*, one which became increasingly popular during and after the war. This was its laicism; never before in the history of the American Church had groups of laymen demonstrated such independence of thought and action. They read the advanced work of European theologians and chose their often unpopular positions independently, by reference to their conscience and their interpretation of the Church's teachings. They refused to rely on authority as a substitute for conscience. They urged the necessity for personal judgment and personal responsibility to act according to their beliefs, ideas which militated against clericalism and against an ideal of Catholic Action as an army under the discipline of the hierarchy. By doing so they challenged the feelings of many Catholics that the Church and all its members must remain united, militant, and disciplined in order to defend its rights and interests against the hostility of the prejudiced American Protestant majority. This could be done only by reliance on the bishops to set the pace and indicate the direction for Catholic Action; lay independence and initiative appeared to threaten the security of the Catholic community. In addition it disturbed the consciences of Catholics who were used to relying on the clergy to give clear directives as to behavior and opinion on matters that involved faith and morals or the interests of the Church. The idea of the Church as the "people of God," with the laity possessed of important functions and responsibilities, had made little headway in the United States; only the liturgical movement contained the seeds of the revolution in lay theology that would take place in Europe after the war.

As for the social problem, Peter and Dorothy attempted to redefine it and, whatever the limitations of their specific proposals, they had a deeper insight into its character than many of their fellow social Catholics in the United States. As one recent commentator has pointed out, they sought to apply the Augustinian notion of the two cities to the "jumbled allegiances of American Catholics." More than any of their contemporaries in active social reform, they recognized the extent of the confusion that had developed between the heavenly and earthly cities, a confusion exemplified in the tendency to locate the sources of social conflict in a person or an institution, rather than within the individual soul. For Dorothy and Peter, as for Virgil Michel, the two cities were not the Church and the world, not Christianity and communism, but the forces of good and evil, of charity and self-love, within each man. The only absolute commitment was to the Church, to "Christ Crucified" in Dorothy's words, an allegiance given in spite of the failings of churchmen. It was a commitment to the Church as the Mystical Body of Christ, the union of all men in Christ, of which the institutional Church was the imperfect, though necessary and divinely ordained, manifestation in this world. The distinguishing characteristic of this devotion to the Church was a refusal to compromise from fear, because the only thing to be feared was the tendency toward self-love. The welfare of the Catholic community, or of the institutional Church was not the primary criterion for action, but the welfare of all men and of each man, of the individuals who possessed ultimate worth, and of the community which shared in all suffering and which was potentially redeemable. Peter's desire for a "green revolution" was a desire to reawaken man's capacity to love both himself and others. The city and the machine destroyed his dignity, frustrated his powers, and separated him from other men. Thus the back-to-the-land movement was "simultaneously a movement toward fellow men in a community bound organically by love." Voluntary poverty was a means to free man for love while avoiding condescension. This social position overcame the tendency to rely on the State and other institutions and shifted responsibility back to the person.[50]

One example of this location of responsibility with the person was graphically expressed by Dorothy Day in her description of the Republic Steel Memorial Day massacre. She attempted to place the blame but found she could not do so, for it took in everyone, the police, the press, the pulpit, the companies, and even the strikers. She concluded: "We are all guilty inasmuch as we have not 'gone to the workingman' as the Holy Father pleads. . . . Inasmuch as we have not inclined our hearts to him, and sought to incline his to us, so that we could work together for peace instead or war, inasmuch as we have not protested such murder as was committed in Chicago—then we are all guilty." [51]

Implicit in Peter Maurin's indictment of industrial capitalism was a perception of many of the problems that disturb contemporary social critics: alienation, the loss of a sense of personal participation in community life, the inability to locate and define responsibility amid the complexities of economic and social organization, the cultural inertia produced by the loss of meaning in work. Peter's defenders deny that he wished to eliminate machines; he was trying to develop a philosophy of work, to restore meaning to the social life of modern man, but he appeared to conclude that this could be done only on the land. Maurin's distributist, agrarian solution offered little hope of a practical resolution of the dilemma of the affluent society that he perceived. As an early disciple, John Cort, later pointed out, Peter tended to identify Christianity "with handicrafts and subsistence farming." [52]

The New Deal years were for many Americans a time of awakening to self-conscious reflection and criticism, stimulated by an outraged sense of justice and equality. Dorothy Day, in her sensitivity to suffering and cruelty, mirrored all of this and became for American Catholics a symbol of these years. She opened the eyes of many Catholics to the existence of suffering, injustice, and the basic materialism of the country's life; conversely, she "opened the portals of the Catholic heart for America to see the Church in a new light." She became a "living and fearless conscience" for the Catholic community, enriching the Church with the best of American radicalism, personal independence and integrity, and a sense of solidarity and human concern.[53] Upholding the perfectionist strain in Catholic thought, she and her followers refused to compromise and sought to incarnate in their lives the charity of the gospel message of love and salvation. They stood apart from the bulk of American Catholics, presenting solidly grounded positions on war, race, the use of goods, and wealth, which challenged dominant opinion. Those who contend that the Christian can live correctly in American society must continually take into account the *Catholic Worker*'s attack upon that society, its values, and its institutions.

It was from a Catholic point of view that the Catholic Worker movement was most important. It held American society up against the basic Christian teachings of love and brotherhood and challenged Catholics to act honestly on the result. By stimulating many to a new awareness of the meaning of the faith, the Catholic Worker helped them attain a sense of detachment and provided a standard by which they could judge their society and work for its improvement. But it was also perfectionist; it raised heroic standards that all could not meet. Its program and its solutions to social problems were unsystematic and unrealistic. Peter Maurin's deprecation of unions and political action, whatever his motives, could be harmful, for as the Popes had recognized, the realization of justice presupposed a framework of justice within which men could operate fairly and freely. In addition, the growth of population made a retreat from urban-industrial society impossible. Mass production, for all its problems, offered a new potential for realizing in practice the ideal of human dignity by overcoming the age-old problem of survival. Maurin's ideas tended to draw men away from the attempt to humanize and Christianize society to a self-righteous retreat from the complexities of the modern world.

The most serious consequence was the tendency to polarize issues around an opposition of the person and the State. Posing questions in these mutually exclusive terms vastly oversimplified the moral problems facing man in society and led the Catholic Workers to underrate and even ignore the problem of power which so disturbed John Ryan. They were correct to question Ryan's reliance on the State, but their alternative of a strict personalism incompatible with governmental power left important, perhaps essential, structural and institutional difficulties untouched. Still, if they erred, they did so on the side of freedom and human dignity and they stirred the American Catholic conscience as no one had done before. In the days of abundance that followed World War II the issues of income distribution, union organization, and industrial government which dominated Catholic social thought during the Depression seemed increasingly irrelevant. The problems that disturbed Peter Maurin and Dorothy Day—depersonalization, bureaucracy, racism, and war—became the great issues confronting the American people. Despite the weaknesses of their thought, the Catholic Workers, far more than their contemporaries, were true prophets of American Catholicism.

It was not surprising that the Catholic Worker movement significantly influenced the generation of young Catholics who grew up in the Depression years.[54] Shocked by the Depression and the rise of totalitarianism, more and more laymen were seeking to express their concern without abandoning the Church. The traditional organizations of American Catholics were usually concerned with such matters as the defense of Catholic interests or the promotion of ethnic solidarity. Catholic Action groups were either strictly educational, neglecting social action, or they were clerically dominated and preoccupied with questions of public morality, parochial schools, birth control, or other matters arising from the supposed conflict of Christian and secular practices and principles. In the face of the moderation, clannishness, and ecclesiastical centralization of the American Church, those who wished to dedicate themselves to their own perfection and to the service of the poor and the worker, often were unable to find an outlet other than the religious life. To these the Catholic Worker offered an alternative. Its lay orientation, its interest in the whole spectrum of Catholic life and thought, its atmosphere of radicalism combined with its loyalty to the Church, all this attracted Catholics disillusioned with their society and with the life of their parish and church organizations. Many of them came to the Catholic Workers' houses, stayed for a period, and went on to active careers in other areas. John Cogley, John Cort, Ed Marciniak, Richard Deverall, and a host of others who would provide leadership to the laymen of the postwar generation were all baptized by the Catholic Worker.[55] As Cort wrote of Dorothy Day: "She was the mother of most of us who today, as lay people, are involved in the Catholic Social Action movement." [56]

IX

Catholicism and Americanism

In the 1930's a remarkable number of Catholics devoted their attention to social and economic problems. The publication of *Quadragesimo Anno* in 1931 provided an authoritative basis for analysis and action, but it was the Depression that caught the attention of Church leaders and made the entire Catholic community more receptive to papal teachings than ever before. Nevertheless, in the United States as elsewhere, acceptance of papal authority did not imply uniformity of opinion on concrete issues. Instead Catholic social thought in the 1930's was characterized by unanimous and enthusiastic approval of official Church teachings and wide, often bitter, disagreement over their meaning and application. This troubled many American Catholics who believed that the Church possessed a distinctive goal and method for reform offering cures for all the nation's ills, a conviction strengthened by Pius XI's prescriptions for Christian social reconstruction. Few thought that the Church possessed no such model of society as it ought to be, that its "answers" could not be translated into solutions for pressing national problems. Yet the necessarily indefinite character of the Church's positive teachings was revealed in the decade by the inability of reform-minded Catholics to agree on the merits of secular programs, or formulate their own alternatives, and in the alacrity with which many responded to a negative anticommunism which possessed the clear and authoritative sanction the reformers lacked.

Some of the most heated controversy centered around the question of federal jurisdiction in national life. In 1932 almost all Catholic spokesmen agreed that the severity of the Depression, the collapse of private charities, and the weakness of state and local authorities necessitated federal intervention. This position represented a sharp break for American Catholics, long accustomed to viewing constitutional limitations on the national government as protective bulwarks against potential anti-Catholic persecution. Those Catholics who were most conscious of the Church's minority status warned that emergency grants of power were temporary and should be rescinded when the crisis had passed. As the pressures of unemployment did subside, such warnings became more frequent until, by 1937, concern over the growth of the federal government was nearly universal among articulate Catholic leaders.

Fear of latent anti-Catholicism was only one reason for such constitutional scruples. American Catholicism had responded to the needs of its immigrant population by constructing an enormous network of schools, hospitals, orphanages, and other benevolent institutions whose existence dictated a policy of caution in dealing with public assistance. William F. Montavon stated this position clearly in his 1933 report to the NCWC administrative board. "The welfare of religion is closely tied up with the problem of federalism," he wrote. "Because of divergent and conflicting views, the larger the scope of any political authority in our country, the more rigidly must it adhere to a policy of minimum interference in controversial matters." At first glance this fact appeared congenial to a religious minority, but Montavon pointed out that it meant, in religious terms, "secularism." "Local authorities," on the other hand, covered a smaller area and were often able to "do things a federal agency could not do," a fact which directly affected "schools, benevolent agencies," and charities.[1] The implication was clear. As long as relief, education, and aid to charitable endeavors were left in local hands, urban Catholic majorities might be translated, if not into direct assistance to private agencies, at least into a benevolent neutrality that would protect them against secular competitors armed with public funds. The interests of the institutional Church thus blended with the fears of the Catholic minority to shape a political outlook hostile to the permanent extension of national power.

This view could find support in papal teachings, but appeals to Church authority posed serious problems. The corporate assumptions of papal social teachings challenged the individualism of American society, the freedom of economic enterprise, and the decentralized structure of American political institutions. The goals and methods of Catholic social action, as outlined in *Quadragesimo Anno*, involved a basic confrontation of the Catholic with his society. Total commitment could well awaken latent anti-Catholicism and revive charges of Catholic disloyalty to American values. More important, such a confrontation would precipitate a crisis for Catholics themselves, for they had long ago accepted as their own many of the principles and practices which Catholic teachings called into question.

The result was that Catholics invariably sought to justify their position by reference not only to Church authorities but to American traditions as well, asserting the compatibility, even the identity, of "true Americanism" and orthodox Catholicism. This assertion had always been a central theme of the American Catholic mind. Since the days when Bishop Carroll organized the American Church, Catholics had never ceased telling Rome and native Protestants that Catholic religious teachings and American political and social beliefs complemented each other perfectly. "To understand the Catholic Church in America," wrote the Church's leading historian in 1926, "one must see how naturally and integrally the spiritual allegiance of its members knits into the national allegiance so as to round each other out." [2] This argument of course required some definition of "true Americanism." Often it seemed merely to denote a consensus on individual natural rights and governmental responsibility for social justice. More frequently it meant a specific assertion that the philosophy of American government was similar to that of traditional Catholic political philosophy. Historical proof could be found in the work of Catholic scholars who demonstrated the influence of the political thought of Robert Bellarmine on the writings of Thomas Jefferson and on the Declaration of Independence, thus providing an historical basis for the argument that America was "Catholic in philosophical principle." [3] The corollary was that, contrary to the slanders of fundamentalist Protestants and secular liberals, the nation had no more ardent or sincere defenders than her Catholic citizens.[4]

Yet in much of the popular writing such arguments were implied and the conclusions assumed, so that professions of loyalty to America and assertions of compatibility of American and Catholic values took the place of detailed argumentation. In either case "Americanism" remained a vague body of values subject to varying interpretations and emphasis; the ideals of the Declaration of Independence and the structure of the Constitution have always been subject to such varying interpretations by all Americans. Catholics were within the American consensus described by so many recent historians, but its acceptance only provided a framework for the discussion of political and social issues; it did not eliminate conflict, or make conflict insignificant. Like Christianity it could provide sanctions for laissez-faire *and* social justice, decentralization *and* federal action, individual rights and liberties *and* the general welfare and the common good. The fact that the balance of these polarities was not struck once and for all by either an authoritative American institution or by the Papacy meant that both "Americanism" and Catholicism easily became sources of support, of emotionally charged symbols to provide a sanction for positions that originated in economic and social conditions. American Catholics wanted to believe that being a Catholic and being an American both had clear, unambiguous meaning—the same meaning—so that they used the terms as if they had that meaning. In so doing, they missed the point that neither was subject to final formulation, at least in political and social terms.

Professions of loyalty to fundamental American values were common in American Catholic history. In the late nineteenth century John Ireland and his followers enthusiastically defended their country against its European detractors. They deplored Catholic separatism and aloofness and urged a policy of Americanization which would simultaneously make the Church a more effective force in society and reform the Church in the spirit of American democracy. More recently this attitude has reawakened with far greater force, expressing itself in a ferment of criticism of Catholic intellectual life, liturgical practice, and Church organization and in a drive to end once and for all the internal preoccupations, moral self-righteousness, and social irresponsibility of "ghetto Catholicism." This emphasis upon assimilation and adaptation depends upon an assumption that the American environment contains nothing that fundamentally conflicts with the principles of Christianity. For liberal Catholics of the 1890's and 1950's this seemed obvious, but it was otherwise for Catholics in the interwar years. In the twenties the strength of anti-Catholicism together with the aftereffects of the condemnations of modernism and Americanism weakened attempts to maintain the liberal policies of Ireland and Cardinal Gibbons and stifled the zeal for reform emanating from the Social Action Department. Yet, while adopting a stance of militant defensiveness, Catholic leaders by no means rejected America. On the contrary they argued that the nativism, materialism, and secularism of the period were untrue to the authentic spirit of American life. Far from denouncing the cry of Americanism so often used by anti-Catholic spokesmen, Catholics adopted it, arguing that, as Father James Gillis wrote after the defeat of Al Smith, "We found ourselves more in harmony with true Americanism than they were who denied our right to be American." [5]

In the 1930's the situation changed. Fundamentalist Protestants no longer posed a serious threat to the Church's freedom, and the political administration gave more recognition to Catholic interests and aspirations than any in history. Men like John Ryan believed that the time had come for Catholics to take their place in the authentic American mainstream now enshrined in the reform administration of Franklin Roosevelt. But many were less sure. Catholic influence on the New Deal was minimal; Roosevelt did seem on occasion to ignore Catholic sensibilities, and the nation's most ardent New Dealers came from the ranks of sophisticated eastern liberals who some Catholics had always regarded as more potent enemies than southern and western fundamentalists. The word "liberal" was a badge of honor for John Ryan, representing to him a position consistent with Catholic natural rights philosophy, the same philosophy which underlay American freedoms. For many others, however, the word summed up the elements in American society they most feared, elements which threatened the autonomy of the Church and challenged the American practices they had always considered most essential.

For those who adopted the latter position, the real establishment in America was not a plutocratic oligarchy, as Ryan seemed to believe, but a liberal elite composed of professors, editors, labor leaders, politicians, and, for some, Jews. The Church remained a besieged garrison, in need of discipline, unity, and vigilance, but her role was not one of simple defense; she had a mission to Christianize and at the same time "re-Americanize" America,[6] an effort sanctioned by the hierarchy's proclamation of a "Catholic Crusade for Christian Democracy" in 1938. The assumptions that shaped this view of the Church in

America were clarified by Father Francis X. Talbot, editor of *America*. Talbot was convinced that Catholics were the largest group in the nation still adhering "to the Constitution and the traditional Americanism that made our country what it was before 1914." Given cohesion by their doctrinal and disciplinary unity, Catholics thought in "almost identical patterns [on] all other matters, social, economic, ethical, moral, cultural (but not political)." Sure that they could "furnish the answer to every national question" Catholics constituted "a tremendous national force" wholly opposed to "the changes coming over American civilization," changes resulting from "American liberals . . . being infected with un-American ideas and the American proletariat being mobilized for redress." [7]

Talbot's view of the Church's situation in the United States was not unusual; many others urged a united "Catholic front" to promote Church interests and teachings, to spread acceptance of Christian moral principles, and defend democratic ideas and institutions against communism and secularism. Education was seen as a crucial battlefield, more critical indeed than national politics. In 1940 the National Catholic Alumni Federation sponsored a symposium on the topic "Man and Modern Secularism." Most of the speakers identified Catholic educational practices with American traditions and denounced secular and progressive education as both unchristian and un-American. The President of Fordham University charged that American public schools were pervaded by a secularism which denied or ignored the supernatural and "degraded" man "to the level of nature." Historians Richard Purcell and Richard Gabel described denominational influence on colonial and early national schools, "a Catholic position on religion in education," which had been destroyed when secularism was "foisted upon American education largely through the adoption of non-sectarian religion." Geoffrey O'Connell, author of *Naturalism in American Education*, described the "atheist" doctrines of the National Educational Association and of leading professors at Columbia Teachers College, while Thomas Woodlock charged that non-Catholic students, because of their lack of religious training, could not defend the principles of the Declaration of Independence. Other speakers went on to praise the Catholic educational system, to urge its extension, and to point out its importance as a force in preserving true American values.

Only a few took issue with the dominant tone of the discussions. Professor Ross Hoffman warned against regarding the advent of a lay society as necessarily harmful to the Church, whose mission was "not to clericalize, but to catholicize society, using whatever means . . . are available to that sublime end." In a lay civilization this meant the sanctification of souls by forming men capable of creative work in the various "secular" areas of human activity, a theme elaborated by Robert C. Pollock, who charged that Catholics were "as one-sided as the secularists." They "one-sidedly affirm the spiritual," Pollock argued, while others "one-sidedly affirm the temporal," at a time when the great need was a reconciliation of the two. Drawing upon traditional Catholic sources he urged a more positive approach to modern life and defended "secularism" as "the temporal order . . . striving after its own rightful form, motivated by the Christian impulse towards the affirmation of the creature and its autonomy." Particularly in America it was imperative that Catholics abandon their condemnations and seek to affirm all values, "wheresoever they be found, in heaven or on earth." Only thus could Catholics "pay off their debt to the modern world for their failures in the past." [8]

Pollock was one of the few American Catholics in the decade to interpret America's challenge to the Church in a manner similar to Hecker and Ireland in the previous century. Economic abundance and political freedom in the United States for the first time made possible the realization in concrete form of the Christian ideal of brotherhood and equality. "When Christianity came into the world the wall of separation between man and man was doomed," Pollock wrote. "American democracy represents in the temporal order man's determination to destroy this wall of separation. Because men are men, we must construct a social order that will emphasize and strengthen, not the differences that divide men, but the common humanity which unites them." America possessed the technical skill and material resources to end the struggle for existence and challenged the Church to forge powerful links with the people and work for the temporal realization of its belief in equality and human dignity.[9]

This view of the positive relation between Christianity and Americanism was not a popular one in the 1930's. By the end of the decade many regarded the dominant trends of their time as antithetical to the doctrines of their Church and the ideals of their nation. The difference between the two positions pivoted upon an assessment of the contemporary scene, and that evaluaton was shaped by sociological more than doctrinal factors. Just as acceptance of the Christian social order brought no consensus on policies or programs, neither did acceptance of "true Americanism" result in any monolithic commitment to particular features of American life and thought. For Americanism, like Catholic social doctrine, turned out to be a magician's hat that produced pre-packaged rabbits. Reformers and conservatives, friends and enemies of the Supreme Court, isolationists and internationalists, all found justification for their positions by reference to what they regarded as accurate interpretations of papal thought and valid references to the authentic American tradition. In the decade the more negative stance dominated Catholic life, despite the efforts of men like John Ryan, George Shuster, Francis Haas, and others to keep open the lines of communication between Catholics and other Americans and to mobilize Catholic support for efforts by men of good will to improve the quality of American society.

There remained still a third option for American Catholics: rejection of America, in theory and in fact, in favor of a whole-hearted commitment to Christian truths transcending the limits of geography, nation, ethnic group, and social class. Before the 1930's this position had been taken only by a small group of Catholic corporatists who understood the antiliberal social philosophy that underlay the social thought of continental Catholicism that ultimately found expression in *Quadragesimo Anno*. Agreeing that America needed to be Christianized, they denied that this could be accomplished by relying on American traditions. Frederick Kenkel, Edward Koch, and others who held this position, belittled the New Deal's efforts to save liberal capitalism, and they attacked moderate Catholics who sought to reconcile the organic, functional theory of Christian social thought with the chaotic individualism of American political and economic life. Relying on education, they patiently awaited the failure of such palliatives as social legislation and trade unionism, confident that eventually, to save itself from totalitarianism or anarchy, America would pay them heed.[10]

In a quite different way the new group of radical Catholics who appeared in the 1930's refused to look for a root American-ism with which to identify. Led by Paul Hanley Furfey, Peter Maurin, and Dorothy Day, they attacked the anxiety of Catholics to be fully Americanized and urged them instead to "think Catholic answers to every problem of their lives." They deplored the influence of American Protestantism and individualism on Catholics whose loyalty to the Church was often coupled with submission to the social and cultural standards of non-Catholic America. Like the Americanizers they fought separatism and aloofness, but because it was unchristian, not because it was un-American. Rather than striving to win recognition and praise, they urged Catholics to "promote the uncompromising advance of supernatural Catholicism along every sector of the Catholic front and around every side of Catholic individual and

social life." [11] Such an approach would build a truly Catholic
culture, win converts, and lead to personalist social action which
would revolutionize American society.

This perfectionism provided a solid basis for self-criticism
within the Catholic community and directly challenged the
implicit self-righteousness of much Catholic opinion. Instead of
focusing on the nation's abandonment of its ideals, the lay Catholics who followed Furfey, Maurin, and Dorothy Day, concentrated on the Catholic community's own failure to live up to the
standards it professed. But, like the group-oriented approach of
Father Talbot, this desire for an integral Catholicism often appeared to assume that the Church did possess answers to all
American problems, that there were social and cultural forms
that would fully express Christian beliefs, that there were such
things as a Catholic society and a Catholic position on every
aspect of life. If all this was true there was no question that
Catholics should unite to promote specifically Catholic objectives in social and political life. However, a few like Pollock and
Hoffman were questioning this assumption at the end of the
decade. Virgil Michel, for example, disagreed with the contention that Catholics should think alike on nonreligious matters.
"As Catholics we agree on essentials of faith and morals," Michel
wrote.

> But there is no earthly (or heavenly) reason why we must
> all agree on any other questions, including public questions.
> Quite the contrary. If, as some seem to hold, we should, in
> spite of legitimate differences, put on a 'united front,' pre-
> tending to agree on every other detailed question, would we
> not be as the scribes and pharisees. . . .[12]

Nevertheless, most American Catholic intellectuals held fast to
the belief that there were specifically Catholic answers to most
of life's problems that should serve as the basis for a mass Catholic social movement. Michel, Hoffman, and Pollock, along with
the Catholic Worker's leaders, only began to question this belief

and to lay the basis for a new approach to Catholic life in America, which would not become powerful for another generation.

For almost two centuries the conditions of what German theologian Karl Rahner calls "the diaspora" had been developing in the United States. Dependence on lay support, lack of cultural dominance, and separation of Church and State were basic features of American religious life. To be sure Americans long regarded their nation as "made by Protestants and cast in a Protestant mold," [13] but their experience and their institutions denied the age-old belief that social and cultural coherence must be based on religious uniformity. The emergence in the twentieth century of large organized blocs of Catholics, Jews, and nonbelievers forced the unfolding of the logic of the American situation, resulting in a real religious pluralism. For American Catholics these same conditions raised the problem of adjusting the claims of religious authority to the demands of a free society and secular State, forcing them to challenge the belief, so strong in the Old World, that "Catholicism could not survive in a *milieu* which did not pay it homage." [14] Whether the need to find a nonreligious basis of social integration resulted in "an idolatrous new religion of Americanism," [15] a "uniform, middle class, liberal secularism," [16] or merely a consensus on political practices which removed ultimate values from the realm of public debate, American Catholics faced a diaspora more clearly defined than elsewhere in the world.

At the end of a decade of controversy, American Catholicism's response to the challenges of American voluntarism remained in many respects unchanged. To be sure there was increased diversity in the Catholic community, and it was less possible to speak of American Catholics as a bloc than it had been in 1929. In addition, there was an increased interest in political and social matters and the influence of Catholics on American life was increasing. But most of the characteristics of American Catholi-

cism remained those of the ghetto, which Rahner describes as
the natural reaction to the coming of the diaspora.

> What, after all, does a person do if he sees the diaspora situ-
> ation coming and thinks of it as something which simply
> and absolutely cannot be? He makes himself a closed circle,
> an artificial situation inside which it looks as if the internal
> and outward diaspora isn't one; he makes a ghetto. . . .
> Here we are, all together, and we can behave as though
> there were nothing in the world but Christians.[17]

The critic who wished to generalize might have found it more
difficult in 1940 than a decade earlier, but he could present solid
evidence that the Church remained unusually rigid in its hierarchical structure and still quite narrow in social outlook. The
passionate, self-righteous identification of Catholicism and Americanism, the preoccupation with questions of private and public
morality, the willingness to use power to impose Christian teachings on society, and the occasional tendency to place institutional interests above the common good remained unpleasant
realities in American Catholic life.

Even the more liberal Catholics remained within boundaries
that appear narrow a generation later. They fully agreed on the
doctrinal and moral teachings of the Church and never criticized
efforts to obtain public recognition of Christian moral standards
through the pressure group activities of the Legion of Decency
or the demands for prohibitive statutes against birth control
propaganda. Within the Church all Catholic spokesmen accepted
the products of the Church's history in the United States, defended the parochial schools and the numerous Catholic organizations, and acknowledged the role of the bishops and the need
for obedience in ill-defined but broad areas of life. On economic
matters too there were boundaries around the sharpest controversy. No important Catholic figure challenged the doctrine of
private property or rejected the wage system and few seriously
questioned the acceptability of profits and competition, so long

as they were limited by the demands of the common good. All supported the program of Pius XI, endorsing the occupational group system and agreeing that justice and charity were the moral and practical guides for reform. Although some Catholics might have doubted the wisdom of the emphasis chosen by some of their leaders, none questioned the importance of opposing communism or striving to provide a religious basis for Americanism by fighting the spread of secularism in all areas of American life.

The exploration of the meaning of work in an industrial society, the awareness of the problems of community and fellowship in modern times, the willingness of many to co-operate with non-Catholics, even with Communists, in securing legitimate objectives, the emphasis upon human dignity and freedom rather than on formal and abstract notions of a Christian social order or negative ideals of anticommunism and defense of the Church— these aspects of Catholic thought in the thirties were important foreshadowings of future developments, but in the decade they remained novelties, overshadowed by the more negative aspects of Catholic life and thought. The desire of the people around the Catholic Worker movement to live fully Christian lives and to find social structures conducive to the realization of personal responsibility and personal dignity was less characteristic of American Catholicism than was the desire to be fully Catholic and fully American without having to confront the realities of either. This desire for a monolithic American Catholicism and an equally integrated Catholic Americanism could be seen in the sharp and bitter reaction of many to George Shuster's attempt at dialogue with American liberals, the sudden loss of circulation by *Commonweal* when it abandoned the Franco cause, the bitter letters that were sent to John Ryan after he attacked Father Coughlin and after he defended the "court-packing" plan, and the collapse of the *Catholic Worker*'s popularity when it refused to abandon pacifism after Pearl Harbor.

Nevertheless American Catholicism did show signs of a new maturity and creativity during the 1930's. The hierarchy, while remaining essentially conservative, did succeed for a time in overcoming the restrictions of Catholic history and presenting a humane and charitable response to the suffering and misery occasioned by unemployment and economic stagnation. Individual bishops appeared who showed foresight and courage in supporting economic reform, labor unions, and social welfare legislation and opposing reaction and isolation within the Catholic community. Many clergymen were willing to depart from strictly parochial concerns to assist their congregations to secure a wider measure of social justice. A few bishops, priests, and laymen began to direct mild criticism at Catholic complacency and self-righteousness. These words seemed to have little effect at the time, but they began a process that would accelerate in the years that followed the war.

Perhaps the most significant aspect of Catholic life in the thirties was the appearance of an awakened laity anxious to realize Christian values in secular life without insisting on uniformity of belief or adherence to the Church. Before the Depression it was possible to speak of American Catholicism almost entirely in terms of the hierarchy and clergy—that is, in terms of the institutional Church as it had developed since the trusteeism episode of the early nineteenth century. In the thirties, however, a significant number of lay Catholics, unable to find meaning and satisfaction in strictly parochial and ethnic organizations, independently sought to find new ways of realizing their religious commitments in their personal lives, at the same time attempting to make Catholicism meaningful within American society.

The Catholic Worker movement, numerically small as it was, presented an effective challenge to the life of American Catholics. From their different backgrounds Dorothy Day and Peter Maurin brought to the American Church a sense of unity of men and of the personal responsibility of each man for the welfare of all. Like the iww she had known in her youth Dorothy Day proclaimed that "an injury to one is an injury to all." From such a standard, supported by the theological concept of the Mystical Body of Christ, the *Catholic Worker* could criticize and challenge American Catholicism on its own grounds of brotherhood and Christian love. It could and did demonstrate to the layman that his desire for social justice and personal involvement could be realized within the Catholic fold. The movement's pioneering interest in religious art, liturgical reform, advanced theological and philosophical speculation, and radical social change, demonstrated the potential richness of the Catholic tradition and anticipated the events of the 1960's. Sensitive laymen had often rebelled against the shallowness and sterility of the cultural milieu of their youth and had felt compelled to leave the Church of their fathers in order to realize their desire for creative activity, intellectual honesty, and personal fulfillment. After the 1930's the situation would no longer be as clear, for the laymen of the *Catholic Worker, Commonweal,* and numerous minor journals and organizations, effectively demonstrated that the Catholic Church could offer far more space, far more depth, and far more freedom than Americans, including Catholics, had suspected.

Notes

CHAPTER I

1. Walter Ong, "The Intellectual Frontier" in Louis Putz, C.S.C., editor, *The Catholic Church, U.S.A.* (Chicago, 1956), p. 414. This represents an "incarnational" as opposed to an "eschatological" approach to the problem of the Church and society. On this and other questions see Peter Riga, *Catholic Thought in Crisis* (Milwaukee, 1962).

2. John Emerich Edward Dalberg Acton, "Ultramontanism" in Douglas Woodruff, editor, *Essays on Church and State* (London, 1952), pp. 50–51. The tragic results of such a closed and exclusive view of the Church are documented in Guenter Lewy, *The Catholic Church and Nazi Germany* (New York, 1964).

3. On this point of view and its dominance in modern times see Michael Novak, *The Open Church* (London, 1964), pp. 52–71, and Hans Kung, *The Council and Reunion* (London, 1961).

4. Pope John XXIII, *Mater et Magistra, America* press edition (New York, 1961), p. 49; Jean-Yves Calvez and Jacques Perrin, *The Church and Social Justice* (Chicago, 1961), p. 62.

5. *Mater et Magistra*, p. 50.

6. Calvez and Perrin, *The Church and Social Justice*, pp. xii–xiii.

7. Leo XIII, *Rerum Novarum* in Etienne Gilson, editor, *The Church Speaks to the Modern World* (New York, 1954), p. 214.

8. Jacques Leclerq, *Christianity and Money* (New York, 1959), p. 57. On the social thought of the Gospels see *Christianity and Money*, chapter 2; Christopher Hollis, *Christianity and Economics*

229

(New York, 1961), chapter 1; Igino Giordani, *The Social Message of the Early Church Fathers* (Paterson, N.J., 1944); John A. Ryan, *The Alleged Socialism of the Church Fathers* (St. Louis, 1913).

9. See Ernst Troeltsch, *The Social Teachings of the Christian Churches*, Harper Torchbook edition, 2 volumes (New York, 1960), I.

10. Frederick Copleston, *A History of Philosophy*, Image Book edition, 3 volumes (New York, 1962), II, 118–43.

11. John A. Ryan, "The Economic Philosophy of St. Thomas" in Robert E. Brennan, editor, *Essays in Thomism* (New York, 1942), pp. 239–60.

12. "Pastoral Constitution on the Church and the Modern World," art. 12, W. Abbott, editor, *Documents of Vatican II* (New York, 1966).

13. William F. Drummond, *Social Justice* (Milwaukee, 1955), chapter 1.

14. John F. Cronin, S.S., *Catholic Social Principles* (Milwaukee, 1957), pp. 128–29.

15. Leclerq, *Christianity and Money*, pp. 70 ff.

16. Pope Pius IX, *Syllabus errorum* in Sidney Z. Ehler and John B. Morrall, editors, *Church and State Through the Centuries* (London, 1954), p. 285.

17. Alec R. Vidler, *The Church in an Age of Revolution* (Harmondsworth, England, 1961), pp. 179–89; Gerald J. O'Brien, S.J., "Integralism: An Historico-Critical Study of the Phenomenon in France as Seen in the Writings of Emmanuel Barbier" (unpublished S.T.D. dissertation, Woodstock College, Maryland, 1962). Riga, *Catholic Thought in Crisis*, describes the impact of these debates on Catholic social thought. Emmanuel Cardinal Suhard of Paris anticipated many of these ideas with his famous postwar pastoral letter "Growth or Decline?" See his collected writings, *The Church Today* (Chicago, 1953), pp. 93–170. For a conservative American reaction which highlights the conflict between modernist and integralist tendencies see Joseph C. Fenton, "Two Currents in Contemporary Catholic Thought," *American Ecclesiastical Review*, CXIX (October 1948), 293–301.

18. Raymond Corrigan, *The Church and the Nineteenth Century* (Milwaukee, 1938), pp. 129–33; Peter N. Stearns, "The Nature of

the Avenir Movement (1830–1831)," *American Historical Review,* LXV (July 1960), 837–47.

19. Henry Somerville, *Studies in the Catholic Social Movement* (London, 1933), pp. 17–29.

20. Matthew H. Elbow, *French Corporate Theory, 1789–1948* (New York, 1953), pp. 49–79; Adrien Dansette, *Religious History of Modern France,* trans. John Dingle (St. Louis, 1961), II, 115–21, 131–35.

21. Pope Leo XIII, *Graves de Communi* in Gilson, *The Church Speaks to the Modern World,* pp. 315–28; Dansette, *Religious History,* II, 125–31, 272–85.

22. Quoted in Somerville, *Catholic Social Movement,* p. 40.

23. Edgar Alexander, "Church and Society in Germany: Social and Political Movements and Ideas in German and Austrian Catholicism, 1789–1950" in Joseph N. Moody, editor, *Church and Society* (New York, 1953), pp. 400–410; Ralph H. Bowen, *German Theories of the Corporative State* (New York, 1947), pp. 83–89; Somerville, *Catholic Social Movement,* pp. 75–89.

24. Quoted in Bowen, *German Theories,* p. 109. On Hitze see *German Theories,* pp. 105–11; Alexander, "Church and Society in Germany," pp. 427–28.

25. Alexander, "Church and Society in Germany," pp. 385–400.

26. *Ibid.,* p. 420. For later developments see Alfred Diamant, *Austrian Catholics and the Social Question, 1918–1933* (Gainesville, Fla., 1959).

27. *Rerum Novarum,* pp. 206–7. The heart of this effort at reconciliation is to be found in the encyclical *Aeterni Patris, On Christian Philosophy* in Gilson, *The Church Speaks to the Modern World,* pp. 29–54. Leo attempted to combine traditional scholasticism with a generous response to modern thought to end the separation of religion from temporal concerns which he believed was at the root of modern problems. See James Collins, "Leo XIII and the Philosophical Approach to Modernity" in Edward T. Gargan, editor, *Leo XIII and the Modern World* (New York, 1961), pp. 179–209.

28. *Ibid.,* pp. 224–25.

29. *Ibid.,* p. 229.

30. *Ibid.,* p. 230.

31. Bowen, *German Theories,* p. 10.

32. Diamant, *Austrian Catholics;* Georgiana Putnam McEntee, *The*

Social Catholic Movement in Great Britain (New York, 1927), pp. 115–17.

33. Mueller, "The Church and the Social Question" in J. G. Lawler and J. N. Moody, editors, *The Challenge of Mater et Magistra* (St. Louis, 1963), pp. 102, 115.

34. Pope Pius XI, *Quadragesimo Anno* in Terence P. McLaughlin, editor, *The Church and the Reconstruction of the Modern World* (New York, 1957), p. 239.

35. For discussion of the term and its application see Calvez and Perrin, *Church and Social Justice*, pp. 138 ff.; Drummond, *Social Justice*, pp. 55, 101–2; and Cronin, *Catholic Social Principles*, p. 112. Each presents a different interpretation of "social justice."

36. *Quadragesimo Anno*, p. 242.

37. On this point see Michael Fogarty, *The Just Wage* (London 1961), p. 274.

38. *Quadragesimo Anno*, p. 246.

39. *Ibid.*, p. 247.

40. *Idem.*

41. *Ibid.*, pp. 247–48.

42. The Latin term *ordines* used by the Pope has been variously translated as "industries and professions," "occupational groups," "vocational groups," or, simply, "orders."

43. *Quadragesimo Anno*, pp. 249–50.

44. *Ibid.*, p. 252.

45. *Ibid.*, pp. 268–69.

46. Calvez and Perrin, *The Church and Social Justice*, pp. 72–73. Cf. Gary Wills, *Politics and Catholic Freedom* (Chicago, 1964).

47. Daniel O'Connor, *Catholic Social Doctrine* (Westminster, Md., 1956), pp. 7–8, 23. See also Mueller, "The Church and the Social Question," p. 73.

48. James J. Burns, "Catholic Social Theory" in Clement S. Mihanovich, editor, *Social Theorists* (Milwaukee, 1953), pp. 334–35.

49. Cronin, *Catholic Social Principles*, p. 92. Father Drummond refers to institutional reform as the *"conditio sine qua non"* of moral reform: *Social Justice*, p. 105.

50. Calvez and Perrin, *The Church and Social Justice*, pp. 58–59.

51. On this point see Diamant, *Austrian Catholics and the Social Question*, pp. 74–81.

52. Aelred Graham, *Christian Thought and Action* (New York, 1957), p. 114.

Notes

53. John F. Cronin, "The Social Economics of Pope Pius XII" in Benjamin Masse, editor, *Fifty Years of the Catholic Mind* (New York, 1953), pp. 517–36.
54. Robert E. Mulcahey, "Government Planning" in Moody and Lawler, editors, *The Challenge of Mater et Magistra*, p. 275.
55. Karl Rahner, *The Christian Commitment* (New York, 1963), pp. 7, 9–10.

CHAPTER II

1. In recent years American Catholics have engaged in rigorous self-criticism on this issue, inaugurated by Monsignor John Tracy Ellis's "American Catholicism and the Intellectual Life," *Thought*, XXX (Autumn 1955), 351–88. The present brief discussion owes much to two books by Walter Ong: *American Catholic Crossroads* (New York, 1959) and *Frontiers in American Catholicism* (New York, 1961).
2. Oscar Handlin, "The Church and the Modern City," *Atlantic*, CCX (August 1962), 102–3. Enlightened analysis of the immigrant character of the American Church is found in Handlin, *The Uprooted* (Boston, 1951); John L. Thomas, "Nationalities and American Catholicism" in Louis Putz, editor, *The Catholic Church, U.S.A.* (Chicago, 1956), pp. 155–76; Joseph Fichter, "The Americanization of Catholicism" in Thomas T. McAvoy, editor, *Roman Catholicism and the American Way of Life* (Notre Dame, 1960), pp. 113–28; Thomas F. O'Dea, *American Catholic Dilemma* (New York, 1958).
3. Richard Hofstadter, *Anti-Intellectualism in American Life* (New York, 1953), p. 136.
4. In addition to the works of Father Ong cited above, see Daniel Callahan, *The Mind of the Catholic Layman* (New York, 1963); John Courtney Murray, *We Hold These Truths* (New York, 1960). Father Joseph Fichter, S.J., has shown remarkable insight into the problems raised for traditional Catholic notions of the relationship between religion and culture by the American experience; see in particular his articles "The Americanization of Catholicism" and "Religion: Integrator of Culture?," *Thought*, XXXIII (September 1958), 361–82.
5. The whole controversy is described in Thomas T. McAvoy, *The Great Crisis in American Catholic History* (Chicago, 1957) and

Robert D. Cross, *The Emergence of Liberal Catholicism in America* (Cambridge, 1958). For a different point of view see Frederick J. Zweirlein, "The Triumph of the Conservative-Progressives in the Catholic Church in the United States," *Social Justice Review*, LI (July-August 1958), 118–23; (September 1958), 154–61; (October 1958), 189–92; (November 1958), 227–30.

6. John Tracy Ellis, editor, *Documents in American Catholic History* (Milwaukee, 1962), pp. 534–43.

7. Ong, *Frontiers*, p. 125. See also Thomas T. McAvoy, "American Catholics: Tradition and Controversy," *Thought*, XXXV (Autumn 1960), 583–600; John Tracy Ellis, *The Life of James Cardinal Gibbons*, 2 volumes (Milwaukee, 1952), II, chapter 16.

8. Fichter, "The Americanization of Catholicism," p. 116; David J. O'Brien, "American Catholicism and the Diaspora," *Cross Currents*, XVI (Summer 1966), 307–23.

9. Quoted in Peter Guilday, *The Life and Times of Bishop John England*, 2 volumes (New York, 1927), II, 498–99.

10. Nathan Glazer and Daniel P. Moynihan, *Beyond the Melting Pot* (Cambridge, 1963), p. 229. See also William V. Shannon, *The American Irish* (New York, 1963), chapters 4, 5.

11. On this point see J. Joseph Huthmacher, "Urban Liberalism and the Age of Reform," *Mississippi Valley Historical Review*, XLIX (September 1962), 231–41. In *Massachusetts: People and Politics, 1919–1933* (Cambridge, 1959), Huthmacher traces the interplay of economic, cultural, and political forces which led to the construction of a liberal coalition of Irish and new immigrant groups, first behind Al Smith and Senator David I. Walsh, then in support of the New Deal.

12. James Edward Roohan, "American Catholics and the Social Question, 1865–1900" (unpublished Ph.D. dissertation, Yale University, 1952); Aaron I. Abell, *American Catholicism and Social Action* (Garden City, 1960), chapter 2; Edward Duff, "Catholic Social Action in the American Environment," *Social Order*, XII (September 1962), 303.

13. Franz H. Mueller, "The Church and the Social Question" in Joseph N. Moody and Justus George Lawler, editors, *The Challenge of Mater et Magistra* (St. Louis, 1963), pp. 85–87, 93–94; Cross, *Liberal Catholicism*, chapter 6; Henry J. Browne, "Catholicism in the United States" in James Ward Smith and A. Leland

Jameson, editors, *The Shaping of American Religion* (Princeton, 1961), pp. 100–103.

14. Quoted by Sister Joan de Lourdes Leonard, "Catholic Attitudes Toward American Labor, 1884–1919" (unpublished M.A. thesis, Columbia University, 1940), p. 48.

15. Irwin G. Wyllie, *The Self Made Man in America: The Myth of Rags to Riches* (New Brunswick, N.J., 1954), p. 57.

16. Glazer and Moynihan, *Beyond the Melting Pot*, p. 234; Bosco D. Cestello, "Catholics in American Commerce and Industry," *American Catholic Sociological Review*, XVII (October 1956), 219–33.

17. Browne, "Catholicism in the United States," pp. 93–100; Roohan, "American Catholics and the Social Question," pp. 161–207.

18. Quoted by Aaron I. Abell, "The Catholic Church and the American Social Question" in Gurian and Fitzsimons, *Catholic Church in World Affairs*, p. 382.

19. Roohan, "American Catholics and the Social Question," pp. 161–331; Abell, *American Catholicism and Social Action*, pp. 47 ff.; Arthur Mann, *Yankee Reformers in an Urban Age* (Cambridge, 1954), chapter 2.

20. Abell, "American Catholic Reaction to Industrial Conflict: The Arbitral Process," *Catholic Historical Review*, XLI (January 1956), 385–407.

21. Henry J. Browne, *The Catholic Church and the Knights of Labor* (Washington, 1949); Ellis, editor, *Documents*, pp. 440–53; Ellis, *Gibbons*, I, chapter 12; Abell, *Catholicism and Social Action*, pp. 66–71.

22. James Cardinal Gibbons, *Our Christian Heritage* (Baltimore, 1890), p. 450.

23. Quoted by Leonard, "Catholic Attitudes Toward American Labor," p. 33.

24. Ellis, *Gibbons*, I, 532.

25. Abell, "The Catholic Church and the American Social Question," p. 386. See also James H. Moynihan, *Life of Archbishop John Ireland* (New York, 1953), pp. 224–30.

26. The work of local labor priests is described in Paul Stroh, "The Catholic Clergy and American Labor Disputes" (unpublished Ph.D. dissertation, Catholic University of America, 1939), and in Bernard C. Cronin, *Father Yorke and the Labor Movement in San Francisco, 1900–1910* (Washington, 1943).

27. The claim is made by Marc Karson, *American Labor Unions and Politics, 1900–1918* (Carbondale, Ill., 1958), chapter 9. The thesis is rebutted by Philip Taft, *The A.F. of L. in the Time of Gompers* (New York, 1959), pp. 334–41, and Henry J. Browne, "Catholicism in the United States," pp. 93–100.
28. Mary Harrita Fox, *Peter E. Dietz, Labor Priest* (Notre Dame, 1953); Henry J. Browne, "Peter E. Dietz, Pioneer Planner of Catholic Social Action," *Catholic Historical Review*, XXXIII (January 1948), 448–56; Mary Adele Francis Gorman, "Peter E. Dietz and the N.C.W.C.," American Catholic Historical Society of Philadelphia, *Historical Records and Studies* (December 1963), pp. 215–26.
29. Fox, *Dietz*, p. vii.
30. Sister Mary Elizabeth Dye, *By Their Fruits: A Social Biography of Frederick B. Kenkel* (New York, 1960), p. 41.
31. *Ibid., passim;* Sister Mary Ligouri Brophy, *The Social Thought of the German Roman Catholic Central Verein* (Washington, 1941); Abell, *American Catholicism and Social Action*, pp. 175–77; Albert Muntsch, "Kenkel of the Central Verein," *Social Order*, II (April 1952), 160–62.
32. Abell, *American Catholicism and Social Action*, pp. 173–74, 179–81.
33. Robert D. Cross, "Catholic Charities," *Atlantic*, CCX (August 1962), 110–14.
34. Donald P. Gavin, *The National Conference of Catholic Charities, 1910–1960* (Milwaukee, 1962); W. H. Russell, "Monsignor Kerby and Social Welfare," *Catholic World*, CXLIV (October 1936), 35–39.
35. Abell, *American Catholicism and Social Action*, chapter 5.
36. C. Joseph Nuesse, "The National Catholic Welfare Conference" in Putz, *Catholic Church*, pp. 138–52.
37. Ellis, *Documents*, pp. 586–603; Abell, *American Catholicism and Social Action*, pp. 199 ff.
38. Guilday, *National Pastorals*, pp. 266–340.
39. Ellis, *Gibbons*, I, 539.
40. Stephen C. Mason of National Association of Manufacturers to Gibbons, February 25, 1919, quoted in Ellis, *American Catholicism*, pp. 142–43.
41. Raphael M. Huber, editor, *Our Bishops Speak* (Milwaukee, 1952), p. 264.

42. Dorothy G. Wayman, *Cardinal O'Connell of Boston* (New York, 1955), 220–22. See also Vincent A. McQuade, *The American Catholic Attitude on Child Labor since 1891* (Washington, 1938).

43. Francis Broderick, *Right Reverend New Dealer: John A. Ryan* (New York, 1963), chapter 6.

44. D.W. Brogan, *The American Character* (New York, 1944), pp. 103–7. On conservatism of decade see Wilfrid Parsons, "The Social Thought of the American Hierarchy: Our Bishops Speak," *Social Order*, II (June 1952), 278–79; Thomas T. McAvoy, "The Catholic Church in the United States Between Two Wars," *Review of Politics*, IV (September 1944), 419. The effects of Catholic efforts to use organized power to protect the Church's interests and win public recognition of Catholic moral positions are analyzed in Robert D. Cross, "The Changing Image of Catholicism in America," *Yale Review*, XLVII (June 1959), 562–75 and Gordon C. Zahn, "The Content of Protestant Tensions: Fears of Catholic Aims and Methods," *American Catholic Sociological Review*, XVIII (October 1957), 205–12.

45. Quoted by Reinhold Niebuhr, "Catholics and the State," *New Republic*, CXLIII (October 17, 1960), 15.

46. Francis J. Lally, *The Catholic Church in a Changing America* (Boston, 1962), p. 48.

CHAPTER III

1. William J. Walsh, "*Quadragesimo Anno*," *Catholic Charities Review*, XV (June 1931), 173.

2. On Coughlin's career see chapter VII. In 1930 the NCWC administrative board of bishops issued a statement on unemployment, which was denounced as an evil greater than famine, "in that men themselves inflict it in the midst of plenty." Raphael M. Huber, editor, *Our Bishops Speak* (Milwaukee, 1951), p. 191.

3. Archbishop John T. McNicholas, "Justice and the Present Crisis," *Catholic Mind*, XXIX (October 22, 1931), 473–81.

4. Paul L. Blakely, "The Schools and *Rerum Novarum*," *America*, XLV (May 9, 1931), 111–12.

5. Speech by O'Connell reported in *Tablet*, December 19, 1931; statement of NCWC administrative board, April 25, 1933, in Huber, *Our Bishops Speak*, p. 298.

6. O'Shaughnessy: "Greed is the Witch," *Commonweal*, XVIII

(November 4, 1931), 9–11; "How Strong Is the World's Industrial Arch?," *America*, XLVI (January 30, 1932), 400–401; "The Catholic League for Social Justice," *ibid.*, LI (September 15, 1934), 537–38. See the files of *Social Justice Bulletin*, organ of O'Shaughnessy's Catholic League for Social Justice, issued monthly from September 1933.

7. "Sursum Corda," *Commonweal*, XVI (April 8, 1931), 619.

8. McNicholas, "Justice and the Present Crisis," 473–81; McNicholas, "Pastoral Letter on Charity," *Catholic Charities Review*, XV (October 1931), 268–69.

9. O'Shaughnessy, *Man or Money?* (New York, 1932), 11, 20–21, 32. Also O'Shaughnessy, "Trade Associations New and Old," *Commonweal*, XVII (January 25, 1933), 351–53.

10. Blakely, "The Marriage Encyclical and Wages," *America*, XLIV (January 24, 1931), 384–86.

11. William F. Montovan, "Legislation in the Making," *Catholic Action*, XIV (March 1932), 21–22; Montovan, "Our Federal System," *ibid.*, XV (January 1933), 5–6.

12. Huber, *Our Bishops Speak*, pp. 194–96. An example of the reasoning behind the turn to federal action is "Federal Relief: The Bridge that Must Be Crossed." *Commonweal*, XV (January 13, 1932), 281–82. In pushing for federal help the hierarchy and the NCWC sought to avoid "stabilization" and "secularization." See semi-annual report of William F. Montovan, head of the Legal Department, for April 1933, in Montovan Papers.

13. Quoted in *Tablet*, January 26, 1932. See also Frank Murphy, "The Moral Law in Government," *Commonweal*, XVIII (May 19, 1933), 63–64.

14. "Two Times Two," *Commonweal*, XVI (September 7, 1932), 442.

15. "The New Cross of Gold," *Commonweal*, XVII (November 2, 1932), 5–6.

16. Wilfrid Parsons, "The Pope, the President and the Governor," *America*, XLVII (September 3, 1932), 517–19; Parsons, "The Parties: Economic Planks," *ibid.* (July 30, 1932), 394–96; William F. Montovan, "New Leadership in the Federal Government," *Catholic Action*, XV (April 1933), 5–6.

17. A public opinion poll in July 1936 showed 66 per cent of Roman Catholics in favor of President Roosevelt, a proportion surpassed only among Jews and Baptists. See Hadley Cantril, editor, *Public*

Opinion, 1935–1946 (Princeton, 1951), p. 755. Samuel Lubell, *The Future of American Politics* (New York, 1952), 220–26; William V. Shannon, *The American Irish* (New York, 1963), chapters 16, 17; William E. Leuchtenberg, *Franklin D. Roosevelt and the New Deal* (New York, 1963), pp. 184, 272; Oscar Handlin, *The American People in the Twentieth Century* (Boston, 1963), pp. 184, 203. George Q. Flynn, "Franklin D. Roosevelt and American Catholics, 1932–1936" (unpublished Ph.D. dissertation, Louisiana State University, 1966) offers further documentation on this point.

18. Patrick Scanlan, "From the Managing Editor's Desk," *Tablet*, July 15, 1933; "President Roosevelt Still Looks Forward," *Sign*, XIII (July 1934), 707–8.

19. Patrick Cardinal Hayes. "The Principles of the Common Good," *Catholic Mind*, XXXI (July 22, 1933), 261. Inviting Roosevelt to the ceremony Hayes congratulated the President on the "marvellous achievements of the past few months." Hayes to Roosevelt, June 16, 1933, Roosevelt Papers.

20. *Toledo Blade*, March 13, 1933, clipping enclosed in letter from William H. Booker to Roosevelt, March 24, 1933, in Roosevelt Papers.

21. Richard D. Skinner to Marvin H. McIntyre, June 13, 1933, Roosevelt Papers.

22. Expression of support came from all sections of the Catholic community: see a summary in "Notes on the Blue Eagle," *Columbia*, XIII (October 1933), 13. Some opponents of centralization who registered support were: Edmund A. Walsh, "Recovery or Disaster," *Commonweal*, XVIII (October 13, 1933), 542–44; James Gillis, "Sursum Corda," *Tablet*, September 16, 1933; "Recovery or State Socialism," *America*, XLIX (July 22, 1933).

23. "Catholic Principles Reflected in Industrial Recovery Act," *Catholic Action*, XV (July 1933), 6.

24. "Dr. Haas Named to U.S. Recovery Committee," *Catholic Action*, XV (July 1933), 6, 17; speech reported in *Tablet*, August 5, 1933.

25. National Catholic Alumni Federation, "A Program for Social Justice," *Catholic Mind*, XXXI (August 8, 1933), 283; National Council of Catholic Women to Roosevelt, October 11, 1933, Roosevelt Papers; "From Social Reform to Social Planning," *Catholic Charities Review*, XVII (June 1933), 163–64; "Recovery and Reformation," *Commonweal*, XIX (November 17, 1933),

56–57; "Beyond the NRA," *ibid.* (November 24, 1933), 87–88; "Is the NRA 'Ideal'?" *America*, L (December 23, 1933), 266; "Neither Fascism nor Communism," *ibid.* (March 17, 1934), 557–58.

26. Edgar Schmiedeler, "Beyond NRA," *Commonweal*, XVIII (September 22, 1933), 485–87; Frederick B. Kenkel, "New Deals Past and Present," *Central Blatt and Social Justice*, XXVIII (April 1935), 7–9.

27. "Economic Planning," *America*, XLIX (April 22, 1933), 52; Editorial, *Catholic Action*, XV (October 1933), 6.

28. William A. Bolger, "Social Legislation," *Catholic Action*, XV (May 1933), 14; "Old Age Pensions," *America*, XLIX (July 1, 1933), 291; Goetz Briefs, "Social Insurance: A Sign of Basic Social Change in the United States," *Catholic Charities Review*, XVIII (May 1935), 134–37; Briefs, "A Non-Contributory System By All Means," *ibid.* (December 1934), 311–12; Francis Haas, *Man and Society* (New York, 1935), p. 244; "Clearing the Air," *Commonweal*, XVII (December 7, 1932), 145–46.

29. John A. Lapp, "Social Security and the Forgotten Man," *Catholic Charities Review*, XVIII (September 1935), 204–6; "Social Security Legislation," *America*, LII (February 2, 1935), 389–90; Patrick Scanlan, "From the Managing Editor's Desk," *Tablet*, October 13, 1933, and August 24, 1935. Michael O'Shaughnessy, on the other hand, regarded the legislation as paternalistic and unnecessary. See his articles "The Constitution and Security," *Commonweal*, XXII (August 9, 1935), 357–58, and "Social Standards Under the Constitution," *America*, LIV (October 12, 1935), 9–10.

30. Paul Kiniery, "Where Are We Going?" *Catholic World*, CXLIII (April 1936), 10–20; Kiniery, "Catholics and the New Deal," *ibid.*, CXLI (April 1935), 10–20.

31. Perhaps the most interesting incident of this sort came in 1935 when the bishops, meeting in Washington, sent Father Burke to the White House with a letter for the President signed on their behalf by Bishop John F. Noll of Fort Wayne. The letter urged Roosevelt to speak out against religious persecution in Mexico, warning that failure to do so would make it increasingly difficult to hold the anger of their people in check. When Roosevelt asked his staff for advice they suggested consulting Father Burke, who accommodated by drafting an evasive reply which was then sent to Bishop Noll verbatim. Noll to Roosevelt, May 13, 1935, Roose-

velt to Marvin H. McIntyre, May 16, 1935, Burke to McIntyre, May 20, 1935, Roosevelt to Noll, May 23, 1935, Roosevelt Papers. See also Flynn, "Roosevelt and American Catholics," *passim*.

32. Roosevelt's extensive correspondence with Cardinal Mundelein is in Roosevelt Papers, President's Personal File 324. Parts of the story of this friendship are contained in *The Secret Diary of Harold L. Ickes*, 3 volumes (New York, 1953), I, pp. 479–80; II, pp. 214–22, 349–50, 538; III, 63–64. Ickes believed Mundelein was the only Catholic prelate friendly to the New Deal. He said Roosevelt felt Mundelein was one of the three greatest men in America. *Ibid.*, III, 28, 53. See also Grace Tully, *F.D.R. My Boss* (New York, 1949), p. 232, Paul R. Martin, *First Cardinal of the West* (Chicago, 1934); *Time*, XXIX (May 31, 1937), 23 and XXXIV (October 9, 1939), 42.

33. Ernest P. Ament, *Industrial Recovery Legislation in the Light of Catholic Principles* (Washington, 1936), p. 88.

34. Edmund A. Walsh to Daniel C. Roper, December 13, 1935, in Roper to Roosevelt, December 14, 1935, Roosevelt Papers. For more directly pro-business critiques see, Elmer Murphy, "The Line of Cleavage," *Commonweal*, XXI (March 8, 1935), 527–28; Gerhard Hershfeld, "Where Is the Money?" *ibid.*, XX (October 4, 1934), 519–20.

35. John A. Ryan to Jerome A. Drolet, February 4, 1936, Ryan Papers. A view which expressed the feelings of many reformers was that of the veteran champion of social justice William J. Kerby, who wrote Father Haas of the "high mission" of NRA made necessary by "the tyranny of the system which is impersonal, deeply rooted, vicious beyond correction by an individual." Kerby to Haas, February 24, 1935, Haas Papers. See also Kerby, "The Old Deal and the New," *Catholic Mind*, XXXI (July 22, 1934), 271–77.

36. "The Distributist Program," *Guildsman*, IV (October 1935), 4–5. Also, Joseph Thorning, "Principles and Practice of NRA," *Catholic Mind*, XXXII (October 8, 1934), 361–69; Frederick B. Kenkel, "New Deals Past and Present," *Central Blatt and Social Justice*, irregularly in 1934 and 1935.

37. "The NRA in the Supreme Court," *America*, LII (January 19, 1935), 341–42; "Exit NRA. Now What?" *Catholic World*, CXLI (July 1935), 385–400; Haas to Roosevelt, October 25, 1935, Haas Papers.

38. "Hold to the Constitution!" *America*, LIII (July 13, 1935), 314.

39. Blakely, "The Textile Labor Code," *ibid.*, XLIX (July 22, 1933), 373–74; Blakely, "Centralized Control of Production and Commerce," *ibid.*, LIII (June 15, 1935), 222–24; Blakely, "The National Public Interest," *ibid.*, LIV (November 23, 1935), 158–59; Blakely, "The Guffey Coal Case," *ibid.*, LV (June 6, 1936), 205–6.

40. Parsons, "The Roosevelt Revolution," *ibid.*, L (January 6, 1934), 322; Parsons, "Philosophy of a New Deal," *ibid.*, LI (May 19, 1934), 126–28; (May 26, 1934), 150–52; (June 2, 1934), 174–76.

41. "Our Unconventional President," *Catholic World*, CXLII (February 1936), 513–23; "Now What, Mr. President?" *ibid.*, CXLIV (December 1936), 258–66; "President Roosevelt's Communist Sympathies?" *ibid.* (November 1936), 129 ff.

42. "A Reply to the President," *Tablet*, October 5, 1935; "The Nestors in Washington," *ibid.*, January 10, 1936; "From the Managing Editor's Desk," *ibid.*, June 22, 1935.

43. "Beware Mr. Roosevelt," *ibid.*, December 1, 1934; "Giving of Degree to Mr. Roosevelt Causes Regret," *ibid.*, December 7, 1935; Scanlan, "From the Managing Editor's Desk," *ibid.*, December 21, 1935.

44. Scanlan, "From the Managing Editor's Desk," *ibid.*, November 2 and December 7, 1935; October 17, 1936.

45. "The Catholic Vote," *ibid.*, August 1, 1936; Scanlan, "From the Managing Editor's Desk," *ibid.*, February 8, 1936, and July 4, 1936.

46. See for example James J. Hoey to John A. Ryan, September 25, 1936, in Ryan Papers; Dean Alfange to James Farley, September 15, 1936, Roosevelt Papers.

47. See chapter VI, 137–138.

48. Bishop Bernard J. Mahoney to Roosevelt, July 21, 1936, Roosevelt Papers; Mahoney to Rev. Maurice Sheehy, July 21, 1936, *ibid.*; Bishop James H. Ryan to Roosevelt, September 25, 1936, *ibid.*, *Chicago Daily News*, September 15, 1936, clipping in Roosevelt Papers.

49. Sheehy to Marguerite LeHand, July 18, 1936; Sheehy to Stephen Early, September 29, 1936; Sheehy to LeHand, October 5, 1936; Sheehy to LeHand, October 8, 1936; Early to Roosevelt, September 30, 1936, Roosevelt Papers.

50. Bosco D. Cestello, "Catholics in American Commerce and Industry," *American Catholic Sociological Review*, XVII (October

1956), 219–55; Nathan Glazer and Daniel P. Moynihan, *Beyond the Melting Pot* (Cambridge, 1963), p. 234.

51. Bishop Bernard Mahoney, "The Mind of the Church on Social Legislation," *Catholic Mind*, XXXII (November 22, 1934), 45–52.

52. Ignatius W. Cox, "Constitutional Liberty and Our Immoral Economic Order," *ibid.*, XXXIV (March 8, 1936), 105–13, also Cox, "The American Liberty League and Our Immoral Economic Order," *ibid.*, 113–21.

53. "Father Cox's Pamphlet," *Commonweal*, XXIII (March 20, 1936), 577.

54. *Organized Social Justice* (New York, n.d.).

55. Alfred Diamant, *Austrian Catholics and the Social Question, 1918–1933* (Gainesville, Fla., 1959), chapter 4. See also Carl H. Carny, "Monsignor John A. Ryan and the Social Action Department" (unpublished Ph.D. dissertation, Yale University, 1954), pp. 213–17 and *passim*. A contemporary critique similar to that presented here is F. A. Hermens's "The Corporative Idea and the Crisis of Democracy," *Central Blatt and Social Justice*, XXXI (March 1939), 372–74.

56. A good example of the conflict between social justice and constitutional liberty was the debate over national health insurance which lasted into the postwar years. A later study of the controversy demonstrates the considerable difficulty Catholics have had in reconciling their desire to achieve social justice for all and to preserve what they conceive to be the liberties guaranteed by the Constitution. William J. Sweeney, "Opinion on Proposals for National Health Insurance in American Catholic Periodicals, 1919–1950" (unpublished M.A. thesis, Catholic University of America, 1950).

57. Sweeney quotes the Jesuit quarterly *Thought*, viewing the problem of health insurance within such a frame of reference: "She (the Church) has high ideals to safeguard and she watches most carefully for the entering wedge of government domination. An apparently innocent law may be packed with educational dynamite and it behooves the Church to be on her guard constantly," *ibid.*, p. 44. This attitude, with its correlative tendency to view all legislative proposals from the perspective of their actual or potential effect on the Church, was powerful in the twenties, was overcome with difficulty for a period of the early thirties, and reappeared strongly after 1936.

CHAPTER IV

1. Father Maurice Sheehy cited a Gallup poll showing that 76 per cent of American Catholics voted for Roosevelt in 1936. Sheehy to Roosevelt, May 13, 1940, Roosevelt Papers.
2. For accounts of Catholic disaffection with the New Deal see Donald R. Campion, "Survey of American Social Catholicism, 1930–1940" (unpublished M.A. thesis, St. Louis University, 1949), pp. 38 ff.; William V. Shannon, *The American Irish* (New York, 1963), chapter 24; Samuel Lubell, *The Future of American Politics* (New York, 1954), pp. 220–26.
3. James Gillis, "Reply to Dr. J. A. Ryan," *Catholic World*, CXVLIII (April 1936), 1–9.
4. *Tablet*, February 13, 1937, and March 13, 1937; "President or Dictator," *America*, LVI (February 20, 1937), 460–69.
5. "The President Slips One Over," *Catholic World*, CXLV (May 1937), 129. Later Gillis rejoiced at the plan's defeat but hoped it would not lead to opposition to all social legislation: "President Loses: How?," *ibid.* (September 1937), 641–48.
6. Paul Blakely, "Young Eyed Cherubins Who Think With the President," *America*, LVI (February 20, 1937), 460–61; Blakely, "Your Rights Under the Constitution," *ibid.* (March 27, 1937), 583.
7. William F. Sands, "The Supreme Court Debate," *Commonweal*, XXV (April 16, 1937), 685–88; Lawrence Lucey, "The Supreme Court and Social Justice," *Catholic World*, CXLVI (October 1937), 34–40.
8. John Ryan, *Declining Liberty and Other Papers* (New York, 1927), 137–45; "The Supreme Court Debate," *Commonweal*, XXV (April 16 and 23, 1937), 683–85 and 701–8.
9. "Revivifying the Supreme Court," *Commonweal*, XXV (March 26, 1937), 593–94. See also Monsignor Robert F. Keegan to Roosevelt, March 6, 1937, Roosevelt Papers.
10. "The Supreme Court Issue," *Sign*, XVI (March 1937), 451; "The Court Reform," *Christian Front*, II (July and August 1937), 107; "Constitutional Crisis," *ibid.* (May 1937), 71–72.
11. John A. Ryan to Dean Alfange, January 18, 1938, Ryan Papers.
12. "Making Black White," *America*, LVIII (October 9, 1937), 12; "Talent Rewarded: Mr. Justice Black," *Catholic World*, CXLVI (November 1937), 1–3; *Tablet*, September 18, 1937.

13. Again Cardinal Mundelein came to Roosevelt's aid, wiring the President that he could not "find that the welfare or freedom of the Catholic Church is in any way menaced by the pending reorganization bill." Mundelein to Roosevelt, April 7, 1938, Roosevelt Papers.

14. "Packing the Senate," *America*, LIX (July 23, 1938).

15. "Fireside Chat in Reverse," *Catholic World*, CXLVII (December 1938), 260–64. For early opposition to third term see "Twelve Years? Too Much," *America*, LXI (June 24, 1939), 253; *Tablet*, July 15, 1939; *Ave Maria*, XLVIII (July 20, 1938), 150.

16. Arthur Stanley Riggs, "American Breakdown," *Catholic World*, CXLVI (February 1938 and March 1938), 550–58, 693–99.

17. "Federal Wages and Hours," *America*, LIX (June 25, 1938), 277–78; Blakely, "A Stirring Year Full of Fear and Anxiety," *ibid.*, LVIII (January 1, 1938), 296–98; "Wages and Hours," *ibid.*, LIX (May 21, 1938), 157–58.

18. Henry M. Wright, "An Economic Gold Brick," *Sign*, XVII (December 1937), 263–65.

19. "What Will Happen Next?," *America*, LVIII (March 19, 1938), 564–65.

20. *Tablet*, October 28, 1939; "Sound Recovery," *Christian Front*, IV (April 1939), 50; John Wiltbye, "Rum, Red Ink, and Emerging Rabbits," *America*, LXI (September 2, 1939), 488–90; "The Selfish Majority," *Commonweal*, XXVII (April 8, 1938), 645–46; Paul Kiniery, "Now What: Another Depression?," *Catholic World*, CXLVI (February 1938), 522–31.

21. "Editorial," *Catholic Charities Review*, XXI (February 1937), 33–34; John A. O'Brien, "Fighting for Social Justice," *Commonweal*, XXVI (June 11, 1937), 179–80.

22. "Return of the Bourbons," *Christian Front*, III (February 1938), 19–20; "Radical Revolution," *ibid.* (January 1938); also see Richard Deverall, "The Way It Was," *Social Order*, XI (December 1961), 452.

23. Francis X. Talbot, "Roosevelt and Revolution," *Thought*, XIV (September 1939), 350–54.

24. Bishop Edwin O'Hara and Bishop Karl J. Alter, "Christian Social Order: Some Basic Principles," *Catholic Mind*, XXXVI (June 8, 1938), 220–22.

25. Raphael M. Huber, editor, *Our Bishops Speak* (Milwaukee, 1952), 324–43.

26. "Something in the Air," *Commonweal*, XIII (August 27, 1930), 411-12; "Recognizing the Russian Danger," *ibid.* (February 11, 1931), 393-95; "Shall We Recognize Russia?," *ibid.* (April 12, 1933), 465; Edmund A. Walsh, "The Basic Issues in Recognition of Soviet Russia," *Catholic Mind* (May 22, 1933), 192-200; *Tablet*, April 8 and October 28, 1933.

27. *Tablet*, throughout 1935, particularly issues of March 16, June 29, and November 23; "Russia and Mexico: Who Cares?," *Catholic World*, CXL (February 1935), 513-23; "The President and Mexico," *America*, LIV (November 9, 1935), 97-98; Martin H. Carmody to Roosevelt, January 12, 1935, and April 22, 1935, Roosevelt Papers. Virtually the sole dissenter was Patrick Callahan, a well-known Louisville, Kentucky, businessman, and friend of Ambassador Daniels. See Callahan to *Michigan Catholic*, March 14, 1935, Callahan Papers.

28. "Child Murder as Entertainment," *Catholic World*, CXI (March 1935), 641-49; Raymond McGowan, "The Yardstick," *Tablet*, February 16, 1935.

29. Elizabeth R. Sweeney, "Principle in World Relations," *Commonweal*, XIX (April 20, 1934), 681-83; "Catholic Association Urges World Parliament," *Literary Digest*, CXVII (March 17, 1934), 19.

30. *Tablet*, July 19, 1930; William Cardinal O'Connell, "The Rule of Chaos," *Columbia*, X (July 1931), 3.

31. John LaFarge, "Causes and Communism," *America*, LII (February 9, 1935), 421-23; LaFarge, "Appeal of Bolshevism," *ibid.*, XLVIII (December 3, 1932), 201-3; "The Battle Against Communism," *ibid.*, LVI (November 7, 1937), 109.

32. Patrick Scanlan, "From the Managing Editor's Desk," *Tablet*, July 26, 1930.

33. Huber, *Our Bishops Speak*, 98-101.

34. Bishop John F. Noll, "Introduction" to James A. Vaughn, editor, *Our Modern Social and Economic Order* (Huntington, Ind., 1939), n.p. See also F. K. Wentz, "American Catholic Periodicals React to Nazism," *Church History*, XXI (December 1962), 400-420.

35. See for example *Tablet*, August 8, 1935, and February 25, 1939.

36. John LaFarge, "Facism or Communism: Which Is the Greater Danger?," *America*, LVI (October 10, 1936), 4-5.

37. "On Communism," *Commonweal*, XXIV (October 9, 1936), 541-42; "The World Revolution," *ibid.* (August 14, 1936), 373-74;

"Catholicism and Communism," *ibid.*, XXV (January 19, 1937), 257.

38. Wilfrid Parsons, S. J., "Fascist-Communist Dilemma," *Commonweal*, XXV (February 12, 1937), 429–31; Parsons, "Popular Fronts and Catholicism," *ibid.* (February 19, 1937), 464–66. John A. Ryan expressed the view that facism was preferable to communism in 1937 but later seemed to regard Hitler as a far greater and more immediate danger than Stalin. Ryan to Daniel M. Welch, October 25, 1937; Ryan to Carl D. Thompson, October 28, 1937; Ryan to C. L. Todd, March 21, 1939, Ryan Papers.

39. George N. Shuster, "Germany Under the Concordat," *Commonweal*, XVIII (September 1, 1933), 420.

40. "The Church in Germany," *ibid.* (July 21, 1933), 295–96; "The German Concordat," *ibid.* (August 11, 1933), 359; "Facing Realities," *ibid.* (September 1, 1933), 419.

41. Allen Guttmann, *The Wound in the Heart: America and the Spanish Civil War* (New York, 1962), pp. 29–52; quote p. 30. See also J. David Valaik, "Catholics, Neutrality, and the Spanish Embargo, 1937–1939," *Journal of American History,*" LIV (June 1967), 73–85.

42. *Tablet*, August 22, 1937.

43. Guttmann, *Wound in the Heart*, p. 46.

44. "Perils of a Communist Victory in Spain," *America*, LV (August 8, 1936), 420–21; "The Real Problem in Spain," *Catholic World*, CXLV (June 1937), 257 ff.

45. Francis X. Talbot, "Clarifying the Issues of the Spanish Civil War," *America*, LVIII (October 23, 1937), 52. For evidence of the anti-Catholic bias of much liberal and Protestant opinion see Guttmann, *Wound in the Heart*, pp. 69, 80, 153–69.

46. Francis X. Talbot, "In Answer to Some Reflections on the Spanish Situation," *America*, LVIX (April 10, 1937), 9–10; John LaFarge, "While Spain Burns They Strum Impartially," *ibid.* (August 20, 1937), 462–63.

47. George N. Shuster, "Some Reflections on Spain," *Commonweal*, XXV (April 2, 1937), 625–27.

48. Shuster, "Some More Reflections," *ibid.* (April 23, 1937), 716–17.

49. "Civil War in Spain and the United States," *ibid.*, XXVIII (June 24, 1938), 229–30.

50. Dorothy Day, "On the Use of Force," *Catholic Worker*, VI (September 1938), 1, 4, 7. Her protégés at the *Christian Front*,

while maintaining a strong pacifist position on the question of American involvement in world war, nevertheless were strongly pro-Franco. See *Christian Front*, II (December 1937), 171–72 and IV (March 1939), 36.

51. "What Is Propaganda?" *New World*, reprinted in *Catholic Worker*, VI (March 5, 1938), 7. Virgil Michel condemned Catholics for "violently emotional thinking" on the Spanish issue, for speaking of a "holy war" and for identifying "the interests of the Church with a particular set of conditions or circumstances." Quoted in Paul Marx, *Virgil Michel and the Liturgical Movement* (Collegeville, Minn., 1957), 316–47.

52. A poll in December 1936 showed 42 per cent of Catholics as expressing pro-Loyalist opinions but noted a large bloc of indifference. A later poll showed 30 per cent pro-Loyalist and 31 per cent neutral. See Hadley Cantril, editor, *Public Opinion 1936–1946* (Princeton, 1951), pp. 807–8; Ralph Lord Ray, *Communism and the Churches* (New York, 1960), p. 112.

53. "Long and Short Views," *Sign*, XI (October 1937), 133; Patrick Scanlan, "From the Managing Editor's Desk," *Tablet*, January 6, 1940, and January 17, 1931.

54. George N. Shuster, "A Catholic Defends His Church," *New Republic*, XCVII (January 4, 1939), 246–48; Shuster, "The Man Without a Country," *Commonweal*, XXIX (December 2, 1938), 147–49; Shuster, "Liberal Qualms," *ibid.*, XXXI (December 29, 1939), 14; *Tablet*, January 14, 1939; "Mr. Shuster's Defense," *New Republic*, XCVII (January 4, 1939), 243.

55. Thomas E. Davitt, "Can We Ally With Russia in Case of War?" *America*, LX (April 1, 1939), 605–6.

56. "Why Quit Our Own?," *ibid.*, LIX (September 24, 1938), 588–89; "Isolation," *ibid.*, LXI (September 30, 1939), 589; "The Still Subsisting War," *ibid.*, LXII (January 6, 1940), 350–51.

57. Many Catholics likewise argued that the papal appeals for international co-operation were not applicable because of the lack of good will on the part of European nations and the primary responsibility of government to watch over the interests of its own citizens. See M. J. Hillenbrand "Our Neutrality Policy Needs Repairing, Not Junking," *ibid.*, LIX (September 3, 1938), 514–15; Bishop Karl J. Alter, "The Lend Lease Bill," in M. J. Reardon, editor, *A Bishop's Rostrum* (Milwaukee, 1946), 190–92; David I.

Walsh, "The United States Must Keep Out of the War," *Catholic Mind*, XXXVII (October 8, 1939), 849–58.

58. "Let the People Decide," *America*, LVIII (November 27, 1937), 180–81; John LaFarge, "Referendum on War," *ibid.* (January 15, 1938), 347; "We Conscientiously Object," *ibid.*, LXI (September 23, 1939), 493–94; "Better Be Slow than Clever," *ibid.* (September 23, 1939), 564–65; "Our Foreign Affairs," *ibid.* (October 7, 1939), 612; Paul Blakely, "America's Responsibility," *ibid.* (September 9, 1939), 508–9; John LaFarge, "Pacifists or Peacemakers," *ibid.*, LX (February 18, 1939), 466–67; LaFarge, "Europe May Be at War While America is at Peace," *ibid.*, LXI (November 11, 1939), 116–19.

59. "Readers of *America* Poll," *ibid.*, LXII (November 18, 1939), 144; "National Catholic College Poll," *ibid.* (November 11, 1939), 116–19.

60. "Come On In; The War Is Fine," *Catholic World*, CXLI (May 1935), 130–37; "The War What Else But the War?" *ibid.*, CL (November 1939), 1–9; "Neutrality," *ibid.*, 129; "Wilson to Chamberlain to Hitler," *ibid.*, CXLVIII (November 1938), 129; "He Who Gets Slapped: Roosevelt," *ibid.*, CXLIX (June 1939), 257.

61. "The Will to Peace," *Christian Front*, I (June 1936), 83–84; "We Too Shall Fight," *ibid.*, III (November 1938), 131; Richard Deverall, "War Fever," *ibid.*, IV (February 1939), 2; Norman McKenna, "Peace Action By All," *ibid.*, II (April 1937), 57–58.

62. Gillis, "Sursum Corda," *Tablet*, August 8, 1931, and May 9, 1938; Archbishop John T. McNicholas, "War: Man's Folly," *Christian Social Action*, IV (November 1939), 164–66. McNicholas's statement on conscription was quoted by Thomas Delaney in a letter to John Ryan August 15, 1940, in Ryan Papers.

63. "Our Foreign Policy," *Commonweal*, XXIX (April 17, 1939), 648–49; Shuster, "The Revolution of Nihilism," *ibid.*, XXX (May 19, 1939), 90–93; *C.A.I.P. Newsletter* (October 1939), pp. 1–2, in Callahan Papers. A press release announcing Taylor's appointment and presenting letters from religious leaders including Archbishop Spellman of New York are in Roosevelt Papers. President's Personal File 4404. Letters in response are in Official file 76B. Maurice Sheehy and Francis Haas were other defenders of Roosevelt's foreign policy: Sheehy to Roosevelt August 10, 1940, and Septem-

ber 12, 1940; Sheehy to Marguerite Le Hand, February 8, 1941, with copy of radio address; Roosevelt Papers; Haas to R. Hillenbrand, October 2, 1939, Haas Papers. Catholic members of the Committee To Defend America by Aiding the Allies are listed in Ryan to Michael Williams, October 26, 1940, Ryan Papers.

64. John A. O'Brien, C.S.C., "Fighting For Social Justice," *ibid.*, XXVI (May 28, June 4, and June 11, 1937), 119, 148–50, 179–80. Quote 119.

65. Virgil Michel, Letter to the Editor, *Catholic Worker*, IV (April 1937), 5.

66. John M. Loughram, "Layman to Layman," *Commonweal* (October 28, 1938), 13–15; Paul Kiniery, "The Catholic Answer to Communism," *Catholic World*, CXLIV (March 1937), 352–60; George Johnson, "Social Justice or Communism," *Catholic Action*, XIX (June 1937), 16–19.

67. Catherine de Hueck, "Communist Techniques," *Sign*, XVI (December 1936), 281–82; Virgil Michel, "The Fight Against Communism," *Catholic Mind*, XXXV (February 22, 1937), 77–80.

68. J.F.T. Prince, *Creative Revolution* (Milwaukee, 1937).

69. Ryan to Deverall, September 27, 1940; Deverall to Ryan, October 8, 1940, Ryan Papers.

CHAPTER V

1. See for example Edward Duff, "Just a Few Things," *Social Order*, XI (March 1961), 97–98.

2. James Edward Roohan, "American Catholics and the Social Question, 1865–1900" (unpublished Ph.D. dissertation, Yale University, 1952), pp. 161–207; Henry J. Browne, *The Catholic Church and the Knights of Labor* (Washington, 1949); Ellis, *The Life of James Cardinal Gibbons*, I (Milwaukee, 1952), chapter 12; Aaron I. Abell, *American Catholicism and Social Action* (Garden City, 1960), pp. 62–71.

3. Ireland "could not believe that the great industralists whose friendship he possessed and who seemed to be 'good men' in all their relations with him and with their neighbors, could stoop to economic oppression of the laborer, the farmer and the consumer." John A. Ryan, *Social Doctrine in Action: A Personal History* (New York, 1941), p. 27. It was Ryan's opinion that Ireland and most of the American clergy were woefully ignorant

of the extent of social and economic injustice. See particularly his *Questions of the Day* (Boston, 1931), pp. 218–31. Dietz's unsuccessful attempts to arouse Catholic interest in the labor movement are described in chapter 2.

4. John A. Ryan, "Social Justice and the State," *Commonweal*, XXX (June 16, 1939), 205–6.

5. Raymond McGowan, "The National Industrial Recovery Act," *Catholic Action*, XV (July 1933), p. 13.

6. These themes run through all McGowan's extensive writings. See in particular "Philosophy of Catholicism in Its Relation to Industry," *NCWC Review*, XIII (May 1931), 9–10; "Property-Organization-Government Action," *ibid.* (November 1931), 28; "Reconstructing the Social Order," American Catholic Philosophical Association, *Proceedings*, IX (1933), 187; *New Guilds: A Conversation* (New York, 1937).

7. Wilfred Parsons, "The Systems of Vocational Groups" in James A. Vaughn, editor, *Our Modern Social and Economic Order* (Huntington, Ind., 1939), p. 268.

8. Carl P. Hensler, Speech to Steel Workers Organizing Committee, reported in *Catholic Worker*, V (July 1937), p. 5.

9. "What of Occupational Groups?," *Guildsman*, II (July 1934), 7–8; "The Unions of *Quadregesimo Anno*," *ibid.* (April 1934), 7–8; "The Occupational Group System," *ibid.* (June 1934), 6–7; "Betraying the True Alternative," *ibid.*, III (November 1934), 5–6; "Must Workers Be Unionized?," *ibid.*, V (June 1937), 8–9.

10. William Cardinal O'Connell, "The Changed Condition of Labor," *Catholic Mind*, XXIX (January 8, 1931), 1–4; *Tablet*, March 23, 1931.

11. Raphael M. Huber, editor, *Our Bishops Speak* (Milwaukee, 1952), p. 191.

12. Ignatius W. Cox, "Wages and Our Immoral Economic Order," *Catholic Mind*, XXXIV (May 8, 1936), 190; John F. Cronin, "A Living Wage Today," *Sign*, XVII (June 1938), 647–51; Richard Deverall, "A Living Wage," *Christian Front*, II (June 1937), 92–93; *Tablet*, December 8, 1934; Arthur E. Gleason, "The Grounds for a Minimum Wage," *America*, LII (October 13, 1934), 12–13; Gleason, "Objections to a Living Wage," *ibid.* (October 27, 1934), 61–62.

13. Haas, quoted in *Tablet*, November 12, 1932; Labor Day speech reported in *Catholic Worker*, I (October 1933), 1. See also his

pamphlets *The American Labor Movement* (Washington, 1937), and *The Wages and Hours of American Labor* (Washington, 1937).

14. "Editor's Introduction," *Commonweal*, XIII (April 22, 1931), 687.

15. "Labor Needs Leaders," *America*, XLVI (November 15, 1930), 126–27; "Mr. Green Takes His Tea Things," *ibid.*, XLIX (August 20, 1932), 425; "Labor Union Progress," *ibid.*, XLVIII (February 11, 1933), 446–47; "Union Racketeers," *ibid.*, LVI (November 7, 1936), 109–10. For similar views see "The Dinner Pail," *Commonweal*, XI (August 20, 1930), 395; G. Hershfeld, "Organized Labor: An Indictment," *ibid.*, XV (March 23, 1932), 567–69.

16. Speeches reported in *Tablet*, September 9 and October 14, 1933.

17. "Religion and the Union," *America*, XLIX (September 30, 1933), 603.

18. "The A.F. of L. and Changing Times," *Catholic Charities Review*, XVII (November 1933), 288–89; George K. McCabe, "Union Labor Takes the Count," *ibid.*, XIX (April 1935), 101–3; "The Gains of Labor," *America*, XLIX (September 2, 1933), 505–6; "The Union or Anarchy," *ibid.*, LI (June 30, 1934), 266; "The Immoral Company Union," *ibid.* (May 19, 1934), 121–22.

19. Huber, *Our Bishops Speak*, pp. 272–300.

20. "Workers Union and the State," *America*, L (March 31, 1934), 605–6; "No Charter for Labor," *ibid.*, LIII (July 13, 1935), 313. See also "Collective Bargaining," *Commonweal*, XXI (March 15, 1935), 560, and for a debate on the legal enforcement of collective bargaining, American Catholic Philosophical Association, *Proceedings*, XI (1935), 119–31.

21. Paul Blakely, "The Twilight Zone of the Labor Relations Act," *America*, LIX (August 6, 1938), 412–13; Blakely, "The One Way Road of the Wagner Labor Relations Act," *ibid.*, LVII (July 17, 1937), 342–43; "A Tribunal of Labor Relations," *Commonweal*, XXV (January 22, 1937), 341–42; John P. Boland, "Labor Relations and the Encyclicals," *Sign*, XVII (January 1938), 336–37. For a description of clerical services in mediation see Stroh, "Catholic Clergy and American Labor Disputes," Chapter 5.

22. Raymond McGowan, "The Yardstick," *Tablet*, July 8 and July 15, 1933, March 3, 1934, and March 30, 1935; National Catholic Alumni Federation, "A Program of Social Justice," *Catholic Mind*, XXXI (August 8, 1933), 283; "Recovery and Reformation,"

Commonweal, XIX (November 24, 1933), 56–57; "Beyond the NRA," *ibid*. (November 24, 1933), 87–88; Wilfred Parsons, S.J., "Philosophy of a New Deal," *America*, LI (May 19 and June 2, 1934), 150–52, 174–76; *Organized Social Justice* (New York, n.d.).

23. John E. Corridan, "Craft versus Industrial Unions," *Commonweal*, XXV (November 13, 1936), 65–66; James E. Norton, "Craft vs. Industrial Unions in the A.F. of L.," *Catholic Charities Review*, XVIII (May 1934), 138–41; "Revolt in the A.F. of L.," *America*, LI (August 18, 1934), 434; "Testing the Vertical Union," *America*, LII (October 27, 1934), 138–41, "The New Labor Union," *ibid.*, LVI (December 7, 1935), 195.

24. Paul Blakely, "Let There Be Peace Twixt the A.F. of L., and the C.I.O.," *America*, LVIII (January 29, 1938), 483–85; "Labor on the March," *Christian Front*, II (April 1937), 51–52; George K. McCabe, "The American Labor Movement," *Catholic Charities Review*, XXI (February 1937), 44–47; William Collins, "Industrial and Craft Unionism," *Commonweal*, XXVI (February 25, 1938), 388–89; Francis Haas to John L. Lewis, March 6, 1936, Haas Papers.

25. *Tablet*, January 16, 1937, and February 27, 1937; Paul Blakely, "Labor Wages a Losing Battle," *America*, LVI (February 6, 1937), 417–18; Blakely, "The Sit Down Strike Harmful to the Union," *ibid*. (March 13, 1937), 532–33; Blakely, "Property Rights in the Workers Job," *Ibid.*, LVII (April 10, 1937), 7–8; Joseph N. Fichter, "What's Wrong with the Sit Down Strike?," *Catholic World*, CXLV (August 1937), 562–72; John A. Ryan, "The Sit-Down Strike," *Ecclesiastical Review*, XCVI (April 1937), 419–20; Ryan to Patrick Callahan, October 29, 1937; Ryan to J.W.R. Maguire, January 21, 1937, Ryan Papers.

26. Jerome D. Hannan, "The Moral Right To Sit-Down," *Ecclesiastical Review*, XCVII (July 1937), 31–39; W.F. Kernan, "*Rerum Novarum* and Labor," *Commonweal*, XXVI (August 6, 1937), 357–58; Virgil Michel, "The Labor Movement," *ibid.*, XXVIII (June 3, 1938), 146–48; "Labor on the March," *Christian Front*, II (April 1937), 51–52.

27. For his views of labor prior to his return to the air see Coughlin, *Eight Lectures on Capital, Labor and Justice* (Royal Oak, 1934), pp. 115–234; *Social Justice*, March 27 and July 20, 1936, and January 18 and February 8, 1937.

28. *Social Justice*, October 5, 1936, and August 2 to September 6, 1937.

29. *Ibid.*, October 18, October 25, and November 1, 1937.

30. *A Series of Lectures on Social Justice* (Royal Oak, 1935), pp. 46–55; *Social Justice*, April 14, April 11, and July 11, 1938.

31. "Mr. Lewis and His Friends," *America*, LV (September 19, 1936), 564–65; "Sit Down Enjoined," *ibid.*, LVI (February 13, 1937), 445–46; "Unions and the Law," *ibid.*, LVII (July 10, 1937), 325–26; "C.I.O. Communism," *ibid.*, LVIII (October 9, 1937), 13–14; "C.I.O. Bargaining," *ibid.* (November 13, 1937), 132; "Comrade Lewis," *ibid.*, LIX (September 25, 1938), 589–90; *Tablet*, January 6, 1937, and September 17, 1938.

32. "Franklin D. Roosevelt and John L. Lewis," *Catholic World*, CXLV (July 1937), 385–93; Eugene Huber, "Socialism, Communism, C.I.O.," *ibid.*, CXLVII (December 1938), 333–39; Arthur Stanley Riggs, "American Breakdown," *ibid.* (February and March 1938), 550–58, 693–99.

33. Arthur M. Murphy, "The State of Labor in a Changing America," National Catholic Social Action Conference, *Proceedings*, II (Cincinnati, 1939), 461–68; "Speaking to John Brophy," *Guildsman*, VI (October 1937), 7–8; "Labor's Right To Organize Today," *ibid.* (February 1938), 4–7.

34. Noll to Brophy, September 1938, Brophy Papers. *Ave Maria* and *America* were among the papers which picked up the charge, Bishop Robert Lucey, Richard Deverall, and John Collins were among those who came to his defense. For correspondence on these matters and copies of Brophy's speeches see Brophy Papers.

35. Huber, *Our Bishops Speak*, pp. 98–101, 305–6.

36. Alter, "Capital and Labor: Rights and Duties," *Catholic Mind*, XXXV (February 22, 1937), 61–64; M.J. Reardon, editor, *A Bishop's Rostrum* (Milwaukee, 1946), 124–34, 186–89; Bishops Edwin O'Hara and Karl J. Alter, "Christian Social Order: Some Basic Principles," *Catholic Mind*, XXXVI (June 8, 1938), 220–22.

37. George Cardinal Mundelein, "Catholic Action for Social Justice," *Catholic Mind*, XXXVI (February 8, 1938), 48. Sheil's speeches are reported in *Labor Leader*, March 2, 1939; *Catholic Worker*, VI (February 1939), 2 and (July and August 1939), 1, 2. See also "The Means of Life," *Commonweal*, 325; "Prelates Plan," *Time*, XXXVI (September 2, 1940), 38–39; "Meat and a Bishop," *ibid.*, XXXIV (July 24, 1939), 12. See also Barbara Wayne Newell, *Chicago and the Labor Movement* (Urbana, 1961), pp. 193, 244–45.

38. Archbishop Edward Mooney, "Duty of the Catholic Worker To

Join Organized Labor," *Catholic Mind*, XXXVIII (March 8, 1939), 569–71; Mooney, "Industry's Great Need: Cooperation not Competition," *Catholic Action*, XIX (January 1937), 9–10; Mooney, "Rethinking Economics," *Christian Front*, III (May 1939), 9–11.

39. Quoted in "New Dealing Archbishop," *Time*, XXXVII (April 7, 1941), 73–74.

40. Bishop Robert J. Lucey, "Economic Disorder and *Quadragesimo Anno*," *Homiletic and Pastoral Review*, XXXV (June 1935), 858–64.

41. Lucey, "Apathy: Our Scourge," *ibid.*, XXXVI (June 1936), 468–77; Lucey, "Are We Fair to the Church?," *Commonweal*, XXVIII (September 9 and 16, 1938), 490–92, 521–23. See also "Labor in the Recession," *ibid.*, XXXVIII (May 6, 1938), 47.

42. John A. Ryan, "Looking Forward II," *Christian Front*, III (April 1938), 58–61; Raymond McGowan, "The Yardstick," *Tablet*, March 6, 1937.

43. John L. Lewis, "Industrial Unionism," *Christian Front*, II (April 1937), 52–54; "Fair Play for Labor," *ibid.* (June 1937), 91; Richard Deverall, "Steel Masters and Slaves," *ibid.*, (April 1937), 42–43.

44. "The March of Labor," *ibid.*, II (September 1937), 123; Richard Deverall, "John Brophy Speaks," *ibid.*, 125–26; "Labor's Awkward Age," *ibid.*, III (January 1938), 4–5; "Catholics and the Unions," *Sign*, XVIII (December 1938), 260; "Catholics and the C.I.O.," *ibid.* (November 1938), 166; "The C.I.O.," *Catholic Digest*, I (July 1937), 89–90.

45. *Catholic Worker*, V (July 1937), 5. See also the *Catholic Worker*, IV (April 1937), 1–6.

46. Noll to Editor, *The Pittsburgh Catholic*, May 14, 1937, copy in Brophy Papers.

47. R. E. Scott and Marie Duff, Letters, *Commonweal*, XXX (July 21, 1939), 318.

48. In addition to Ryan and McGowan a number of others supported profit sharing. See for example "Toward Industrial Democracy," *Commonweal*, XXIX (January 27, 1939), 369–70 and Joseph Thorning, "Labor's Share," *Sign*, XVI (July 1937), 731–32.

49. Defense of the duty to join the union came from Bishop Sheil and Lucey and Archbishop Mooney, the latter a strong supporter of the A.C.T.U. Others who supported this principle included Ryan and McGowan and Norman McKenna, "Catholics and Labor

Unions," *Catholic Mind,* XXXVII (August 22, 1939), 794–803;
Arthur E. Gleason, "Labor's Obligation: To Join or Not To
Join?," *America,* LVII (September 11, 1937), 532–33. For a mild
dissent see Paul Blakely, "A New Mortal Sin," *ibid.,* LIX (August
20, 1938), 465.

50. The philosophy of the A.C.T.U. can be gleaned from the following articles: John Cort, "Catholics in Trade Unions," *Commonweal,* XXX (May 5 and June 30, 1939), 34–36, 256; Cort, "This
Tremendous Job," *ibid.* (October 20, 1939), 588–89; Cort, "Labor
and Violence," *ibid.,* XXXI (November 10, 1939), 68–70; Thomas
F. Reilly, "The ACTU," *Catholic Digest,* III (February 1939), 17–
20; Paul Weber, "ACTU," *Christian Front,* III (December 1938),
153–54. In New York the A.C.T.U. published a bi-weekly paper,
The Labor Leader, while the Detroit branch published its own
Michigan Labor Leader.

51. Quote is from Hensler's speech to the Steel Workers Organizing
Committee reported in *Catholic Worker,* V (July 1937), 5. See
also "Catholic Radical Alliance," *Commonweal,* XXVI (May 14,
1937), 77; Richard Deverall, "Catholic Radical Alliance," *Christian
Front,* II (October 1937), 141–43; Hensler, "Bloodless Revolution," *ibid.,* III (October 1938), 105–6; Rice, "A Priest on Labor,"
ibid. (September 1938), 116–17.

52. *Catholic Worker,* I (July and August 1933), 1.

53. *Catholic Worker,* III (February 1936), 4; *ibid.,* IV (July 1939),
1, 2.

54. The history of the Catholic Worker is best followed in the books
of Dorothy Day, which are heavily autobiographical. See in particular *Loaves and Fishes* (New York, 1963).

55. This view was clearly expressed by John Ryan, who frequently
refuted charges that labor was becoming too powerful. On the
contrary, Ryan insisted, the balance remained clearly on the side
of management. See Ryan to Bishop John F. Noll, March 8, 1938,
and March 31, 1941, Ryan Papers.

CHAPTER VI

1. William F. Montavon, Report of the Legal Department of the
National Catholic Welfare Conference for the Six-Month Period
Ending April 20, 1933. Montavon Papers.

2. Address to Seventieth Birthday Celebration, *Congressional Record*, LXXXIV, Part 13, 76th Congress, First Session, May 26, 1939, 2254–56. Sources for Ryan's life include his autobiography, *Social Doctrine in Action* (New York, 1941); Francis L. Broderick, *Right Reverend New Dealer: John A. Ryan* (New York, 1963); and Aaron I. Abell, "Monsignor John A. Ryan: An Historical Appreciation," *Review of Politics*, VIII (July 1945), 128–34.

3. *Social Doctrine in Action*, p. 27. Ryan's views on clerical reaction to *Rerum Novarum* can be found in his articles: "Some Effects of *Rerum Novarum*," *America*, XLV (February 25, 1931), 58–60; *The Church and Socialism and Other Esssays* (Washington, 1917), pp. 152–63. On the clergy's lack of empirical knowledge see Ryan's *Questions of the Day* (Boston, 1931), pp. 218–31; *Social Doctrine in Action*, p. 298.

4. Ryan to John Maurice Clark, June 20, 1940, Ryan Papers. Also see Patrick W. Gearty, *The Economic Thought of Monsignor John A. Ryan* (Washington, 1953).

5. Ryan paid tribute to Ely in a number of places, including *Social Doctrine in Action*, pp. 53–54. Ely wrote a preface and found a publisher for Ryan's first book, *A Living Wage* (New York, 1906). In his autobiography Ely praised Ryan and the latter appended a section on the encyclicals at Ely's request; Richard B. Ely, *Ground Under Our Feet* (New York, 1942), pp. 93–94. Marc Perlman draws a close parallel between Ely and Ryan in *Labor Union Theories in America* (Evanston, 1958), pp. 55–64.

6. Francis J. Haas, Sermon at Ryan's Funeral, *Congressional Record*, XCI, Part 12, 79th Congress, 1st Session, September 26, 1945, App. 4055–57. Ryan described his methodology in *Social Reconstruction* (New York, 1920), pp. 200–216. See also Broderick, *Right Reverend New Dealer*, pp. 27–33.

7. Ryan's major theoretical works were *A Living Wage* and *Distributive Justice* (New York, 1916). Quotes from *A Living Wage*, pp. 16–17; "Social Objectives of Catholics," *Catholic Charities Review*, XIII (April 1929), 116.

8. "Puritanism, Prohibition, and Catholicism," *New Republic*, LX (September 11, 1929), 102. See also Gearty, *Economic Thought*, pp. 100–105.

9. *The State and the Church* (New York, 1922), p. 196.

10. *A Living Wage*, pp. 3–4. Ryan's role in popularizing the idea of a legislated minimum wage is discussed by Joseph Dorfman, *The*

Economic Mind in American Civilization, 5 volumes (New York, 1949), III, p. 324.

11. *Ibid.*, p. 103; in 1920 edition also pp. 104–8.

12. *Distributive Justice*, pp. 18, 35, 36, 150, 180, 278. See also *Social Reconstruction*, pp. 182–200, "Objectives of Catholics," p. 116.

13. See Dorfman, *Economic Mind*, III, 324; *Social Reconstruction*, pp. 59, 161–62; *Distributive Justice*, pp. 213–30.

14. *Social Doctrine in Action*, p. 70; *The Church and Socialism*; pp. 100–152; *Social Reconstruction*, pp. 121–41; *Declining Liberty and Other Papers* (New York, 1927), pp. 213–23; *A Living Wage*, p. 165.

15. *Social Reconstruction*, pp. 101–2; *Social Doctrine in Action*, p. 39. As late as 1928 he wrote; "The greater the proportion of our population that lives on farms, the sounder will be American life as a whole." Farm people, he continued, have "more independence, more self-reliance, more room for children, saner ideas of what constitutes welfare, and better opportunities for decent home life, than city families with equivalent incomes." "Looking Forward II," *Christian Front*, III (April 1938), 58–61. Robert D. Cross, "The Changing Image of the City Among American Catholics," *Catholic Historical Review*, XLVIII (April 1962), 33–52.

16. Ryan's views on these matters can be followed in his collected essays, *Declining Liberty and Other Papers* and *Questions of the Day*. Ryan had an interesting exchange of letters with Norman Thomas on the Mexican issue: Thomas to Ryan, February 10 and February 25, 1927; Ryan to Thomas, February 15 and February 17, 1927, Ryan Papers.

17. Ryan to William Hard, January 28, 1927, Ryan Papers. Yet Ryan eventually quit the A.C.L.U. over its absolute interpretation of free speech and academic freedom. See Ryan to Roger Baldwin, November 5 and November 6, 1931, Ryan Papers.

18. *The State and the Church*, pp. 30–40; *Questions of the Day*, pp. 57–90. On the episode see Francis L. Broderick, "But Constitutions Can Be Changed," *Catholic Historical Review*, XLIX (October 1963), 390–93.

19. *Questions of the Day*, pp. 91–99. The passage in question permanently damaged Ryan's image among Protestants and Liberals. In 1945 *Christian Century* noted Ryan's death by praising his social views but added that in politics "he defended the most rigid concepts of Roman Catholic authority and exclusiveness." *Christian Century*, LXII (September 26, 1945), 1084.

20. Broderick, *Right Reverend New Dealer*, pp. 153–60. Ryan's position on the amendment was unchanged a decade later: Letter to the Editor, *Commonweal*, XX (May 25, 1934), 104–5. Among his most vocal Catholic critics was Conde Pallen of The National Civic Federation who charged Ryan with being socialistic because of his views on the 1919 steel strike. See Margueritte Green, *The National Civic Federation and the American Labor Movement, 1900–1925* (Washington, 1956), pp. 400–401, 410–11. Ryan's difficulties with O'Connell continued in the 1930's: Rev. P. J. Waters to Ryan, November 27, 1930; Ryan to Waters, December 1930; Rev. F. A. Burke to Ryan, April 15, 1932; Ryan to Burke, April 19, 1932. Ryan Papers.

21. *Declining Liberty*, pp. 224–38, 209–12, 258–67; *The Ethics of Public Utility Valuation* (Washington, 1928), p. 30.

22. "Poverty in the United States," *Studies*, XIX (March 1930), 80–81; "The Necessity of Federal Relief for the Unemployed," *Catholic Charities Review*, XV (November 1931), 290.

23. "International Aspects of Unemployment," *Catholic World*, CXXXIV (November 1931), 129–36; *Seven Troubled Years* (Ann Arbor, 1937), p. 51.

24. Ryan's analysis of the Depression is summed up in *A Better Economic Order* (New York, 1935), pp. 62–74. See also "High Wages and Unemployment," *Commonweal*, XIII (January 7, 1931), 260; "Unemployment and the Coming Winter," *Catholic Charities Review*, XIV (November 1930), 223–25; "The Responsibility of Congress Toward Unemployment," *ibid.*, XVI (December 1932), 306–8.

25. Ryan to Mrs. S. N. Warren, September 26, 1930, Ryan Papers; "Mr. Hoover and the Depression," *Commonweal*, XII (September 3, 1930), 436–38; "Mr. Hoover and the National Welfare," *ibid.* (September 10, 1930), 457–59; "Our Bankrupt Leadership," *Tablet*, May 10, 1931; *Seven Troubled Years*, pp. 14–15.

26. "Social Justice and the State," *Commonweal*, XXX (June 16, 1939), 205–6. Ryan's views on the encyclical are found in "Papal Encyclical on Labor," *Survey*, LXVI (June 15, 1931), 307; "The New Things in the New Encyclical," *Ecclesiastical Review*, LXXXV (July 1931), 1–13; "The New Deal and Social Justice," *ibid.*, XIX (April 13, 1934), 657; *A Better Economic Order*, cited above, is his description of the occupational group system.

27. "Economics and Ethics," *Commonweal*, XVIII (October 6, 1933), 521–23. Ryan to Newton D. Baker, June 10, 1932; Franklin D.

Roosevelt to Ryan, September 1, 1932, Ryan to Roosevelt, September 7, 1932, Ryan Papers. Joseph Dorfman described the 1919 Bishops' Program: "It reads like a blueprint for the New Deal legislation enacted in the 1930s." *Economic Mind*, IV, 107.

28. *Seven Troubled Years*, p. 130. See also Ryan to M. L. Wilson, September 17, 1932; Ryan to P. J. Connolly, June 30, 1933, Ryan Papers; "President Roosevelt's Economic Program," *Studies*, XXII (June 1933), 194–204.

29. "The American Presidential Campaign," *Studies*, XXV (September 1936), 379–89.

30. "Are We On the Right Road?," *Commonweal*, XX (October 12, 1934), 547–49. Ryan never lost his admiration for Roosevelt and the New Deal. See Ryan to Roosevelt, June 17, 1944, Roosevelt Papers.

31. Ryan to Michael Williams, June 10, 1935; Ryan to E. J. O'Connor, January 10, 1935; Ryan to William Hard, January 7, 1935; Ryan to John F. Cronin, March 9, 1936, Ryan Papers; Review of Hugh Johnson, *The Blue Eagle from Egg to Earth*, *Commonweal*, XXII (September 20, 1935), 503–5. Ryan also was Chairman of the Advisory Council of the United States Employment Service and a member of the President's Committee on Farm Tenancy. He delivered the invocation at the 1937 and 1945 inaugurals.

32. "President Roosevelt's Economic Program," p. 198; Ryan to William Hard, January 7, 1935; Ryan to Franklin Roosevelt, September 24, 1935, Ryan Papers; *A Better Economic Order*, pp. 74–116; "What About Industrial Recovery?," *Catholic Action*, XVII (March 1935), 7–8; *Seven Troubled Years*, pp. 66–72, 192–95.

33. Ryan to F. T. Sullivan, May 17, 1934. See also Ryan to W. C. Earle, February 18, 1936, Ryan Papers; *Seven Troubled Years*, pp. 154–64, 287–88.

34. Speech in *Seven Troubled Years*, pp. 295–99. On background see James J. Hoey to Ryan, September 25, 1936, October 1, 1936, October 2, 1936, and Ryan to Hoey, September 26, 1936, and October 5, 1936, Ryan Papers; Broderick, *Right Reverend New Dealer*, p. 225.

35. Letter to the editor, *Commonweal*, XXV (November 6, 1936), 44–45. For support of Ryan see "Ryan-Coughlin Controversy," *ibid.*, XIV (October 23, 1936), 597–98. The most serious criticism came from Archbishop Curley's Baltimore *Catholic Review*, October 16, 1936, Clipping in Ryan Papers.

36. "An Open Letter to the Editor," *Catholic World,* CXLIII (April 1936), 22–25. There are numerous letters to Coughlin supporters in the Ryan Papers in which Ryan criticized Coughlin's monetary theories.

37. Ryan to Franklin D. Roosevelt, September 24, 1935, Ryan Papers. See also *Declining Liberty,* pp. 137, 239–50; *Seven Troubled Years,* pp. 198–99; "The Supreme Court Debate," *Commonweal,* XXV (April 16, 1937), 683–85; *Social Doctrine in Action,* p. 251.

38. Quoted in Broderick, *Right Reverend New Dealer,* pp. 230–31.

39. "The Revival of Minimum Wage Legislation," *Catholic Charities Review,* XVII (May 1933), 133–35; "Labor Organization Today," *ibid.* (November 1933), 291–93; *Seven Troubled Years,* pp. 192–95; "The 'Sit-Down' Strike," *Ecclesiastical Review,* XCVI (April 1937), pp. 419–20; "Looking Forward II," *Christian Front,* III (April 1938), 58–61.

40. "A Program for Recovery and Reform," National Catholic Social Action Conference, *Proceedings,* I (Milwaukee, 1938), 372; *Social Doctrine in Action,* p. 261. See also *The Constitution and Catholic Industrial Teaching* (New York, 1937), pp. 10–26.

41. Michael J. Ready (General Secretary, NCWC) to Ryan, July 13, 1940, Ryan Papers. See also "Political Causes of International Disorder," *Commonweal,* XXVII (October 21, 1938), 667. "Shall We Repeal the Arms Embargo?," *Congressional Record,* LXXXV, Part 2, October 26, 1939, 513–14; *Social Doctrine in Action,* p. 263.

42. "Labor and Economic Construction After the War," *Vital Speeches,* LXXVI (February 15, 1943), 266–69. See also "Roosevelt and Social Justice," *Review of Politics,* VII (July 1945), 297–305.

43. Ryan to C. T. O'Keefe, March 9, 1937, quoted in Broderick, *Right Reverend New Dealer,* pp. 242–43.

44. "Ethics and Political Intervention in the Field of Social Action," *Review of Politics,* III (July 1941), 300–305. For a perceptive critique see Karl H. Cerny, "Monsignor John A. Ryan and the Social Action Department" (unpublished Ph.D. dissertation, Yale University, 1954), pp. 196, 273–77 and Broderick, *Right Reverend New Dealer, passim.*

45. McGowan, Review of Herbert Agar and Allen Tate, editors, *Who Owns America?, Commonweal,* XXIV (June 12, 1936), 14; *Catholic Action,* XVIII (August 1936), 7–8.

46. McGowan, "Outside the Protestant Garrison," *American Review,* III (April 1934), 48–49. For a comparison with Ryan's interpreta-

tion of the encyclicals see "American Contributions to the Implementation of the Industry Council Plan," *American Catholic Sociological Review*, XIII (March, 1952), 10–24.

47. McGowan, "Causes of Unemployment: A Study," *NCWC Review*, XII (November 1930), 29.

48. McGowan, *New Guilds: A Conversation* (New York, 1937), p. 10. See also McGowan, "Philosophy of Catholicism in its Relation to Industry," *NCWC Review*, XIII (May 1931), 9–10, 31.

49. McGowan, "Property-Organization-Government Action," *Catholic Action*, XIV (January 1932), 25. See also same title, *NCWC Review*, XIII (November 1931), 28; "Reconstructing the Social Order," American Catholic Philosophical Association, *Proceedings*, IX (1933), 187; "Government and Social Justice," *Catholic Mind*, XXVI (June 8, 1938), 222–26.

50. McGowan, *New Guilds*, p. 13; "The Papal Economic Encyclicals" in J. A. Vaughn, editor, *Our Modern Social and Economic Order* (Huntington, Ind., 1939), p. 157; "The Yardstick," *Tablet*, March 30, 1935.

51. McGowan, "The National Industrial Recovery Act," *Catholic Action*, XV (July 1933), 31; "The Priest and the Industrial Crisis," *Ecclesiastical Review*, LXXXIX (September 1933), 225–34; "Reconstructing the Social Order," p. 188.

52. McGowan, "The Yardstick," *Tablet*, August 4, 1934.

53. As an example see Frederick B. Kenkel, "New Deals, Past and Present," *Central Blatt and Social Justice*, XXVII (July, August, 1935), 115–18; (October 1935), 200–203.

54. Ryan to Russell Wilbur, October 14, 1935, Ryan Papers; Paul Marx, *Virgil Michel and the Liturgical Movement* (Collegeville, Minn., 1957), pp. 216–17.

55. Broderick, *Right Reverend New Dealer*, p. 242.

56. George N. Shuster, Review of Broderick, *Right Reverend New Dealer* in *New York Times Book Review*, April 15, 1963.

CHAPTER VII

1. Father Coughlin allows no one to examine his papers and he seldom grants interviews. What little is known of his early life is derived from the work of admiring authorized biographers or hostile journalists. A scholarly biography by Charles Tull draws on printed sources, newspapers, periodicals, and New Deal manu-

script collections to describe the career of Father Coughlin: Charles J. Tull, *Father Coughlin and the New Deal* (Syracuse, 1965). Two earlier works by Coughlin followers are Louis B. Ward, *Father Charles E. Coughlin: An Authorized Biography* (Detroit, 1933) and Ruth Mugglebee, *Father Coughlin: The Radio Priest of the Shrine of the Little Flower* (Garden City, 1935). One of the better accounts by an opponent is in Raymond Graham Swing, *Forerunners of American Fascism* (New York, 1935). A perceptive secondary account is Wallace Stegner, "The Radio Priest and His Flock" in Isabel Leighton, editor, *The Aspirin Age* (New York, 1949), pp. 233–57.

2. Quoted in Mugglebee, *Coughlin*, p. 169.
3. An interesting suggestion on the question of Coughlin's motivation was offered by journalist Forrest Davis. He argued that the strong-willed bishop Michael Gallagher, far from being the mere passive supporter of his subordinate, was actually the source and inspiration of his work. Educated in Austria, Gallagher was a close friend of that country's Catholic leaders, Ignaz Seipal and Engelbert Dollfuss, and visited the latter twice in the early thirties. Coughlin's ideas have a vague resemblence to those of the Austrian school, particularly his anti-Semitism and his later proposals for a corporate State. But there were important differences as well which seem far more significant, at least until 1936. See Forrest Davis, "Father Coughlin," *Atlantic*, CLVI (November 1935), 659–68. For Gallagher's support of Coughlin, even against fellow bishops, see Louis Ward, *Coughlin*, chapters 29, 30; *Tablet*, April 27, 1935, and *Social Justice*, August 3, 1936. Open disagreement between the bishop and the priest took place during the election of 1936. See *Social Justice*, November 9, 1936.
4. Walter Davenport, "The Shepherd of Discontent," *Colliers*, XCV (May 14, 1935), 12–13, 57.
5. *Father Coughlin's Radio Sermons, October 1930–April, 1931* (Baltimore, 1931), p. 16.
6. *Father Coughlin's Radio Discourses, 1931–1932* (Royal Oak, Mich., 1932), p. 218 also pp. 118–31.
7. Quoted from Congressional Committee Hearings on Communism in Detroit by Arthur Schlesinger, Jr., *The Politics of Upheaval* (Boston, 1960), p. 23.
8. *Social Justice*, March 13, 1936; *Sermons, 1930–1931*, p. 162.
9. Speech defending monetary policy in New York quoted by

Schlesinger, *Politics of Upheaval*, p. 23. On relations with the New Deal, see Tull, *Father Coughlin, passim,* and James P. Shenton, "The Coughlin Movement and the New Deal," *Political Science Quarterly*, LXXXIII (June 1953), 352–73.

10. *The New Deal in Money* (Royal Oak, Mich., 1933), p. 127.

11. *A series of Lectures on Social Justice* (Royal Oak, Mich., 1935), pp. 84–96, 122–51. See also *The Secret Diaries of Harold L. Ickes,* 3 volumes (New York, 1953), I, 285, John M. Blum, *From the Morganthau Diaries* (Boston, 1959), pp. 186–87, 255, Schlesinger, *Coming of the New Deal* (Boston, 1959), p. 251.

12. *A Series of Lectures on Social Justice* (Royal Oak, Mich., 1936), p. 41, also p. 11. Hereafter cited as *Series of Lectures, 1936.* See also *Series of Lectures, 1935,* pp. 155, 193–96, 197–99.

13. *Series of Lectures, 1935,* pp. 17–18 and *Social Justice,* July 13, 1936.

14. These developments can be followed in *Social Justice* and *Series of Lectures, 1936.* On Lemke see Edward C. Blackorby, *Prairie Rebel* (Lincoln, 1963).

15. *Social Justice,* May 29, June 5, July 6, September 21, September 28, October 19, 26, 1936.

16. *Ibid.,* November 16, 1936, Coughlin, "Pope Pius XI and Social Justice," *Catholic Digest,* I (February 1937), 46.

17. Attorney General Francis Biddle recounts the events leading to Coughlin's silencing, which was brought about with the aid of Leo T. Crowley, a friend of both Archbishop Mooney and President Roosevelt. Biddle, In *Brief Authority* (Garden City, 1962), pp. 238, 246–47.

18. Charles and Mary Beard, *America in Midpassage* (New York, 1939), p. 197. See also Aaron I. Abell, *American Catholicism and Social Action* (Garden City, 1960), pp. 240–41.

19. Joseph E. Reeve, *Monetary Reform Movements* (Washington, 1943), p. 3.

20. *Ibid.,* pp. 132, 134, 146–47. See also Davenport, "Shepherd of Discontent," p. 57, Schlesinger, *Politics of Upheaval*, p. 20, and Ward, *Father Charles E. Coughlin,* chapter 14.

21. *Series of Lectures, 1935,* p. 146. The clearest exposition of Coughlin's views is in *Money: Questions and Answers* (Royal Oak, Mich., 1936) which draws heavily on the writings of Gertrude Coogan, an early Coughlin ally whom the priest later repudiated. See Reeve, *Monetary Reform,* p. 144 and *Social Justice,* October 5, 1936.

22. Coughlin to Roosevelt, September 24, 1933, Roosevelt Papers. See also *Eight Lectures on Capital Labor and Justice* (Royal Oak, Mich., 1934), pp. 7–20, 85, 100–115.

23. See *The New Deal in Money; Questions and Answers,* especially, pp. 119–31; *Eight Lectures,* pp. 90–100; *Series of Lectures, 1935,* pp. 60–68, 166–78.

24. Reeve, *Monetary Reform,* pp. 94–95, 99.

25. *Sermons, 1930–1931,* pp. 90–91; Schlesinger, *Coming of the New Deal,* p. 245.

26. *Series of Lectures, 1936,* p. 37.

27. *Ibid.,* p. 23.

28. *Social Justice,* April 3, 1936.

29. *Sermons, 1930–1931,* pp. 137–53; *Series of Lectures, 1936,* pp. 59–60. Reeve describes how many of these themes were common to most of the currency reformers: *Monetary Reform,* chapter 8.

30. *Social Justice,* March 27, 1936; *Money: Question and Answers,* pp. 20–21, 31; *Series of Lectures, 1936,* p. 14.

31. *Series of Lectures, 1935,* p. 17.

32. *Sermons, 1930–1931,* p. 177.

33. *Series of Lectures, 1936,* p. 113; *Social Justice,* March 20, 1936.

34. On the agrarian myth and its themes of natural values, xenophobia, and conspiracy, see Richard Hofstadter, *The Age of Reform,* (New York, 1956), chapters 1, 2.

35. While Coughlin's congressional supporters for the appointment to the London Economic Conference delegation in 1933 were heavily Western, the National Union for Social Justice and the later Christian Front were even more heavily centered in the northeast. See Shenton, "Coughlin Movement," pp. 352–62 and Schlesinger, *Politics of Upheaval,* p. 26.

36. *Series of Lectures, 1935,* pp. 69–71.

37. *Series of Lectures, 1935,* pp. 16, 58; *New Deal in Money,* p. 8.

38. Mugglebee, *Coughlin,* pp. 196–97. When the Baltimore *Catholic Review* stated that it could not accept all the National Union's sixteen points, *Social Justice* replied that all Catholics must accept them as they were based upon *Quadragesimo Anno.* The Coughlinite paper also stated that Catholics who said that they could either support or oppose the New Deal while remaining faithful to the Church were incorrect and had to be ignorant either of the encyclical teachings or of the anti-Christian policies of the administration. See *Social Justice,* June 5, 1936.

39. *Sermons, 1930–1931,* p. 132.

40. Wilfrid Parsons, "Father Coughlin and Social Justice," *America* LIII (May 18, 1935), 129–31; Parsons, "Father Coughlin and the Banks," *ibid.* (May 25, 1935), 150–52. Edward Koch, who presented German and Austrian Catholic social thought in the United States, deplored Coughlin's loyalty to American individualism and to a "pure and reformed capitalism," although he sympathized with his hostility to the New Deal, the unions, and the Jews. Koch concluded that the radio priest did not understand the Catholic program. See comments in *Guildsman*, III (January 1935), 9; V (November 1937), 5–6.

41. Parsons, "Coughlin and Social Justice," p. 131.

42. *Sermons, 1930–1931*, p. 134; *Radio Discourses, 1931–1932*, p. 80.

43. Forrest Davis, "Father Coughlin," p. 688; also Raymond Graham Swing, *Forerunners of American Fascism*, chapter 2. See also James P. Shenton, "Fascism and Father Coughlin," *Wisconsin Magazine of History*, XLIV (Autumn 1960), 6–11.

44. *Social Justice*, November 20, 1936. Actually, Coughlin had called upon the Jews to reject communism and the law of "an eye for an eye" and to accept the teachings of Christ much earlier. *Social Justice*, October 26, 1936, and August 31, 1936. William E. Leuchtenberg found in a letter from Coughlin to Elmer Thomas, dated February 15, 1933, and located in the Thomas Papers, statements as viciously anti-Semitic as any Coughlin made later. See William E. Leuchtenberg, *Franklin D. Roosevelt and the New Deal* (New York, 1964), p. 103n.

45. *Social Justice*, December 19, 1938.

46. *Ibid.*, December 5, 1938.

47. The Protocols began appearing in *Social Justice*, July 18, 1938. The distinction between religious and nonreligious Jews was spurious. Coughlin admitted that the real need was for Jews to "openly profess the divinity of Christ" and that there would always be a "Jewish problem" as long as they would not accept the "Spiritual brotherhood of Christ." *Social Justice*, June 28, 1937, and August 22, 1937. Viereck's articles appeared in May 1938. For an account of the whole episode of anti-Semitism see Gustavus Myers, *History of Bigotry in the United States* (New York, 1943), chapters 33, 34, 35 and Donald S. Strong, *Organized Anti-Semitism in America* (Washington, 1941).

48. Editorial, *Guildsman*, IX (April 1941), 8. Such views appeared in the paper regularly in mid-1938. See in particular "Some Facts Concerning Jews," *ibid.*, VI (September 1938), 11–12.

49. *Social Justice*, August 1, 1938. In answering his critics "Father Coughlin's Friends" cited several popes and a number of contemporary European bishops to defend the priest's position. See *An Answer to Father Coughlin's Critics by Father Coughlin's Friends* (Royal Oak, Mich., 1940).

50. *Why Leave Our Own?* (n.p., 1939), p. 155.

51. *Social Justice*, April 11, 1938, and throughout his speeches.

52. National Union for Social Justice," *Commonweal*, XXIV (August 8, 1936), 426; "Father Coughlin and the Jews," *ibid.*, XXIX (December 9, 1938), 169–70; "Anti-Anti-Semitism," *ibid.*, XXX (July 21, 1938), 305–6; "The Hypnotized," *ibid.*, XXXI (January 26, 1940), 293; "The Real Christian Fronters," *ibid.* (February 23, 1940), 375; George N. Shuster, "The Jews and Two Revolutions," *ibid.*, XXIX (December 30, 1938), 262–64; John A. Ryan, "Anti-Semitism in the Air," *ibid.*, 260–62. For other refutations see General Jewish Council, *Father Coughlin; His 'Facts and Arguments'* (n.p., 1939); W. C. Kernan, "Coughlin, the Jews and Communism," *Nation*, CXLVII (December 17, 1938), 655–58; open letter of David Goldstein to Coughlin, April 21, 1938, copy in Ryan Papers.

53. "Testimony Against Anti-Semitism," *Commonweal*, XXX (July 7, 1939), 265; Michael Williams, "Views and Reviews," *ibid.*, XXVIII (May 27, 1939), 129; "Father Coughlin and the Press," *ibid.*, XXIX (December 16, 1938), 213–14; *Catholic Action*, XXI (August 1939), 3–4 and XX (August 1938), 5–6; Dr. Emmanuel Chapman to Ryan, July 12, 1939, Ryan Papers.

54. James Gillis, "Sursum Corda," *Tablet*, June 9, 1934, and December 10, 1938; "Comment," *America*, LXII (February 10, 1940), 478–79. Opinion polls showed that 58 per cent of the American people thought that Nazi persecution was at least partly the Jews' own fault. Another poll reported 31.8 per cent favoring some restrictions to prevent the Jews from gaining too much power in the business world in the United States while an additional 10.1 per cent favored deporting them to a new Jewish homeland if it could be done humanely. Hadley Cantril, editor, *Public Opinion, 1935–1946* (Princeton, 1951), pp. 381–83.

55. These views appear in the *Tablet* throughout the decade. See in particular *Tablet*, March 21, 1936, and September 30 and October 7, 1939. Also Patrick Scanlan "From the Managing Editor's Desk," *ibid.*, September 19, 1936. For the paper's endorsement of Coughlin see *Tablet*, October 19, 1936, and November 13, 1937. For

Ave Maria see "A Letter from Austria," *Ave Maria*, XLVII (July 9, 1938), 52; "The Jews Must Answer This," *ibid.* (August 27, 1938), 280–81; "The Anti-Christian Wave," *ibid.* (October 22, 1938), 534–35; "Stopping Anti-Semitism," *ibid.*, LII (July 20, 1940), 69.

56. *Social Justice*, December 5, 1938. John A. Ryan recognized that an important source of indifference to anti-Semitism was the apparent disregard of others of persecution of Catholics. Ryan to Philip Stevenson, November 30, 1938, Ryan Papers.

57. See the detailed analysis in Shenton, "Coughlin Movement," pp. 352–69. On the election Samuel Lubell, *The Future of American Politics* (New York, 1952), pp. 220–26. See also Wilfrid Parsons, "Father Coughlin; The Aftermath," *America*, LIII (June 29, 1935), 275–77.

58. *Social Justice*, May 15, 1936. On Cardinal O'Connell see *Series of Lectures, 1935*, pp. 69–71. James Michael Curley reported that O'Connell ordered his priests not to listen to Coughlin but that, despite the Cardinal's efforts, Boston was "the strongest Coughlinite city in America." *I'd Do It Again* (Englewood Cliffs, 1957), p. 296.

59. *Social Justice*, November 22, 1937. See also *Social Justice*, July 5, 1937; November 8, 1937.

60. William V. Shannon, *The American Irish* (New York, 1963), p. 296.

61. Wilfrid Parsons, "Coughlin and Social Justice," p. 129; "Father Coughlin, Al Smith, and the Popular Mind," *Catholic World*, CXXXVII (March 1934) 641–45; "Comment," *Commonweal* (January 28, 1931), 343.

62. *Social Justice*, June 14, 1937. For samples of criticism, see "Exploiting the Ego," *Catholic World*, CXLI (August 1935), 513–32; "The Trend of Events," *Commonweal*, XXIV (July 31, 1936), 334–35; "Father Coughlin Again," *ibid.* (August 7, 1936) 355–56; "Father Coughlin's Position," *ibid.* (October 9, 1936), 553–54; "What the Cardinal Said," *America*, LII (December 22, 1934), 245; The Pilgrim "Father Coughlin and Reluctant Catholics," *ibid.*, LV (August 15, 1936), 443.

63. See discussions of 1936 election, particularly; "Ryan Coughlin Controversy," *Commonweal*, XXIV (October 23, 1936), 597–98; Edward V. Dargin, "Father Coughlin and Canon Law," *Ecclesiastical Review*, XCIII (June 1935), 29–35; and summary of criti-

cism on Coughlin's intemperate remarks in *Guildsman*, V (October 1936), 10–11. Also Shenton, "Coughlin Movement," pp. 362–65 and Shannon, *American Irish*, pp. 312–14.

64. One poll showed that 30 per cent had listened regularly to Coughlin's broadcasts before 1936 but only 9 per cent in April 1938. Of the 1938 listeners, however, 83 per cent approved of his ideas. Cantril, *Public Opinion*, pp. 147–48.

65. Noll to James McMullen, October 26, 1936, copy in Roosevelt Papers; *Tablet*, August 6, 1938; *Social Justice*, March 13, 1936, September 12, 1938, Shenton, "Coughlin Movement," p. 364.

66. Patrick Scanlan, "From the Managing Editor's Desk," *Tablet*, July 8, 1939; Strong, *Organized Anti-Semitism*, pp. 67–69. See also Nathan Glazer and Daniel P. Moynihan, *Beyond the Melting Pot* (Cambridge, Mass., 1963), pp. 217–87; Richard Robbins, "American Jews and American Catholics: Two Types of Social Change," *Sociological Analysis*, XXVI (Spring 1965), 1–18. Scanlan wrote Patrick Callahan, July 9, 1935: "As for our fellow citizens being suspicious of what would happen if we got control, I bid them look at New York. We were supposed to control this city for years, but I must confess the Protestants got a much better deal than they do now when we no longer control." Callahan Papers.

67. Richard Deverall, "The Way It Was," *Social Order*, XI (May 1961), 195–200. Deverall described his subsequent career in the other articles in the series which ran in *Social Order* until June 1962.

CHAPTER VIII

1. Paul Kiniery to John A. Ryan, March 3, 1937, Ryan Papers.

2. In a semi-official *Manual of Catholic Action* (New York, 1936) Msgr. Luigi Civardi set as objectives the protection of the Church's schools and the "Christianization of all the rest," and the inspiration of social life "indirectly, by way of intervention with the public powers for the safe-guarding of the rights of the religious conscience, and by the realization of Catholic principles in laws and public institutions." He stated that the laity had "not of themselves any powers in the Church. . . . They constitute the Church that learns and obeys," pp. 27, 34, 145. Richard Deverall said that the Detroit branch of the A.C.T.U. was "com-

pletely subject" to Archbishop Mooney's judgment. *Michigan Labor Leader*, January 12, 1940. For a personalist criticism see Norman McKenna, "A Manual of Catholic Action," *Christian Front*, I (April 1936), 53–54.

3. Raymond J. Champion, "Catholic Action," *Catholic Mind*, XXIX (March 8, 1931), 117–24.

4. Francis J. Weber, "John J. Cantwell and the Legion of Decency," *American Ecclesiastical Review*, CLI (October 6, 1964), 237–47.

5. McGowan, "Working for a New Social Order," *Catholic Action*, XLV (May 1932), 22–23 and throughout issues of the NCWC journal. See also, Norman McKenna, "Fortitude Preferred," *Commonweal*, XXVI (August 20, 1937), 397–98 and Ed Willock, "Catholic Radicalism in America," in *Catholicism in America* (New York, 1953), p. 134.

6. In addition see Mary Elizabeth Walsh, "The Saints and Social Work," *Catholic Digest*, I (February 1937), 28–38 and Paul R. Martin, *The Gospels in Action* (Milwaukee, 1932). The former, a student of Furfey, attempted to apply the supernatural methods of the saints to modern social problems, while the latter attempted the same application of the teachings and methods of Saint Francis of Assisi.

7. Furfey, *Fire on the Earth* (New York, 1936); and *This Way to Heaven* (Silver Springs, Md., 1939).

8. Furfey, "The Positive Society," *Commonweal*, XXV (January 22, 1937), 353–54.

9. Furfey, *This Way*, pp. 70–71, 181; Furfey, "Voluntary Poverty," *Christian Social Action*, V (February 1940), 49–53.

10. Furfey, *This Way*, pp. 181–82.

11. Furfey, "The Challenge of Modern Thought to Neo-Scholasticism," American Catholic Philosophical Association, *Proceedings*, XII (1936), 45–58, quote 58; Furfey, *Three Theories of Society* (New York, 1937), p. 217.

12. Furfey, "Personalist Social Action in *Rerum Novarum* and *Quadragesimo Anno*," *American Catholic Sociological Review*, II (December 1941), 204–16, quote 212.

13. Thomas E. Davitt, "Labor and Ownership," *Christian Front*, III (February 1938), 23–25.

14. Norman McKenna, "Fortitude Preferred," p. 398. See also Charles Bruehl, "The Relativity of the Ideas," *Central Blatt and Social Justice*, XXIX (December 1936), 263–64.

15. Furfey, "The New Social Catholicism," *Christian Front*, I (December 1936), 181–84; Michel, "Social Aspects of the Liturgy," *Catholic Action*, XVI (May 1934), 9–11; Michel, "The Liturgical Movement and the Future," *America*, LIV (October 12, 1935), 6–7; Michel, "The Layman in the Church," *Commonweal*, XIV (June 4, 1930), 123–25.

16. Quoted in Paul B. Marx, *Virgil Michel and the Liturgical Movement* (Collegeville, Minn., 1957), p. 218.

17. *Ibid.*, p. 205. Michel's views were elaborated in the journal *Orate Fratres*.

18. *Ibid.*, p. 208.

19. See for example Fulton J. Sheen, "The Mystical Body," *Commonweal*, XXIII (November 1, 1935), 7–9.

20. Marx, *Virgil Michel, passim* Leo R. Ward and Emerson Hynes, "Virgil Michel," *Commonweal*, XXIX (December 23, 1938), 237.

21. Arthur Sheehan, *Peter Maurin, Gay Believer* (Garden City, 1959); Joseph A. Brieg, "Apostle on the Bum," *Commonweal*, XXVIII (April 29, 1938), 9–12.

22. Most of Dorothy Day's writings are heavily autobiographical. *From Union Square to Rome* (Silver Springs, Md., 1939) and *The Long Loneliness* (Garden City, 1960) contain the story of her conversion. *Houses of Hospitality* (New York, 1939) is a collection of articles from the *Catholic Worker* while *Loaves and Fishes* is the story of the movement from 1933 to 1960.

23. *Long Loneliness*, p. 9; Joseph McSorley, Review of *From Union Square to Rome*, *Catholic World*, CXLIII (January 1939), 498–99.

24. *Catholic Worker*, IV (January 1937) 1; Maurin's "Easy Essays" were collected and published, as *Catholic Radicalism*, edited by David Mason (New York, 1949).

25. *Ibid.*, I (September 1933), 12; II (April 1935), 1, 8; *Long Loneliness*, p. 166; Julian Pleasants, "Personal Responsibility" in Leo R. Ward, editor, *The American Apostolate* (Westminister, Md., 1953), pp. 83–93.

26. *Catholic Worker*, I (July and August 1933), 1; (April 1934), 3; (February 1934), 8; *Long Loneliness*, p. 219.

27. *Catholic Worker* (September 1933), 12.

28. *Ibid.*, IV (November 1936), 1, 6.

29. Dorothy Day, "Day With An End," *ibid.*, 1 (April 1934), 3.

30. Day, *Houses of Hospitality*, p. 54.

31. *Catholic Worker*, I (July and August 1933), 8 and III (November 1935), 1, 8, and (January 1936), 1, 2 and V (February 1938), 8.
32. Furfey, "There are Two Kinds of Agrarianism," *Catholic Worker*, VII (December 1939), 7, 8; Furfey, "Unemployment on the Land," *ibid.*, VII (October 1939), 8; John J. Hugo, "In Defense of the Romantic Agrarians," *ibid.*, VII (November 1939), 8. Cyrile Echele, "An Idea of a Farming Commune," *ibid.*, III (February 1936), 2, 6. Ade Bethune, "Technological Tenuousness," *ibid.*, VI (June 1938), 7.
33. Thomas Coddington, "Catholic Class Consciousness," *ibid.*, II (February 1935), 3; T. L. Burke, "The Catholic Social Movement Is Anti-Bourgeoise," *ibid.*, III (June 1935), 6; editorial comment, *ibid.* (July and August 1935), 4.
34. *Catholic Worker*, III (January 1936), 3; IV (May 1936), 8; III (July and August 1935), 5; V (June 1937), 4.
35. *Ibid.* VII (February 1940), 7.
36. Day, *Union Square*, p. 104.
37. Quoted in McDonald, *Memoirs*, p. 115.
38. *Catholic Worker*, II (December 1934), 3; Day, *Union Square*, p. 140.
39. *Catholic Worker*, IV (November 1936), 4.
40. *Ibid.* (November 1933), 1, 7; also I (September 1933), 6; (February 1934), 7; (March 1934), 1.
41. *Ibid.*, II (September 1934), 1, 6; (June 1936), 1, 5.
42. *Ibid.*, V (May 1937), 1, 2; *ibid.*, IV (May 1936), 1, 6.
43. *Ibid.* (September 1936), 1.
44. *Ibid.* (May 1936), 4.
45. Day, *Long Loneliness*, pp. 145–46.
46. John LaFarge, S.J., "Peter the Agitator Quotes the Prophets of Israel," *America*, LV (August 1, 1936), 395; LaFarge "Some Reflections on the Catholic Worker," *ibid.*, LVII (June 26, 1937), 275.
47. For example see *Guildsman*, III (April 1935), 7.
48. Scanlan, "From the Managing Editor's Desk," *Tablet*, June 5, 1937, p. 11; Edward Lodge Curran, Letter, *Tablet*, July 31, 1937, p. 8; Curran, Letter, *ibid.*, August 7, 1937, 6; Curran, Letter, *Catholic Worker*, VI (March 1939), 3.
49. *Ibid.*, V (May 1937), 1, 3; (July 1937), 1.
50. James W. Douglass, "Dorothy Day and the City of God," *Social Justice Review*, LIV (May 1961), 40–48.

51. Day, *Houses of Hospitality*, pp. 207–8.
52. Cort, "The Catholic Worker and the Workers," *Commonweal*, LV (April 4, 1952), 635 ff.; Cort "Memories of Peter Maurin," *Commonweal*, LXXI (January 22, 1960), 462–64; Arthur Sheehan, "In Defense of Peter Maurin," *Ave Maria*, XCV (March 17, 1962), 3.
53. H. A. Reinhold, "The Long Loneliness of Dorothy Day," *Commonweal*, LV (February 29, 1952), 521–22.
54. Edward Duff, "Catholic Social Action in the American Environment," *Social Order*, XII (September 1962), 306–7.
55. John Cogley, "Store Front Catholicism," *America*, LXXIX (August 21, 1948), 79 ff. Cogley himself is one of the best examples of this; he describes vividly the impact of the Catholic Worker on his generation and on himself. After heading up the Chicago house he went on to edit *Commonweal*, to serve as staff director of the Center for the Study of Democratic Institutions and finally to become religion editor of *The New York Times*.
56. Cort, "The Catholic Worker and the Workers," p. 635.

CHAPTER IX

1. William F. Montovan, Report of the Legal Department, National Catholic Welfare Conference, for six-month period ending April 20, 1935, in Montovan Papers.
2. Peter Guilday, "The Catholic Church in the United States," *Thought*, I (June 1926), 7.
3. William F. Sands, "The Return of the New Deal," *Catholic Digest*, I (May 1937), 1–7.
4. Louis J. A. Mercier, "Catholic Thought and the Nation," *Catholic Mind*, XXXII (July 22, 1934), 261–70. The Bellarmine argument is outlined in John C. Rager, "Catholic Sources and the Declaration of Independence," *ibid.*, XXVIII (July 8, 1930), 253–68. Examples of the uses to which it could be put can be seen in James Gillis, *This Our Day* (New York, 1933) pp. 5–7; Gillis, "The President as Philosopher," *Catholic World*, CXLVIII (February 1939), 513. Merrill D. Peterson discusses the literature on the "Bellarmine-Jefferson Legend" in *The Jeffersonian Image in the American Mind* (New York, 1960), pp. 306, 307, 500, 501. Cf. Dorothy Dohen, *Nationalism and American Catholicism* (New York, 1966).

5. Gillis, *This Our Day*, p. 141.

6. Joseph M. Corrigan, "The American Tradition," National Catholic Social Action Conference, *Proceedings*, 1, 387.

7. Francis X. Talbot, "Catholicism in America" in Harold E. Stearns, editor, *America Now* (New York, 1938), pp. 528–42.

8. National Catholic Alumni Federation, *Man and Modern Secularism* (New York, 1940), pp. 1–82.

9. Pollock, "Catholicism and the American Way," *Commonweal*, XXX (June 20, 1939), 248–50 and (August 11, 1939), 371–75.

10. Americans "refuse . . . to recognize their choice at present lies between a totalitarian State on the one hand and the corporative society on the other." F. P. Kenkel, "On the Threshold of a New Order?," *Central Blatt and Social Justice*, XXXI (January 1939), 299–301.

11. John E. Reardon, "Active Leadership in American Catholic Culture," *America*, LXI (May 6, 1939), 82–83.

12. Letter to Edward Skillen, July 11, 1938, quoted in Paul Marx, *Virgil Michel and the Liturgical Movement* (Collegeville, Minn., 1957), p. 32.

13. Denis W. Brogan, "The Catholic Politician," *Atlantic*, CCX (August 1962), 84; Karl Rahner, *The Christian Commitment* (New York, 1963), pp. 23–26.

14. Daniel Callahan, *The Mind of the Catholic Layman* (New York, 1963), p. 191; Callahan, "The New Pluralism: From Nostalgia to Reality," *Commonweal*, LXXIX (September 6, 1963), 527–31.

15. Christopher Dawson, interview in *The Moral Curve* (New York, 1961), p. 27.

16. Will Herberg, "Religion and Culture in Present Day America" in Thomas T. McAvoy, editor, *Roman Catholicism and the American Way of Life* (Notre Dame, 1960), p. 15. See also Herberg, *Protestant, Catholic, Jew* (New York, 1960).

17. Rahner, *Christian Commitment*, pp. 28–29. As late as 1959 John Cogley wrote of his fellow Catholics: "We content ourselves with standing in judgement on (our age) as if its problems were not our problems, as if *its* failures were not our own, as if the challenges confronting it were not confronting *us*." "The Catholic and the Liberal Society," *America*, CI (July 7, 1959), p. 495.

Index